IF I'M SO WONDERFUL, WHY AM I STILL SINGLE?

"This superb, practical, compassionate book really answers the question asked in the title. Single people who lose self-confidence and are ready to give up could profit from keeping this book at their bedside. The chapter on 'Commitmentphobes' is a masterpiece and well worth the price of the book ten times over. Altogether a wise and valuable book."
—Penelope Russianoff, author of
  Why Do I Think I Am Nothing Without a Man?

"Finally we have a singles' book that goes beyond what to say at parties, how to write a personal ad, and how women ought to tolerate this pathetic opposite sex. Not only does Susan Page not antagonize and blame men, she directly addresses our needs as well as women's. Susan Page has a vision that reaches beyond our present quagmire. Here is the refreshing new voice that singles have been longing to hear."
  —Paul Reese, director of Trellis,
    San Francisco Bay Area Singles Organization

"Men and women who want permanent partners will benefit from her '10 strategies that will change your life forever,' as set forth in this engaging guide."
  —*Publishers Weekly*

If I'm So Wonderful, Why Am I Still Single?

TEN STRATEGIES THAT WILL CHANGE YOUR LOVE LIFE FOREVER

Susan Page

BANTAM BOOKS
NEW YORK · TORONTO · LONDON · SYDNEY · AUCKLAND

*Dedicated with deepest love and affection
to my parents, Edwin and Helen Hammock*

*This edition contains the complete text
of the original hardcover edition.
NOT ONE WORD HAS BEEN OMITTED.*

IF I'M SO WONDERFUL, WHY AM I STILL SINGLE?
A Bantam Book / published by arrangement with Viking Penguin Inc.

PRINTING HISTORY
Viking edition published April 1988

*Grateful acknowledgment is made for permission to use the following
copyrighted material:*
*Two "Cathy" cartoons by Cathy Guisewite. Copyright 1983 Universal Press
Syndicate.*
Reprinted with permission. All rights reserved.
Self-esteem meditation by Dr. Emmett Miller.

Bantam edition / January 1990

*Bantam Books are published by Bantam Books, a division of
Bantam Doubleday Dell Publishing Group, Inc. Its trademark,
consisting of the words "Bantam Books" and the portrayal of
a rooster, is Registered in U.S. Patent and Trademark Office
and in other countries. Marca Registrada. Bantam Books,
666 Fifth Avenue, New York, New York 10103.*

Preface

This book grew out of my own experience as a single woman. I had been quite happily married for eight years and, after a shattering divorce and painful but enlightening recovery, had been single for six. Now, I longed to fall in love with a man who was also in love with me and who, I felt, "deserved me." Perhaps partly because my own parents are still very happy together after fifty years, I kept alive a vision of building my life together with someone else. I knew that such relationships were possible, and I wanted to be a part of one myself.

But I wasn't having much luck. My mother kept telling me I'd find a "normal" man if I moved back to Ohio. I dated men who were married, men who were gay, men who wouldn't even discuss "the 'C' word" (commitment), and men who would discuss it long enough to tell me they were against it. Once, I videotaped a PBS documentary I had been dying to see so I could go on a date. By the end of the evening, I decided I had made a mistake: I should have videotaped my date and stayed home and watched TV!

And I read. I used to linger at the "relationships" and "psychology" sections of bookstores looking for a book that might tell me what I could do differently to find the relationship I knew I wanted. I found lots of books on how to love living alone; how to feel strong and independent, even though I'm a woman; how to make the best of relationships that won't last forever; and how to fix tantalizing dishes to eat by candlelight—alone!

My desire to fall in love did not distinguish me from most of the lively, attractive single women I knew. We all felt lonely sometimes; we all went through cycles of optimism and pessimism. And we all had trouble figuring out a way to date that didn't make us feel we were back in high school.

But the longer I was single, the more I began to sense a difference between me and my other single friends. For one thing, I seemed to be more determined and systematic in my search for love. And for another, I was quite certain I would succeed.

I actually carried around in my purse a list of all the qualities I was looking for in my ideal man. And I put the word out in as many ways as I could dream up. I tried personal ads and dating services. I attended singles events and stepped up my participation in my "hobbies," such as folk dancing and theater. I actively encouraged all my friends to think of men who might be suitable for me.

All this went on for some time, although I did not have a frantic or urgent feeling about it. I *knew* I would meet the right person; I just didn't know when. How I came by this confidence, I can't say exactly, although I believe it was critical to my success, and it is a feeling I have tried to conceptualize and pass along in this book. I simply knew I was not a person who would spend my life alone; it wasn't my self-image. Also, I knew I was not capable of "settling" for someone who did not fulfill my ideals. I believed that all I had to do was keep looking and hold out until I was certain I had what I wanted. There were discouraging, depressing times to be sure, but I never really doubted that I would achieve my goal.

One evening, my dear friend Roseann called to say that her husband's cousin, Mayer, had recently moved to the area and had invited her whole family over for a delicious dinner. Roseann was impressed by his hospitality—and his cooking. Also, she said he had talked about what he sought in a woman and had mentioned that he liked to cuddle and snuggle—something that, Roseann knew, was also important to me. She invited me over that very evening to meet him, but, alas, I already had plans.

"Cancel your plans!" Roseann told me. "I don't know when I'm going to see him again, and I *really* want you to meet him. Where are your priorities?"

I knew she was right. I managed to alter my appointment so I could spend an hour with them.

As I approached Roseann's house, I could see through the window that the back of this man's head was bald—*not* part of my image of Mr. Ideal. The conversation was pleasant, however, until I asked him what he did for a living.

"I'm a ceramic artist," he said brightly.

That really cooled my interest. Mr. Ideal was going to be

a university professor or a minister or a politician—maybe the ambassador to France—something like that.

I thought I'd give it one more try.

"Where did you go to school?"

"Los Angeles City College." (What? Not Harvard or Yale or Stanford?) "But I dropped out after a year."

That was the *coup de grace*. I was very friendly, but I hurried on to my previous engagement.

Mayer later said of that short encounter that I was putting out such a strong signal—not with anything I *said*, but with my general demeanor—that it was clear to him I would either scare him off or get what I wanted. Though I was completely unaware of this at that time, I realized when he said it that the message was deliberate. If a man was going to be intimidated by me, I wanted it to happen right away so we wouldn't waste each other's time.

Mayer was *not* intimidated. I guess that alone impressed me enough to say yes to a second date.

To make a short story even shorter, on our fourth date, we guessed aloud to each other that we would probably get married. We didn't *decide* to; we just recognized—joyfully—that we had both found what we wanted.

I learned once and for all that fortune rarely comes in the form you expect it. In fact, if you work out the details of your dream—a perfectly harmless and pleasurable activity —you can be certain that's *not* the way it will happen. If you dream hard, you will achieve the substance of your dream, but probably not in any specific form you ever imagined.

Mayer and I did get married six months later. We are still living happily ever after, and our prognosis is excellent.

As I was working on my personal "campaign," it became clear to me that my approach to looking for love was somewhat distinctive, and I began conducting workshops for other singles who felt they were wonderful and couldn't figure out why they were still single. My professional background made the workshops a natural step for me. As a Protestant campus minister, the founder of a human sexuality counseling program at a large university, the director of a domestic violence prevention agency, and a management consultant, I had done a great deal of teaching and counseling. In addition, although I am not a licensed therapist, I had had years of training and experience in Gestalt and Bioenergetic therapies.

The theory behind Gestalt (a German word meaning, roughly, "whole") is that through the process of ordinary living, most individuals become fragmented; that is, they become alienated from certain aspects of themselves. For example, a woman who grew up in a family where anger was severely punished and politeness was maintained at all costs may be completely unaware of her buried anger. Or, a man who was taught never to cry and always to maintain an "in-control" attitude may be altogether unconscious of his soft, vulnerable feelings. Using a variety of techniques, Gestalt, which was developed by Fritz Perls, assists individuals to reclaim lost aspects of themselves and, thereby, to become more integrated, more "whole," and more fully functioning human beings.

My workshops depart from strict Gestalt techniques, but they are based on the principle that singles don't see how they are standing in their own way of finding love. Together, we fill out questionnaires and discuss our responses. We play games that are informative and surprising—as well as fun. We ask and answer tough questions. We discuss ideas and tell personal stories.

Throughout all these activities, insights emerge and friendships develop. We laugh a lot; now and then there are tears. Occasionally we spar. Sometimes the sharing becomes incredibly courageous.

I began conducting workshops for women only, but soon realized that what both women and men needed most was to talk to *each other*. The co-ed workshops that I have held ever since are charged with excitement, always educational, and at times, quite moving.

Much of what we have learned in these workshops I have presented in the chapters that follow. I have also drawn upon the experiences of over two hundred men and women whom I interviewed during the course of the writing, and upon my own personal odyssey from singlehood to marriage.

Many knowledgeable people have assured me that only women will read this book. I am convinced they are wrong. I know men are interested in relationship issues because they have been lively participants in my workshops for years. Fully as many men as women have told me, "I can't wait to read your book!" At least let me go on record as saying that I invite and encourage men to read this book, that I believe men need to be involved in discussing all these issues if they are ever to be resolved, and that although I haven't succeeded entirely I have worked very hard to use gender-inclusive language throughout the book. Most of the ideas and strategies presented are *not* gender-specific, but apply equally to men and women.

Similarly, I believe both hetero- and homosexuals will find the material useful, though I have not been so successful in making my language inclusive of homosexual relationships, and I have used heterosexual case studies.

Throughout the book, when I use the term "single," I am not referring to marital status. What I mean is "unattached" or "alone." Some unmarried people are attached, and some married people are unattached. "Available for a relationship" is the critical factor in my use of the term "single," not "unmarried."

I frequently use the term "involuntary single" to emphasize that I am addressing singles *who would prefer to be in a committed intimate relationship.* Individuals who are single by choice, that is, "voluntary singles," will not find this book relevant. However, I have no intention of offending them or of belittling their single lifestyle. I regret very much that this book's title inadvertently implies that there is something wrong with being single. The implication is entirely unintentional, and I surely do not believe any such thing.

While I recognize the advantages of singlehood and know it is a preferred lifestyle for many people, at the same time, I am to some degree an "intimacy advocate." An intimate connection of the highest quality can enrich life immeasurably, yet for too many people, love seems like more trouble than it's worth. In its eagerness to rectify injustices in the workplace, feminism has neglected an equally urgent task: creating models for "liberated" intimate relationships. Beside the symbol of the lone woman of high achievement, feminism must encourage the symbol of the woman whose achievements include creating a successful love relationship. Intimate relationships are in trouble right now. Feminism must provide leadership in helping men and women to find common ground without sacrificing feminist principles.

Some involuntary singles date frequently, and some have not had a date for months or even years. I have tried to take all of these states of singlehood into account, to discuss how to get started dating as well as how to get out of counterproductive dating patterns. The book is divided into four sections. Part I is about the importance of *attitudes*, and suggests a basic plan and guidelines to get you started dating regularly. Part II is about *strategies* to keep in mind *as you date*. Part III addresses *issues* you have to find a way to cope with as a single person, dating or not. And Part IV assists you in pulling together from the foregoing chapters the information which is most relevant *for you*. By the end of it, you will have a specific, step-by-step program tailored to your own needs, desires, and goals for your own love life, and you will have the tools you need to implement your plan.

If you would like to be in a loving partnership but you are tired of dating and of the whole singles scene, read on. You will discover, as my workshop participants have, that you can view it all in a new light; abandon useless old myths you thought were "truth"; and above all, get the results you long for.

As I write this, I am imagining *you*, a person I've never met but yet with whom, as of now, I have a kind of relationship. I hope we have a good time together in the pages that follow. I'm certain you won't agree with everything I say, but I hope you find it provocative, and that some of it is genuinely helpful. As I identified and began to use these ten strategies in my own life, I found I felt much better about myself as well as about my love life. I very much hope the same happens for you.

August 1987

Susan Page
Oakland, California

Acknowledgments

From the earliest stages of this project, I have received unswerving encouragement and support from Carolyn Newman, Roseann Packard, Jean Keeshin, and Susana Valadez. Nancy Peterson showed me how to get started; Roland Tapp was the first editor to give me a green light; and Sybil Baker offered advice and hand-holding at a difficult moment.

Malcolm Lubliner took such a personal interest in this book that I came to view him as a consultant. His perspicacity improved many passages.

As my running partner, Diane Blacker couldn't escape hearing the daily ups and downs of struggling with a manuscript. Her suggestions and encouragement were invaluable.

All of the following people read at least a portion of the manuscript at one or another of its many stages, and made valuable suggestions, which I have included in the final text: Lorraine Bahrick, Loren Cole, Bonnie Davis, Lucy Fine, Paul Hammock, Carol Hyland, Dorothy Kruse, Paul Ramshaw, Janet Roach, Peter Schattner, and Dorothy Wall.

Clive Cazes, Craig Comstock, Judye Hess, Coille Hooven, John McKenzie, Gertrude Schattner, Paul Schulze, Martin Schwartz, Diane Singer, Joyce Snapp, and Bonnie Weiss have also made noteworthy contributions.

The publishing industry is a formidable labyrinth. Standing at various dark corners with a welcome lantern were Harriett Blacker, David Cole, and Michael McTwigan. I will be forever grateful to Arthur Ollman for introducing me to my literary agent.

Glenna Goulet typed early versions of the manuscript and was a pleasure to work with. Elizabeth Adjen gave an extra measure of devotion at a critical time; I am deeply grateful for her loyalty and tenacity. And Mary Strads is everything a writer wants in a typist. She's the modern-day elf who took my messy straw and, quickly and cheerfully, turned it into gold.

This book is the culmination of a lifetime of learning, and I see my debt to my teachers on every page. These people bring love and skill to their task, do their work, and then move on, but not without profoundly changing the people whose lives they touch. I have had the good fortune to work with Michael Conant, Abe Levitsky, Jim Simkin, Mari Krieger, and Eliana Gil.

My in-laws, Florence and David Shacter, and my parents, Edwin and Helen Hammock, are among the few people who never offered the advice so many of my friends kindly gave: "Susan, don't you think you ought to go back to work?" Not only that, but they came through at our most destitute moments with the kind of support that pays the rent. I—quite literally—could not have finished the book without their help, for which I am deeply appreciative.

Every writer should be lucky enough to have a literary agent like Sandra Dijkstra. She made critical contributions to the manuscript, and is gifted at every aspect of her craft. If I am the mother of this book, Sandra is its loving nanny! It is also a great pleasure to thank my editor at Viking, Mindy Werner, who was willing to take quite a risk on an unknown writer. I am grateful for her confidence in me and for her outstanding skill in doctoring the manuscript. Working with her has been an education and a delight.

Finally, to my extraordinary husband, Mayer, and my loyal son, Gabe, I owe my deepest gratitude. Not only did Mayer believe in me, even when I lost faith in myself, he willingly gave the toughest type of support: living on the financial edge. "It's okay," he would tell me. "We have riches of our own, the kind that matter." Gabe found those riches much less appealing, but he stuck by me, too. Thanks, guys. I love you.

Contents

PART II—GUIDELINES FOR KISSING FROGS

Part I

Powerful But Overlooked Attitudes to Set the Stage for Love

Introduction

The Great Emotional Depression

Finding Love in an Unloving World

Mother Teresa commented that the United States was the most loveless country she ever visited.

I won't presume to say what she might have meant, but the statement hit home with me, for I have long experienced this culture as loveless. Our preoccupation with money and consumerism seems to me far more dominant an influence in our lives than our desire for pleasurable human relationships. We *say* we seek love and belonging, but we spend far more time and energy acquiring money and the things it buys. Love is an extracurricular activity—relegated to "off-hours."

The real problem is the extent to which love and work are incompatible activities. Too often, time spent on one is time unavailable for the other. Worse, love and work require opposite types of behavior. For example, to succeed in the "marketplace," you have to be competitive, "businesslike," wary of others, and committed above all else to the bottom line. To succeed in an intimate relationship, you need to be cooperative, flexible, emotionally available, honest, and committed above all else to the welfare of your loved one.

Such different skills are required for love and work that it is difficult to be good at *both* of them. And when a society values visible affluence as much as ours does, most people are going to spend their energy becoming good at work. Love takes a backseat.

Our education and socialization as good Americans is geared almost exclusively toward making us good business and professional people or good workers. The "skills" required for a successful intimate relationship—such as active listening, empathy, "fair" fighting, generosity, the apprehension and expression of emotions—are generally more difficult to learn than professional or business skills and far more neglected in our education.

Where are we taught—or socialized—to listen with empathy, to communicate consciously, to look at ourselves honestly, to feel and express emotions appropriately? An occasional eighth-grade family-life class? One hour of Sunday school a week? An eight- or ten-hour parenting class?

In the seventies, a group of therapists, encounter group leaders, body and movement specialists, and philosophers formed a loose coalition that came to be known as the Human Potential Movement. This "movement" looked briefly as though it might become a balancing force emerging on the fringes of our society. It was designed to assist people in becoming acquainted with the feelings and desires that were buried under their drive to succeed. Using a variety of techniques, it encouraged participants to expand the options for their lives, to enrich their emotional and spiritual selves, and to tap into their full potential as humans rather than settling only for their working selves.

But the Human Potential Movement was short-lived. Perhaps it was too threatening. What would happen to our economy if workers went on weekend retreats where they opened up to other people and felt alive and then returned to work wanting some of that quality in their daily lives? The Human Potential Movement valued "aliveness" more than achievement, pleasure more than profit, quality human relationships more than status or affluence. It simply wasn't the American Way.

Efforts to soften the clash between human-oriented values and production-oriented values have emerged in recent years. A few enlightened corporations are providing child care services, flex-time scheduling, parental leaves, "personal" days off. Women in positions of power—and occasionally even men—can now be found making career "sacrifices" in order to improve the quality of their personal lives. But these changes remain the exception rather than the rule and serve to underscore the presence of a value clash more than to indicate that it is disappearing on any widespread scale.

Work and love—that is, production-oriented values and

human-oriented values—are *not* mutually exclusive. Indeed, both are critical. Our problem is that we do not have them in good balance. The policies and procedures that govern most work settings are excellent evidence of this value imbalance.

Here is another interesting fact to ponder:

In the sixties, a major concern of sociologists as they looked ahead to the seventies and eighties was how we would manage the extra leisure time we would have as a result of time-saving technologies. They were right about time-saving technologies. But they couldn't have been more wrong about the leisure time. *The Wall Street Journal* said recently that, according to their poll, Americans had 33.4 percent less leisure time in 1984 than they had in 1974.

What happened? Why didn't that leisure time materialize? What did we replace it with?

Stress.

It wasn't leisure time but stress that turned out to be the major management problem of the eighties. Virtually every management consulting firm teaches techniques for stress management. But when did you last see a course entitled "Managing Your Leisure Time"?

Stress and intimacy are virtually incompatible. When you are preoccupied with anxiety or exhausted from overcommitment, you can't be available to become fully invested in the welfare of another human being. And you can't find the unstructured, leisurely time in which intimate relationships thrive.

Why do most Americans choose to manage stress rather than reduce it? Why do we end up with far more stress than leisure time?

It's because we fear that the price we will pay for reducing stress is sacrificing achievement, falling behind our fellow workers. And for most of us, this is too great a price to pay. Again, we value money and the things it buys more than we value a calm, pleasurable, loving lifestyle. We would rather have stress than leisure time.

We have set up a competitive, work-oriented society for ourselves. It is a setting in which love and rich emotional connections between people have a hard time flourishing. I call it the Great Emotional Depression.

In the 1930s, this country underwent the Great Depression. Money was scarce, and people searched in vain for jobs that didn't exist.

We are now in the throes of a second Great Depression—of the emotions. We are witnessing a shortage of emotional maturity, an apathy about healthy human relationships, an aversion to intimacy, and people search in vain for appropriate mates who—they believe—don't exist.

But this is not a sociological book. Rather, it is about what you as an individual can do to find a satisfying intimate relationship. I want to make only one point here: in your search for love, you need to recognize that society is *not with you.* Singles looking for love today are like workers in search of jobs in the thirties: The forces around you are subtly but certainly working against love in your life. In his book *New Rules,* researcher Daniel Yankelovich summed it up when he reported that "most people choose financial gain over a more creative, self-fulfilling life."

So do not blame yourself for your "failure" at love; the values surrounding you are powerful, and you are fitting right in. Just be aware that if you value "aliveness" and pleasure as much as you value achievement and material success, you may need to become something of a rebel. It is *not* your imagination that societal conditions in general make love hard to come by. We are in the midst of an Emotional Depression. But if you recognize this and factor it into your search, it doesn't need to defeat you every time you come up against it. Forewarned is forearmed.

Men vs. Women

A second set of circumstances also contributes to the Great Emotional Depression: We are smack in the middle of a revolution in the relationship between the sexes, and we have to cope with all of the confusion that goes with mid-revolutionary times.

I like to use the metaphor of a giant seesaw to characterize in very general terms what is happening. In the fifties, men were on the top end and women were on the bottom end. Men maintained their upper position by providing for women and setting up societal rules that seemed to benefit all.

But then, when the contemporary women's movement

began, the women decided they didn't like the game anymore, and they got up and walked away. When the seesaw moved, the men went flying. They were shocked and confused. They *liked* the old game. Some laughed and teased the "women's libbers" and said, "You'll see." Some got really angry. Others backed off and hid for a while or tried to pretend nothing had changed. Still others cheered the women on but then found that when they tried to date one of them, it just wasn't the same.

Women weren't sure what they wanted to do about men either. Some became separatists and went through a "man-hating" stage. Others tried to hate all men but love individual men. In general, women prevailed upon men to adapt, to forsake their patriarchal ways, and to join in forming an egalitarian society. This process continues, slowly, steadily.

In their confusion, most of the men tumbled around on their own; they didn't talk to other men about their new experiences. A lot of men still think that their confusion is entirely personal and, therefore, unique.

The women, on the other hand, got together in groups right away and discovered power in mutual support. At first, they focused on joining the White Male Club. They learned the Club language, dress codes, and rules for advancement. Later on, they realized that the White Male Club as it was had serious problems, and they began the even bigger task of transforming the Club.

While all this was going on, we all, both men and women, saw that the old nuclear family idea was limited and began experimenting with new models for living together. In the radical decade of the sixties, we experimented with open marriage, cohabitation, communal living, group marriage, partner swapping, and non-monogamy. In the seventies, we realized that these new models by themselves weren't delivering the richer relationships we sought, and we began to break away from our dependence on each other as men and women. "I am not in this world to meet your needs," went Fritz Perls's Gestalt Prayer, and we had the Me Decade. It was a critical step in our collective consciousness, for never before had we asked on such a widespread scale, "What do I want?"

Finally, in the eighties, we have discovered that we want more than "space" in our relationships. What we want, after all, is each other, but on wholly new terms. We are struggling to forge relationships that provide security and intimacy without robbing us of the freedom from traditional roles and the self-sufficiency we worked so hard to gain in the sixties and seventies, relationships which provide closeness without limiting who we are.

We are still in the middle of all this chaos. As pioneers, we are continuing to shape our respective men's, women's, and human movements, and trying to hammer out new models for relating to each other in egalitarian, mutually enhancing, and deeply pleasurable relationships.

The movements of recent decades have heightened our expectations about what is possible between two people. We want deep intimacy, equality, enlightened communication, and pleasurable sex. At the same time, because of the factors which shape the Great Emotional Depression, these qualities seem harder than ever before to achieve. Those of us who are still without the love we seek are in a kind of Emotional Third World in which images of ecstatic, liberated relationships tantalize us but are exasperatingly elusive.

I don't know how men and women will resolve their impasse. But I'm confident we will. Only very recently has the balance of the seesaw been upset. In a few decades, we will look back on this tumultuous time and see it as an early stage in the resolution we will then be embracing. I believe we are in a short period of history, now, during which men and women are at different phases of their social and psychological evolution. It's difficult right now, and like the Depression of the 1930s, we can't see how we'll ever move on. But we did then, and we will this time. Somehow, we'll forge an emotional "New Deal," and men and women will find the common ground they now seek.

But that brings us to a critical question: What do we do in the meantime, those of us who want love now and can't wait around for the next phase of the revolution?

That is the topic of this book.

Descriptions of our times abound. Much has already been written about the dilemmas women face, the confusion men feel, and the specific problems that our times have spawned, such as misogyny and addictive behavior.

In this book, rather than describing them one more time, I want to accept certain sociological and psychological factors as *given* and discuss what you as an individual can do if you want to overcome them. In my observation, singles use "the hard facts" as excuses for staying single rather than viewing them as obstacles to be overcome.

So before we get started, let's agree on some of the facts of our current situation. Virtually all the singles I spoke to agree—based only on their own experience—that these conditions exist. (Everyone also agrees there are welcome exceptions to these broad generalizations.) I am making no attempt to be scientific here, nor to present shocking new information. These are axioms. In this book we will not discuss *why* these conditions are as they are, and we will not lament them. Rather, we will talk only about how you can get around these unfortunate difficulties if you would prefer to share your life with an intimate partner rather than go it alone.

Finding love is a challenge today because:

- In general, work-place skills are taught, valued, and reinforced, and intimacy skills are not. Thus, it's hard to find time for love, and when we do, we are ill-prepared for the demands an intimate relationship makes. We are good at work, but we aren't as good at love.
- Men and women are at different phases of their political and social evolution. Women have learned about and become a part of "men's world" faster than men have learned about and become a part of "women's world." Women have gained professional and work-place skills faster than men have gained interpersonal, emotional, nurturing skills. Men and women both become frustrated about what the other sex wants and what the other sex is able to give.
- In most geographical areas, the women who are available and looking for a relationship slightly outnumber the men who are available and looking.
- Fear of commitment is rampant among both men and women, but especially, it seems, among men. Large numbers of otherwise wonderful single men are resolutely opposed to—or somehow incapable of—making a commitment to a woman for a long-term, intimate relationship.

- Meeting eligible members of the opposite sex is not as easy as it was in college. Indeed, it is not easy at all.
- The rise of sexually transmitted diseases has introduced caution and awkwardness into the early stages of romantic encounters.

In the thirties, people wrote books about how to make a living despite adverse conditions. This book is about how to find love despite the adverse conditions of the Great Emotional Depression.

These are troubled times for lovers. The question is, are you going to let this defeat you? Or are you going to take it as all the more reason to become systematic and deliberate in your search for love?

A Final Question to Get You Started

So why are you still single anyway?

Just unlucky?

Both to people who have found love and to those who have not, it *feels* like luck plays a large role:

> God, we were so lucky to find each other! What if one of us hadn't gone to that party? It's scary to think we might never have met!

Or:

> How did *they* get so lucky? Why can't I find someone like that? Why not me???

Luck may be a factor. But it is the purpose of this book to suggest that the harder you work, the luckier you will get. Luck needs help. And luck has a hard time breaking through if you continually stand in its way.

Besides luck, then, why are you still single?

Let me invite you to do an experiment.

Throughout the book, I have occasionally suggested "experiments" you might want to try. Since the purpose of an experiment is to gather data, it can never fail. If you try one, you will find out *something* about yourself, and that is the spirit in which I suggest them. Usually, I have no specific outcome in mind but hope that the process itself will be educational. In my personal life, whenever I find myself at an impasse, I devise an experiment as a way to move off dead center and get a new perspective. Often, I am very surprised and could never have predicted what I end up discovering. I hope that you have a similar experience with some of the experiments I propose.

You may wish to get a little notebook or journal in which to do your experiments, since many, though not all, of them require some writing. That way you can keep them together and refer back to the ones you found meaningful. Also, whenever you do an experiment, date it. One of the most educational ways to use an experiment is to repeat it after several months or years. It can be enlightening to see what changes and what doesn't.

For the first experiment, I invite you to answer for yourself the question "Why am I still single?" before you begin to read my theories about what the reasons might be. That way, as you read through my reasons, you will have a gauge. Is this a reason you already realized was a factor in your life? Is this a reason that doesn't apply to you? Or is it a reason that *does* apply to you but that you had not been aware of? It may be interesting for you to see whether the reasons I suggest in the chapters that follow already showed up on your list in one form or another. We will use the list you make now in another experiment at the end of the book.

EXPERIMENT #1

In your experiments notebook, list *everything* that is a factor in your current relationship status. Let your mind wander, and list every reason: historical, psychological, circumstantial, attitudinal: Why are you single?

After you make your own list, compare it with the following "reasons I am still single" often given by participants in my workshops:

- I want to be alone.
- I haven't found the right person.
- I'm still hurting from my last relationship.

- I'm working on myself; I don't feel ready yet.
- I'm too busy.
- I see my friends pouring out their emotions on losing relationships. I don't want to waste my time.
- I enjoy my privacy; I value my independence.
- My standards are too high. I'm too fussy, too critical.
- I don't have the energy because my work is too important to me.
- I don't have the skills to meet new people.
- Whenever I get close to someone, I back off.
- I don't want to deal with the hassles.
- I keep hooking up with people who don't want to become committed.
- I'm too hard to live with, too set in my ways.
- I don't want *to want* love too much because what if I never find it? I need to prepare myself for that possibility.
- I'm afraid I'll get into a relationship and later discover I don't like it. Then I'll feel trapped.
- I don't feel as if I'm any good as a potential partner. I wouldn't respect anyone who would choose me.
- I'm too needy. My desire for a relationship is too strong.
- I hate dating and looking.
- There's a wall around my heart.
- I'm furious with the opposite sex and every member of it I meet makes me angrier.
- I'm afraid of failing a second time. One failed marriage is enough.
- I don't want anyone to become too dependent on me.
- I don't want to become too dependent on anyone else.
- I want to get my career together first.
- If I make a commitment, I'll lose myself.
- I'm afraid of being confined to a role.
- I've put in years convincing myself that it's okay to be single!

Whatever your reasons are for being single, if you want to be in a relationship, *no reason is good enough!*

Here, then, are ten strategies that many involuntary singles overlook *without realizing it,* ten powerful but invisible ways in which singles can keep the Great Emotional Depression from defeating them in their search for love. This book will identify the strategies and show you how to put them into action. As one who found love during the Great Emotional Depression using the very means I am about to suggest, I invite you to take control of your dream and make it come true, for, as people who are in truly happy relationships seem to agree, love is a corner worth painting yourself into!

Chapter 1

The First Strategy: Examine Your Hidden Ambivalence

Wishful thinking has not brought you love.

Neither has apathy, depression, denial, anger, panic, analyzing the problem, blaming the opposite sex, or cursing the bleak demographics.

So if you still want love in your life, the question is, what will bring you love?

Perseverance.

The way to achieve any goal is first to know what the goal is and then to proceed unswervingly toward it, patiently but persistently overcoming any obstacles which present themselves—with perseverance, tenacity, and determination.

Yet in spite of all our obsessing about the state of relationships today, perseverance is one of the rarest qualities to be found among singles. We've all heard about the tortoise and the hare, but we failed to learn the lesson of the tortoise. Instead, we dash about like the hare, trying relationships that don't work, tormenting ourselves with theories, believing our excuses, following one false lead, then another, and finally, like the hare, simply falling asleep in the middle of the race.

Why?

Why do we long for love, yet fail to proceed in a determined fashion toward this goal? Why do we get sidetracked?

Ambivalence is one major reason. We aren't sure which race we want to be in or whether we want to be in any race at all.

Is love worth it?

Am I better off alone?

Is there anyone out there I could even tolerate?

Will I lose my independence?

Will I be too vulnerable?

Will I have to compromise too much?

Will my career suffer?

This book is about perseverance. But we can't talk about *staying* in the race until we talk about whether to race at all. That is the main stumbling block for most singles: not *getting* what we want in love, but *knowing* what we want. We keep ourselves from moving forward because we aren't sure which way we want to move.

The most important prerequisite for finding a satisfying intimate relationship is wanting one. Wholeheartedly, genuinely, earnestly, single-mindedly, and without reservation.

If you sincerely want an intimate partner, you are already beyond the roughest hurdle. But if you aren't altogether certain, then you need to take a close look at the issue of ambivalence and how to move beyond it.

Involuntary singles fall into two categories: singles who want a relationship but haven't met the right person yet; and singles who, whether consciously or unconsciously, are ambivalent. Distinguishing between the two types is difficult because their language is identical. Both kinds say, "I *really* want a wonderful relationship in my life." But the first type *really* means it. And the second type, as it turns out, doesn't. What the second type actually means is something more like, "I want a relationship, but equally or more important to me is

- not having to take risks
- progressing in my career
- hanging on to my great lifestyle
- avoiding pain
- keeping my secrets to myself
- proving I'm right that the opposite sex is the problem.

The ambivalent person is one who wants a relationship but who values something else equally—or more. The competing value will demand allegiance and will surreptitiously sabotage anything that stands in its way—like love.

Some singles are well aware of their ambivalence. They make statements like these:

- I want to be in a relationship, but I don't want to give up all I love about being single.
- I want to be in love, but I'm afraid of losing control.
- I'm torn between my career and my love life.
- My lover is wonderful, but maybe I can do better.
- I want to be married, but I'm terrified of another divorce.
- I'm afraid what I'll gain won't be worth what I'll have to give up.

Ambivalence is especially powerful in its ability to keep you single when it remains unconscious. Many singles genuinely believe they want a relationship and are unaware of the injunctions which rule their lives and demand total compliance: "Thou shalt not risk. Thou shalt not reveal thy secrets." These rules of survival, partly because they are unconscious, are far more influential in our lives than our conscious desire for love and connection.

I received a phone call from a woman named Michelle. She knew I was interviewing people and wanted the opportunity to tell me her story. She had participated in one of my workshops six months before. Michelle told me:

I totally discounted the issue of ambivalence when you talked about it. I couldn't think of any reason why I didn't want a man in my life. I felt ready! But after your workshop, I realized that in spite of all my new determination, I still wasn't doing anything about it. Whenever I planned to go to a singles event or answer an ad, I found a reason not to. I finally realized, I *hate* meeting men for the first time—under any circumstance. And I think avoiding those situations—which I dread—was a higher priority for me than finding someone. When I understood that that's what was going on, it really shocked me. Now, it takes a monumental effort every time, but I am forcing myself to meet men. I still don't like it, but it's getting easier, and I feel *so good* that I'm doing this. The way I force myself, by the way, is I always make my plans *with* a woman friend. Then it's much harder to back out.

Another woman spoke up during a workshop. She was thirty-nine and had her own successful public relations firm. She reported:

> I *know* what my competing priority is! My career, my lifestyle. I don't know how I'd fit a man in! And I'm not sure I want to. I guess that's why I'm here. I think if I could find the *right man,* I'd want to make a commitment to him, but finding the right man seems so remote. But then, I don't do anything to try to meet him either. Ambivalent? Who, me?

Whether conscious or unconscious, ambivalence is one of the most common and most powerful reasons why singles who would like to be in a relationship still aren't. Reluctant to relinquish the advantages of singlehood, at the same time they fear they may be missing out on something wonderful in a committed relationship. Often, they are conducting an active search for a mate while secretly hoping inside that they don't find one. Or, they may be talking about how much they want love, but doing nothing toward that end.

If you are not wholeheartedly committed to love, and if you do not hold finding love as a top priority, you may be talking and behaving as though you want love but holding back on your follow-through.

Before we talk more about ambivalence in general, let me give you the opportunity to think about your own. How certain are you about what you *most* want in your life? How high a priority is love for you? What are your competing priorities?

EXPERIMENT #2

Ask yourself this question: What is more compelling for you right now than finding a good relationship? List in your notebook anything in your life which seems to be a higher priority for you *at this time*.

With regard to each item on this list, ask yourself this question: How long will this continue to be a priority for me?

Some of your higher priorities may seem reasonable to you, and some may seem irrational. Search hard, and list everything which may be a competing priority.

To help you get started on this experiment, here is a sampling of responses that have been shared during my workshops:

Higher priorities for me right now than finding a relationship, and how long I expect each to be a higher priority:

Finding a job—three to six months
Paying off my debts—one year
Building my house—eighteen months
Getting my China fellowship—two years
Finishing my dissertation—six months
Not having to date and do the singles scene—forever
Keeping my life the way it is: career, kids, house, friends
    —five years???
Keeping my options open—forever
Nursing my hurt over my divorce—short time, *I hope*
Spending time with my kids—six years
Not having to waste time on mediocre relationships—
    forever
Retaining my independence, freedom to travel, etc.—a
    few more years?

The Age of Ambivalence

If you found in the above experiment that you have several competing priorities, or one very strong one, then you are not alone, for ours is the Age of Ambivalence.

Intimacy is both appealing and intimidating. Singlehood is both freeing and lonely. Men are supposed to be successful *and* family-oriented. Women are supposed to eschew patriarchy but love men.

In the sixties and seventies, singles banded together to stand up to the larger society that viewed singles as flawed human beings. This "singles movement" has, fortunately, largely succeeded in achieving general acceptance of the single lifestyle. But it also created an attractive alternative to coupling up, leaving a generation caught between two appealing choices. Now, both men and women search for love with one hand and sabotage it with the other. They come to my seminars on how to find love, yet spend the whole day convincing us all that love is restricting. Or they fall in love with married people. Or they keep themselves too busy to date but then complain about how hard it is to meet people. They dance around relentlessly on the edge of the pool, not willing to dive in and not willing to walk away, get dressed, and forget it.

The Living-Together Trap

Perhaps nothing symbolizes the ambivalence of our era better than the institution of living together. I am not referring here to couples who have a clear commitment to each other but have chosen not to get married. Rather, I refer to the couples who date for a while and then, because they don't want either to give it up or to commit to each other, decide to live together. Side by side, they stand on the edge of the pool, prolonging their mutual ambivalence rather than helping each other to move through it.

Janice and David, whom I met because they attended my workshops, are a case in point. David is a corporate attorney and Janice is the director of public relations and marketing at David's firm. They had worked at the same place for five years but met and began to date shortly after Janice got a divorce. David is a real romantic and pursued Janice steadily but gently. She responded cautiously but soon found she was very much in love. Yet every time I saw Janice, she was reporting another fight. It seemed David was more committed to the relationship than she was. Also, she had a hard time with David's two young boys and didn't like the way he treated them. They fought about other things, too. For example, Janice was critical of the way David dressed, and David would finally get tired of her nagging and blow up at her.

Months would go by before I saw one or the other of them, but each time the story was similar. They loved each other, but they were "having problems."

One day, Janice called me, all excited: she and David were buying a house together. "Oh!" I replied. "Are you getting married?"

"Heavens no!" she cried out. "I'm not ready for that. Living together is the best of both worlds. I still feel independent, but I have intimacy and companionship. This way, we'll know that we aren't staying together because of some vow, but because we choose to be together every day."

"And you know you can still choose to split every day, too," I wanted to add. That seemed to me to be the real advantage of their plan, but it remained unspoken. I also wanted to ask her, "Have you considered a trial separation?" but it seemed the wrong question to ask at that moment. Besides, I knew it would be useless.

David and Janice were *both* ambivalent about their relationship, and they were not willing to face their ambivalence directly and resolve it. Instead, they institutionalized it. They actually agreed with each other to remain on the fence for as long as they could both stand it.

The epilogue to this story is that David and Janice lived together for two years, spent a small fortune on couple counseling, and then, with a great deal of mutual resentment and pain and two angry little boys, broke up.

Living together is a fundamentally ambiguous partnership which represents the worst of both worlds rather than the best. As a single, you lose the freedom of exploring new relationships, having your own place to bring people home to, making your own decisions, setting your own schedule. You're not really single anymore.

But you aren't able to explore genuine intimacy either, because the cloud of uncertainty that hangs over the relationship precludes it. You never get to experience the unfolding that begins to occur in a relationship of complete trust. You may feel inhibited about releasing tension in a great gush of anger because every time you fight, the entire relationship could be up for grabs. Rather than furthering exploration of the subtle reaches of deep intimacy, moving in together usually shifts the focus to mundane issues like who's going to do the shopping. Neither singlehood nor an intimate bond is served by institutionalizing the ambivalence no one has the courage to resolve. All you get is more information about your daily habits— one of the easiest things to work out eventually if genuine, unabridged love is there in the first place.

When it became popular in the sixties, living together looked like a revolutionary solution to the problem of marrying prematurely for logistical reasons. The idea was to have a "trial marriage" before making the big commitment. But too often it has turned out to help couples postpone decisions that would serve them far better in the long run than living for months with one foot in the relationship and one foot out the door.

The "I'm Trying" Trap

Ambivalence kept Janice and David *in* a difficult relationship. But for many singles, ambivalence keeps them alone. They institutionalize their ambivalence by "trying" to find love.

I once told a Gestalt therapist that I was trying to lose weight.

"Trying isn't enough," she told me. "Here." She threw a pencil on the floor. "Try to pick up this pencil."

I bent over and picked it up.

"No," she said. "I didn't say pick it up. I said *try* to pick it up." Then I reached and reached for the pencil. I touched it; I moved it. "I'm trying," I said. But the pencil never got picked up.

I got the message: Committing oneself to trying to accomplish a goal is very different from committing oneself to accomplishing the goal.

But ambivalent singles try a lot. They may *think* they are committed to the goal of finding a lover, but they are not at all committed to the process they must go through to achieve the goal.

Annie, a forty-five-year-old professional photographer, told me she had been trying to find a long-term relationship for twenty years. "I really want to be married," were her exact words. When I met her, she was dating a fellow photographer of whom she seemed to be very fond. "What are your hesitations about him?" I asked her.

She thought for a while. "I guess he's moving too fast for me. He likes to spend four or five nights a week together. I feel crowded. And he's almost too sweet. He's real tolerant of my needs. But I don't know, I feel like backing away from him. Something doesn't feel right."

When you really want to get married, having your lover eager to spend time with you is a welcome development, not a problem. Yet Annie genuinely believed she wanted permanent love. She didn't pay attention to her strong inner need to remain alone. Precisely because she didn't pay attention to it, and therefore was unaware of its strength, it controlled her life. For twenty years, she had been "trying" to find love, and for twenty years she had been alone. She was confused because her desire to find love seemed real to her.

Much later, through a coincidence, I had the pleasure of meeting the man in question, Peter. By then he was married to a social worker and they seemed genuinely happy. I found out their courtship had lasted only four months. Peter was not ambivalent about what he wanted, and he kept looking until he found someone who was equally clear-headed about her desires.

Betsy teaches math and statistics at a junior college. She told me:

> I really am trying! I hate personals ads but I answer one a month. I've never met anyone that way. I hate singles groups too, but I make myself go to one a month. I've tried dozens of methods over the years. I joined a dating service but dropped it after two months of lousy results.

Betsy wanted a relationship. But through my conversations with her, it became clear that she also had a need to prove that all men are "emotional cripples," that the singles scene is dreadful, and that her single status was not "her fault." And again, because she didn't pay attention to those inner needs, they were the needs that always got met in the end.

Betsy's competing priority was subtle: she wanted to be right about how awful the singles scene is. She had unconsciously committed herself to trying to find a relationship —but never actually finding one. That way, she could be right in all her claims about the man shortage, the gaps between men and women, and the unfair predicament of single women.

After Betsy became aware of how she was sabotaging herself, she began to pay closer attention to her behavior and her conversation. She gradually realized that her negativity was toxic—even to her, and she was able to give it up. She stopped *trying* to find a relationship, and began to work seriously on making one happen. She did connect with a man, and she told me later, she probably would not have taken a close look at this man had she not become aware of her ambivalence and paid attention to how it was defeating her.

Ambivalence: Pros and Cons

Ambivalence is not all bad. In fact, remaining on the fence has some distinct advantages, and people stay there for very compelling reasons.

For one thing, you never have to go through the agony of deciding anything. Some decisions are pretty earthshaking and avoiding them is certainly the safest route. That was the reason David and Janice prolonged their ambivalence by moving in together. They didn't want to make a final decision about whether to get married or split up.

For another thing, you never have to give up anything, but can instead keep a little of everything you want. For example, if you *want* to stop smoking but you also *don't* want to, you get to be what one psychologist calls a "class B member" of the Non-Smokers Club. You get to identify with non-smokers (it helps if you feel guilty), but you still get to smoke! It works the same way with relationships: if you are always looking, you get to be a class B member of the Intimacy Club. You *want* intimacy, but you get to stay single!

Ambivalence is an easy way out of some tough choices. But remaining ambivalent exacts a hideous price: You never get to experience anything fully. Whether you are alone or with a partner, part of you will always be gazing out the window at what you fear may be greener pastures.

If you are alone and ambivalent, you are likely to remain that way. Since it is easy to keep your life just as it is, there you shall remain, surrounded by your rationalizations, your explanations, your excuses, and all the other people you blame.

If you have no doubt that you want an intimate partner, there are plenty of things you can do to find one. If you aren't doing them, chances are you aren't altogether certain you want one.

What to Do About Ambivalence

It is not possible to undo ambivalence by an act of will.

The only thing you *can* do is pay attention to it. *As long as ambivalence remains unconscious it remains in control.* It becomes a little voice inside you saying, "Careful. Don't go too far. You'll have to give up too much. Don't move in together; you are moving too fast. On the other hand, don't hesitate forever or you'll lose out completely."

But if you can identify your ambivalence and bring it out in the open, then you can begin to make choices about it. And clarity will begin to emerge all by itself.

So don't push yourself; don't try to force yourself not to be ambivalent. Rather, begin to identify the sources of your ambivalence and become increasingly aware of them.

Pay attention to signs of confusion: fears, doubts, hesitations, endless debates in your head, obsessive conversations with your friends. Recognize that if you never make up your mind about what you want, you may never get it.

Ambivalence is normal and reasonable, so be careful not to berate yourself. Your ambivalence doesn't make you "weak" or "wrong," so don't judge it. Just notice it.

Be realistic about your goals. You will not be able to eliminate all the voices within you which compete for attention. The real point is not to be without ambivalence—a nearly impossible goal. What you want to strive for instead is the ability to act decisively in the presence of ambivalence.

If you want love in your life, but your desire for love is not wholehearted, genuine, earnest, singleminded, and without reservation, that is, you want love but you are also ambivalent and have competing priorities, one option is that you can *behave as though* you have a strong, *un*ambivalent desire for love. Your *behavior* is what will bring you results, as we shall see in the chapters that follow. If you can make yourself *behave as though* a love relationship is a strong desire for you, you will be overcoming your ambivalence—not eliminating it, but acting decisively in the presence of it.

The decision whether to build your life alone or together with an intimate partner is momentous. Yet, in the face of ambivalence, you may be failing to make any decision at all about what to strive for. The way your life turns out is not an accident; you have a great deal of control over it. If you don't decide what you want, you are leaving some pretty important things up to fate!

All important decisions are made on the basis of insufficient data because you can't be sure what will result from your decision until you make it. If you wait until you are absolutely positive, you'll wait forever, and a non-decision will become a decision by default.

Do you want an intimate partner in your life?

The secret to making a decision when you are ambivalent is to consider carefully all the information you do have, make an informed decision, and then commit yourself to the decision you have made. You are not deciding between right and wrong or good and bad, but between several options, all of which may be good and right. So make a decision even though you are still ambivalent and then trust that you and the universe working together will make it a good, right decision. You can't take all the paths in the woods, but once you select one, throw yourself fully into that journey and don't keep thinking about the path you didn't take.

Remember, ambivalence is not good or bad, it just is. If you recognize that you have ambivalence, do not judge it. You cannot change your ambivalence by feeling bad about it or by ordering it away. Both of these tactics will be counterproductive for you.

Rather, simply live with your ambivalence. Think about and honor all the values that are competing within you. Accept your ambivalence as an old friend, a part of you that is familiar and that has served you well for a long time. If you want to act in spite of your ambivalence by moving toward one choice or another, you will.

The following experiments will help you get started on a program of paying attention to what you want *most.*

EXPERIMENT #3
a. On one page, list everything you would gain—all the positive ways in which your life would change—if you got into a primary, committed relationship today.

b. Next, on a separate page, list all that you would lose—
negative ways in which your life would change—if you got into
this kind of a relationship now.

Which list is longer? Which items are more important to
you? One strong consideration could outweigh a whole string
of more minor ones.

Now write a statement in your notebook saying what you
learned by doing this experiment.

EXPERIMENT #4

Place yourself somewhere on the continuum below. If none of
the statements fits you exactly, write your own and put it in the
appropriate spot.

Many people choose to occupy two positions: one is what
they want for themselves now; the other, what they would
eventually like for themselves.

1	2	3	4	5
I would never marry or commit myself to one person under any circumstance.	I think I want to remain single and date around, but I'm not sure.	I'm ambivalent. A part of me wants to be with someone, but I have lots of doubts and fears.	I'm fairly sure I want to be in a relationship but my doubts are _____.	I know I want a committed, long-term relationship. I have not a shred of doubt.

One woman who was working on this exercise in a workshop
threw up her hands in frustration, declaring, "I'm ambivalent
about where to place myself on the ambivalence scale!"

EXPERIMENT #5

If you are genuinely undecided about what you want—with
regard to a specific relationship or in general—try this experi-

ment. The purpose of it is to give you more data about where you stand.

Give yourself an uninterrupted half hour. Sit comfortably. Close your eyes. Breathe easily for a minute to quiet yourself. Now, for ten minutes, try believing that you want to get married (to a specific person or in general). Really throw yourself into it and cast away all doubts. Pretend just as hard as you can.

Then for another ten minutes, believe the opposite and throw yourself fully into that option. Act as though the decision has already been made.

The important thing to observe during this experiment is how you feel, *not* what you think. Your thoughts are what keep you ambivalent. Rationally weighing all your alternatives and assessing your pros and cons can be an endless and ultimately confusing endeavor.

But if you pay attention to what you are feeling, you may discover that a decision has already been made, and that you are obscuring it with all your data!

Thoughts occur in your head. Feelings occur in your body. So while you are doing this experiment, pay close attention to various parts of your body. Where do you feel sensation? It may be subtle, so focus your attention. Do you feel any emotion in your eyes? Is your jaw tight? Are your shoulders tense? Does your stomach ache? Do you feel tearful? Can you sense relief sweeping over you? Does your heart feel warm and open?

As you imagine that you have already made a decision, do you feel tense and anxious or relieved or excited or afraid?

The information you want is how you *feel* about your hypothetical decision. You will not get this by listening to the rational pros and cons of your dilemma. You must quiet your thoughts and focus on what you feel in your body.

Experiments 2, 3, 4, and 5 are designed to increase your awareness about your own state of ambivalence. Let me reiterate, whatever you discover, simply begin to pay closer attention to it. You may want to repeat the experiments in a few weeks to see whether any movement has occurred. Keep in mind your ambivalence; awareness of it can make a very big difference in your life. On the other hand, if you are ambivalent and you don't pay any attention to it, what we say in the rest of this book will have very little impact; your ambivalence will take precedence over it.

A Word to the Non-Ambivalent

We have discussed ambivalence at length. But we should also take a look at what freedom from ambivalence looks like, for certainty, it turns out, has its own set of problems.

Let us return briefly to the two groups we identified at the beginning of this chapter: (1) involuntary singles who know what they want but haven't found the right person yet, and (2) involuntary singles who are ambivalent about what they want.

The first group is composed of those rare singles among us who are *not* ambivalent. They are certain about what they want and determined to find it. And they will.

Not all these people want marriage. Within this group are people who want a whole range of relationship styles. But they all know exactly what they want, and they know with certainty that they want it.

How can you tell whether you are in this group? For one thing, as you read this, you will find it validating. You will have the feeling "See? It *can* be true. It *is* possible that my only real problem is that I haven't found the right person yet!"

If you are unambivalent, but your perseverance hasn't produced yet, your challenge is to maintain your clarity in the face of a barrage of books, articles, and well-wishers whose aim is to convince you that something else is wrong.

Most books and articles directed at singles tell you either that there is something wrong with you for wanting a relationship and that you ought to be basking in the joys of singlehood, or that there is some pathological reason why

you are still single. You make foolish choices or you love too much or you haven't gotten your own act together or you are addictive or you repeat counterproductive behavior of your parents—or you have hidden ambivalence. You must have enough faith in your convictions not to get sidetracked by all these scenarios—which are surely valid for many people, but not for you.

You are in a minority, and you will not find many soul mates on this subject. But if you are convinced deep inside that you will find the right person and you will know when you have found him or her, then simply persevere. Knowing what you want is the hard part, and you are already there. But getting what you want still requires action, tenacity, and time.

More About Perseverance

Now we are ready to say more about how to pursue your goal of finding love without getting sidetracked, how to commit yourself to the process, and persevere until your goal is achieved.

We have spoken about the importance of knowing what you want. And in the chapters that follow, we will examine the obstacles that present themselves to involuntary singles. But I want to pause now to look more closely at the two aspects of perseverance: patience and persistence, for they are both critical.

Patience without persistence is apathy, laziness, or indifference.

Persistence without patience can easily lead to desperation, panic, anxiety, or depression.

But the combination of persistence and patience leads to *results,* with pleasure and good self-esteem on the way to the results, however long they are in coming: a rich journey and a certain destination.

You can't stop working for what you want. But at the same time, you can't become frantic in your activity either. Your motto must be Determination Without Desperation.

"Determination" means that you systematically and deliberately do things which will further your cause, move you closer to your goal. It also means that you stop doing things which prevent you from reaching your goal. This book contains many specific strategies for a determined involuntary single in search of love, things to do and to stop doing.

"Without desperation" means that you operate with trust. You believe that doing the right things will work for you *given enough time.* You realize that fortune seldom comes in the form or at the time you expect it. You can't *make* love happen for you. You can make certain that if it wants to happen, you aren't standing in its way. You have to accept that doing the most you can do for yourself is all you can do. Take an active role in the things you can control and let go of the things you cannot control. As *The Book of Runes,* ancient oracles from the Vikings, says, "set your house in order, tend to business, be clear, and wait on the Will of Heaven."

Persistence and patience.

Determination without desperation.

Let us now proceed to consider *how* to persevere, how to proceed steadily toward your goal of an intimate partnership in your life, trusting as you go that the Fates are on your side.

The search for a person with whom to share your life does not have to be difficult or discouraging. *The way you go about conducting your search makes all the difference.* As we shall see, if you do it right, the search for love can enrich your life, contribute to your self-esteem, *and* make your fondest dreams come true.

Chapter 2

The Second Strategy: Ignore the Dread Statistics

The first obstacle singles in search of love must overcome is the seemingly horrendous numbers problem. One single woman I spoke with put it this way:

> I'm not sure why I should even bother to read your book. Nothing it says can alter the *facts: There aren't any men left.* I've waited too long, and now—it says so in *Newsweek*—the odds that I will marry are *smaller* that the odds than I will be killed by a terrorist!

The study of census data which created the Summer of Panic in '86 was only one of a long line of doomsday reports which emerge regularly from the drawing boards of statisticians and writers. They paint a picture of a vast game of musical chairs, with a hundred women in a room and only four chairs. They would have you believe that finding a man to marry is about as likely as winning the state lottery.

On and on these articles go, citing actual numbers and percentages and always the "shocking" ratios: five single women for every available man figured one way; three to one if you factor in gays. Thoughtful writers will tell you which cities have better odds and which age brackets to avoid—as though you had any choice in the matter.

Singles emerge from this thicket of statistics feeling as though they've been hit in the solar plexus. They start with, "See? That's why I'm not married. It's not my fault!" Then they move through "This isn't fair!" and "What am I going to do" to, finally, "I'm doomed."

Remember the oil shortage? We suspected all along that it was artificially created, and we were right. Just so with the man shortage: it has sold a lot of books and magazines.

But if you are serious about finding intimacy in your life, you can relax.

Here's why.

The Bennett-Bloom-Craig study that created such a fracas in 1986 actually zeroed in on two facts: that, from 1947 to 1964, more babies were born each year than were born in the previous year; and that women usually marry older men. Thus, the authors of the study concluded that women born in 1950 are looking for mates among the smaller pool of men born in 1947. And each year a woman postpones marriage, more of the older men she presumably seeks are married or molded into immutable bachelors. According to this logic, the older she gets, the smaller her pool of available men becomes.

Other studies tease out other isolated "facts." Between 1970 and 1980, they will tell you, the number of never-married women between twenty-five and twenty-nine doubled, from one in ten to one in five. Women outnumber men in the general population to begin with, and women outlive men by eight years. Divorced men marry sooner after splitting up than women do. There are more gay men than gay women, and more men in prison than women.

If we plotted all these figures together on a graph, we would probably discover that the number of men available for marriage is minus a half million! So where do all those men come from who flock to singles bars and dating services by the hundreds?

Here is what the number-mongers *don't* tell you, and I assure you, it changes the picture considerably:

1. The shortage that the Bennett-Bloom-Craig study identified is a shortage of *older* men only. Baby-boom women who marry same-age or younger men are not included in the dismal picture this study painted. (And, as long as we raised the subject of age, there is a lot to be said in favor of younger men. They tend to be more interested in egalitarian marriages, involved fatherhood, and shared housework than those allegedly more desirable older men. They are less threatened by successful career women and more available for genuine intimacy, too. And since men die younger than women, your chances of having companionship in your golden years are greater if you marry a younger man.)

Already, the image of the hooded terrorist bursting out

of your closet in the middle of the night with a submachine gun is beginning to fade, isn't it?

2. If you were born before 1947 or after 1964, you are also not included in the grim picture, even if you want to marry "up." After 1964, the number of births declined each year. For you, the pool of older men right now is larger than the pool of women your age.

3. The categories most demographers study are decidedly inadequate. Bennett, Bloom, and Craig measured only "married" and "single," failing to acknowledge that "single" includes (a) women who are happily cohabiting with male lovers, (b) lesbians, (c) women who are part of a committed, intimate partnership but living alone, and (d) women who remain alone by choice. "Single *and looking*" is the figure that would be of interest to study, but because statisticians don't go out and interview the women they count, they end up describing groups which are irrelevant to us real people. What we care about is people who are available for relationships. Some singles are not available, and some available people are not single, so counting all singles and only singles gives a misleading picture.

The news media that base their crisis reports on these studies would apparently love to have us believe that *all* the single women the census counts are involuntarily alone and miserable about it. Alongside their stories they run illustrations of women with paperback romances on their laps and teddy bears on their beds staring plaintively off into space! But in fact, many of the women who will never marry have freshly dry-cleaned suits lying on their Ralph Lauren–covered beds and they are poring intently over computer printouts, medical journals, or legal briefs.

So, if you are an unattached woman who does want an intimate connection in your life, you should already be feeling much better on the basis of statistics alone. If you are open to meeting younger men and you eliminate from all your alleged competitors those who are *voluntarily* unmarried because they are lesbian, living with a man, or single by choice, then your "odds" are considerably brighter than they were a few paragraphs ago.

And that's not even the best news!

4. The real point is that statistics about "a population" are irrelevant with regard to your personal life. Even the statisticians would agree that their "averages" and

"trends" say nothing about your individual odds of marrying. Numbers by themselves, without interviews or polls, say nothing about your inner desires, your motivation, your fears, your ability to flirt, or a hundred other factors that have more to do with your own chances of finding love than the numbers someone printed on a page in a magazine.

The day I first heard about the report that doomed women over forty to eternal singlehood, I gave the keynote address at a conference for single men and women. I found myself facing over two hundred eligible single men. How could anyone convince me that the supply of single men had simply dried up! A singles magazine in the San Francisco area prints more than eight hundred personal ads every month, half of them from men—men who care enough about connecting with a woman that they go to the trouble of placing an ad. Speaking of odds, the odds that among those four hundred there aren't at least a dozen "good" men, whatever that may mean to you, must be minuscule.

The bar graphs that newspapers print to show how dismal the "man shortage" is always looks positively encouraging to me. Suppose the bar graph for your city looked like this:

Number of single men and women in your town

| WOMEN | 100,000 |
| MEN | 70,000 |

Look at how long the area on the women's bar is that *does* match up with the men's bar. A single woman in your town has 70,000 men to choose from!

If you are searching for love, your problem is not numbers. You should behave as though these silly articles don't exist. *Your chances of finding a good relationship are what you make them.* There are men out there. And all you have to find for yourself is one. Whether or not you find that man has nothing to do with statistics and everything to do with how serious you are about wanting a good relationship and what you are willing to do to make it happen. If you are highly motivated and quite active in your search, you will increase your odds dramatically over your sisters who do nothing to promote their cause.

So don't let the statistics discourage you. Women of all ages are connecting with terrific men all the time. There is no reason why you can't be one of them if you want to be and if you are willing to do something about it—persistently and patiently!

Chapter 3

The Third Strategy: Abandon the Myth That There Are No Good Ways to Meet People

One day, a very polite-sounding gentleman, Walter, called to ask me if he could skip some portions of my workshop and come only to the part on how to meet people. I told him yes, even though I thought it a somewhat strange request.

On the appointed day, Walter did show up, just in time to receive my handout—a long list of methods for meeting people—everything from personal ads to hanging out in Porsche showrooms! Walter couldn't wait to get his hands on it, and for the next hour, he dominated the group discussion explaining to us in detail why each method on the list was a bad suggestion, hadn't worked in the past, and wouldn't work in the future.

Walter was a caricature of himself, but what he did in the extreme I have seen to a lesser extent in many "normal" singles: they don't want to relinquish their precious belief that there are no good ways to meet people. Always eager to hear about new methods, they breathe a sigh of relief when they can show that this too is an unworkable idea—for them.

So what's going on here? Why do singles often seem to take a perverse delight in placing limits on their arenas of opportunity?

No-good-ways-to-meet-people is a wonderful excuse to stay single without having to take responsibility for it. By relying on this explanation, singles can protect themselves from falling in love and either being rejected or having to face all the fears and dangers they imagine love entails. They are a little like the overweight woman who obsessively searches out every diet she can find, tries each one for two days, and then proudly tells everyone that diets don't work for her and that she will just always be fat.

But something even more subtle may be going on, too: the no-good-ways-to-meet-people excuse lets a single person keep hope alive, for all that stands between him or her and eternal bliss is some brilliant new magic method. That's why meeting people is such a popular subject. It is one of those topics—like dieting—on which one can never get enough information. We eagerly snatch up every new article on how to meet people in the hope of finding some elusive secret, something other people know but that we somehow missed out on. No-way-to-meet-people keeps many singles right where they want to be: single but hopeful. They get the safety of singlehood and the excitement of looking.

So before you launch further into this chapter, you should ask yourself whether you are genuinely interested in finding ways to meet people.

If you are, this is your lucky day, for I am about to give you that elusive secret you were fervently hoping for when you saw this chapter title on the contents page. I am about to fulfill your wish that someone would show you exactly where to go and what to do to meet the intimate partner you've always longed for.

Here is the secret. Ready?

It doesn't matter.

It doesn't matter what method or methods you use. All that matters is that you *do something*.

That's it. That's the entire secret.

It is simply untrue that there are no ways to meet people. This is just as untrue as that there are no people left to meet. There are enough people and enough ways to meet them. You can choose any "method." But you can't just read about it or plan to do it; you have to *do it* if you want it to be effective.

I realize, of course, that "doing something" is not necessarily all that easy. So I hereby offer a foolproof, five-part formula—including a list of places and methods for meeting people—which I call "How to Go Mate Shopping and

Still Be Able to Read Epic Novels." My method got its name from Jan, who told me,

> I love a cozy evening at home with the wood stove going, a glass of sherry, and a good novel. But I can't enjoy these evening anymore because there is always a voice in my head saying, "You should be out where you'll meet people. Go to a movie, go to a bar, go out for dessert." Every time I turn a page the voice says, "Okay, *now*, get out of the house!"

Most singles have a binge/purge mentality about dating, like Deborah, a thirty-two-year-old budget analyst:

> I get all caught up in my life and everything's going great and suddenly I'll realize I haven't had a date for six months. Then I panic and start going to three singles events a week and answer ten personal ads all at once—and in four weeks, I'm completely burned out and want to give up on the whole plan. Then I don't do anything for another six months.

A critical part of the five-part formula I'm about to suggest is maintaining a balance between doing nothing, on the one hand, and letting your life be controlled by your need to meet people, on the other. Neither extreme works; moderation is the key.

Here, then, is my tried and true five-part formula for mate seeking:

1. Recognize that mate shopping is not necessarily fun.
2. Establish a master plan.
3. Go for volume.
4. Use the Two-Hour Date.
5. Screen for "relationship-style-preference" first.

Part One: Recognize That Mate Shopping Is Not Necessarily Fun

Common wisdom is that you should seek out only those activities that you enjoy anyway when you are "looking."

Don't plan your life around meeting someone. If you like to hike, go on hikes. If you like to bowl, bowl. If you like to dance, attend dances. You will enjoy life more, and anyone you meet is likely to have interests compatible with yours.

There's absolutely nothing wrong with this approach *if you do it.* But it can be limiting. Too often it is a myopic guideline that serves primarily to keep you in a rut.

In a perfect world, we could all go about our daily routines and meet plenty of people to go out with. But it's not a perfect world. In the one we're stuck with, if you want an intimate partner, you have to go looking for one. Often that looking is not very pleasant, but that is no reason *not* to do it.

Unfortunately but undeniably, partner shopping has certain similarities to job hunting. When you are looking for a job, you spend time at it; you're organized and systematic; you both advertise yourself and respond to companies that are advertising; you go to interviews that may be scary, intimidating, or disappointing; you get rejected; and often, because you are unemployed, your self-esteem, which is at a low point to begin with, bottoms out. But successful job seekers do not let any of this stop them. Even if they feel miserable, they dress up and put on a good face for the interview. And they keep answering ads.

All of this is—at least sometimes—true of the search for love and intimacy. I don't mean to imply that it *has* to be disagreeable. But far too many singles give up on the whole enterprise simply because, as they say, "It's a drag!" A lot of times it *is* a drag. Factor this in, and don't let it stop you! If you insist on enjoying every episode in your search for the right person, you will pay a big price: greatly reduced opportunities to meet people.

Many singles allow loneliness, depression, and low self-esteem to keep them out of circulation. Yet you wouldn't cancel a job interview just because you were feeling rotten. It's an unfortunate irony that when you most *need* your good feelings about yourself—when you are out of work or out of love—that is when they are most likely to abandon you. But consider this: if you can force yourself to act anyway, you may have quite a positive experience which can make you feel a lot better.

If you can keep your search active without doing anything that sounds like—or turns out to be—a drag, super!

Do it! Try to look upon your "shopping" as an adventure, an opportunity to meet new friends, to develop new interests.

But don't be unrealistic. It is far more important to be deliberate and systematic in looking for your dream love relationship than it is to enjoy thoroughly every moment of your continuing search. Don't *anticipate* misery, but don't give up just because you have some mediocre experiences.

Part Two: Establish a Master Plan

First: Sit down and make a list of a dozen or so activities for meeting people. At the end of this chapter is a list of suggestions to get you started, but don't let it limit you. Be imaginative. Talk with your friends about what they do. Together, create novel approaches.

Try to choose activities you think you might genuinely enjoy. But if you can't find enough of those, list ones you are willing to do—and discard the idea once and for all that mate shopping has to be enjoyable. Don't eliminate an idea because someone else had a bad experience with it. Try for yourself before you decide.

Next: now that you have a list of a dozen or more activities, select a few of your favorite ideas and *put them on your calendar.*

Choose a manageable, comfortable pace for yourself. You may schedule one activity a week, one a month, or one every two or three months. The advantage of having scheduled events on your calendar is that you can relax. Planning, an old trick borrowed from time-management experts, allows you to let go of the worry that you are not doing enough to meet new people. Instead, when your "voices" tell you to get out of the house, you can reassure yourself that you will when the calendar calls for it!

Of course, a plan is something to work from, not to hold yourself rigidly to. But when you come to an activity on your calendar, try to do it.

See whether you are willing to experiment, to stretch your limits a bit. For example, suppose you have never gone browsing in a bookstore, looking for interesting people as well as interesting books. Suppose that even sounds like a preposterous idea to you, manipulative and disgusting. *Try it anyway.* See what it's really like before you knock it. If you are willing to explore new avenues, you have no idea what you may discover.

Part Three: Go for Volume

When you are mate shopping, operate out of a sense of abundance, not scarcity. Deliberately increase the flow of people through your life.

If you were searching for the perfect wallpaper, you wouldn't bring home one sample, live with it for six months, and then take it back and try another sample for six months. Yet that is how many people treat their search for a mate. They finally get one date. If they like the person even a little, they begin evaluating this individual against their highest standards, struggling to make the relationship work. They behave as though this is the last person they will ever have a chance to meet. They may even date the person for six months knowing full well that he or she is far from ideal.

A secretary looking for work is advised to go to twenty interviews and only then make a choice—or decide to go to twenty more interviews. She knows what she wants in a job, and she keeps looking until she finds it. She is ill-advised to take the first job she comes across—unless it is everything she is looking for. An infinite number of secretarial jobs are out there for her to explore.

If you live in an urban area of any size and if after reading this chapter you are able to divest yourself of the erroneous notion that there are no good ways to meet people, then you, too, have an infinite variety of people to choose from. Don't linger with anyone whose company you do not fully enjoy.

A friend of mine told me a story about a woman he knows. He insists it is true.

Alice is a high-school teacher. When she turned forty, she realized that, more than anything else, she wanted to share the rest of her life with someone. She wanted a husband. She determined that she did not have time or energy to work hard at her goal during the school year, so she decided to devote her summers to it. She placed personal ads in several publications every week, using several different ads, and she kept busy attending events that interested her. She stayed with this program for two summers, realizing that it was a higher priority for her than traveling, which is what she usually did. She told me, "I interviewed sixty-eight men. I married the sixty-eighth, and we are very happy together. We are each other's dream come true."

Alice understood the principle of going for volume! Most of us are not as aggressive as she was; we may be content to meet ten new people over the course of a summer. But the principle still applies.

On the other hand, I asked one man to tell me why he was against using want ads. He explained, "I tried it once and got fifteen letters. I chose to meet five of the women and they were all real bores. It was awful. I just don't want to put myself through that again."

Suppose this man met these women for an hour for coffee. If he isn't willing to commit five more possibly unpleasant hours to his search for an intimate partner, he may never find one. I don't mean to lobby for personal ads as a method, but rather to suggest that a certain number of awkward or boring hours may have to be factored into the business of looking for love, because you have to meet lots of people.

Let's apply some logic.

If you seek a partner who wants to be monogamous, does not want children (and does not have children), agrees with you politically, has a reasonable level of self-awareness, and hates traveling as much as you do, the subset of people who will interest you is quite small. And for every criterion you add, the subset gets smaller.

In general, we seek partners who we feel are emotional and intellectual equals. If you are a person who has risen to the top of your field or who has developed a high degree of sophistication in some intellectual, emotional, or spiritual area, then you probably desire a mate who has a similar level of achievement or sophistication.

High level of achievement or sophistication

Medium level of achievement or sophistication

Low level of achievement or sophistication

Ironically, if you have worked hard in life to place yourself into the top little triangle and you seek a mate who is there, too, your search may be more difficult than other people's. Don't be discouraged, but do realize you will need to screen many people to find your ideal mate. If the person you seek is one in a hundred, then screen a hundred.

It is simply good logic that, in an era when there are many obstacles to overcome in forming a good relationship, the more people you meet, the greater are your chances of finding one person who suits you. In other words, if we assume it is true that you have to kiss a lot of frogs before you meet your prince or princess, then it makes sense to get on with the process of kissing frogs.

CATHY by Cathy Guisewite

CATHY COPYRIGHT 1983 UNIVERSAL PRESS SYNDICATE

Part Four: The Two-Hour Date

The whole system of going for volume depends on the invaluable institution of the Two-Hour Date.

When you are seeing a new person for the first time, never agree to meet for longer than two hours. Even one hour is okay. You don't have to announce your time limit;

just arrange it. Meet the person for breakfast before work, or for cocktails—and make it clear you have dinner plans. You can even meet for dinner if you have a rehearsal or meeting at 8:00.

The advantages of the Two-Hour Date are obvious. Never again will you have the dreadful experience of realizing in the first ten minutes of an evening that a person is not your type, and still have to endure the whole evening.

Of course, if you are enjoying your Two-Hour Date, you always have the option of skipping your rehearsal or meeting or setting up another occasion very soon. Two hours may not be enough to tell whether you have found your soul mate, but it is often enough to tell when you haven't. And when you have committed only two hours, saying no to a second date is relatively easy.

A less obvious benefit of the Two-Hour Date is that if you are enjoying each other, the brevity of your initial rendezvous automatically sustains the titillation and builds the drama, drawing out those extremely pleasurable initial stages of falling in love.

If you are not certain what you feel about your new acquaintance, set up another Two-Hour Date. First impressions can be misleading. You probably want to give anyone who interests you at all a second chance—assuming the other person wants one. Don't be *too* efficient or protective.

Part Five: Screen for "Relationship-Style Preference" First

I continue to be amazed at the numbers of relationships I see in which a big problem is the partners' disagreement about what the relationship itself ought to be. "Why," I ask myself, "didn't they clear that up in the first month and split when they saw they were so far apart?"

Of course, I know why. Love is blind. Incompatibilities are overlooked in the excitement of new love. And each partner becomes convinced that the other will change. Also most singles are operating from a scarcity mentality that tells them, "You better hang onto this one; it's the last compatible partner left in the universe."

If you know what your goals for your own life are, it

seems to me foolish to put that information away when you date.

Marne was a thirty-seven-year-old management consultant who understood the principle of screening for relationship-style preference *early*. Here is her story:

Between my marriages, I was single for six years. During the first four, I had several "serious" relationships, each of which ended after a few months or years, or drifted into a less-intense phase.

By the end of four years, I was quite certain that I wanted to marry again. I longed to share myself with someone who *wanted* to build his life together with me.

So I simply resolved to have no more short-term relationships.

One day a friend told me she had someone for me to meet. She invited him to an afternoon performance of the *Messiah* in which I was singing, and then had us both over for dinner.

My heart skipped a beat when I first met this man; he was gorgeous. And the first thing he said was that he fell in love with me watching me sing. There were six people at this dinner, so we had to wink and smile at each other in between holding up our share of the conversation. Finally, he offered to drive me home, and we spent several delicious hours in front of my fireplace. But we both agreed not to rush things, which delighted me, since I very much enjoy the pleasures of the "anticipation" phase.

We saw a lot of each other in the next two weeks, including several nights together, and they were wonderful times. We cooked Chinese, did some Christmas shopping, spent a glorious day in the park. Then I went to Iowa to visit my family over Christmas. One day my parents' doorbell rang and a deliveryman presented me with a dozen long-stemmed roses—and a little note: "Thinking of you." I melted. And now, not only I but my entire family was excited.

We had an airport reunion right out of Hollywood.

The next week, I told him I was eager to meet his two children, four and six, who lived in the next county.

He was very hesitant.

I was crushed. I probed for his reasons. By reading between the lines, I could tell he was still very attached to his recently divorced wife and not at all certain where I fit into the picture. He told me he was very unsure about ever marrying again.

It was all I needed to hear. The next day, I called and told him I needed a cooling-off period, an indefinite one. He begged and pleaded with me to be willing to "just date." I was careful not to blame him; I just knew what I needed to do for myself. Not ever again was I willing to pour energy—and months—into a relationship that would never meet my needs.

Believe me, the next weeks were painful. I missed him terribly. I kept counting up all his virtues and dwelling on the tragedy of what a near miss this was. But I never doubted that I had done the right thing for myself.

When I met the man I eventually married, months later, I was unencumbered, and my heart was open. I shudder when I think that if I hadn't had the courage to get out, I might still be hanging around in that dead-end relationship and have missed the wonderful man I'm married to.

Personal ads should be classified by what sort of relationship the advertisers seek. "Seeking intimacy, commitment, and monogamy"; "Ambivalent"; "Looking for someone to enjoy and see what happens"; "Dead set against commitment"; "Desire intimacy but fear it." This seems to me to be critical information, and having it to begin with would save everyone's time. But until this enlightened approach is used, you can always do the screening yourself. I recommend it.

Discovering what a new friend's relationship plans and preferences are may seem like an awkward task, especially early in the relationship when the information is the most critical for you. But you can do it without being obvious. Bring it up as a general topic, not specifically about the two of you. Trends in the singles scene is a popular, easy topic on which almost everyone has an opinion. You don't need to ask your partner questions point-blank; rather, talk about your own general opinions and your own desires.

You can tell a great deal from the responses you get. Actually, if you are serious about not wanting to date people whose needs vary greatly from your own, it may be okay to be "obvious." You don't have to bring the subject up on the first date—or even the second. But especially if this person is getting your juices flowing, don't wait forever. If you know people who know your new acquaintance, ask around. "Commitmentphobia" is very common; don't walk right into it if you can help it. Find out what the person's relationship history is. No matter how much you like a person, if you want a committed relationship and your new flame is dead set against commitment, you are better off not starting a relationship at all. Indeed, the more you like each other, the more heartbreaking your incompatibility in this area will be.

I spoke with Katherine, a thirty-six-year-old San Francisco area artist who was quite successful with her business. Katherine had never heard of my five-part formula, but she was doing it all anyway. She was highly motivated to find a partner; she knew what she wanted; she devoted time and energy to her search; and when she found someone, she investigated his relationship-style preferences right away. Her story is delightful—and informative.

I had been through two relationships, one for three years and one for four. But they were not satisfying. I had picked wrong—men who weren't willing to make a commitment. In other ways, they were fine, but their fear of commitment was a fatal flaw. Because I really wanted commitment, I was determined this time not to make a bad choice. It had been really painful breaking up with these guys.

So after suffering for about three months after my breakup with Rick, I decided, "I'm making a list this time of exactly what I want and need." One night I sat down and wrote three pages—right off the top of my head. The next day I put in a few more things, and then I put it away. But I was really driven to find a partner, so I spent a lot of energy looking. I think I probably went out every day with that in mind. I went to bookstores. I went to the grocery store often. I'd go to coffee shops. And I did meet people. But if I could see it wasn't right after one date—or even after a five-minute conversation—I didn't pursue it.

When I finally met the guy I'm now married to, I had been invited to two parties the same evening. One was a house-warming party for Rick, with whom I had ended my relationship about ten months before. It was still painful for me. But I was determined to go and look good, so people wouldn't think I was a lost cause. All my friends were going to be there. So I went, and it was okay for the first couple of hours—I really did feel good about having the courage to go. But then something happened that upset me, and it got horrible. I just left. I got in the car and sobbed and screamed, thinking, "Why am I still crying over this guy? I'm going to that other party!" So through my tears, I drove across town and went to the other party at 11:30 at night. I went in and looked around the dining room—there was no one interesting there. So I went into the hallway and saw a couple of real attractive guys there. I liked the energy from the one guy—so I started talking to the other one. I sensed the guy I was attracted to had the kind of personality I was looking for. He was sparkling! I could tell he was checking me out, too. Then I went into the bathroom, which was right off the hallway, and was able to hear through the door. David, the guy I was interested in, starting asking the other guy, "Who is she? What does she do?" I loved it! So then, when I came out, I started talking directly to him. I really liked him; it was exciting! I knew I had found someone who was possible.

After about an hour, I realized—wait a minute—I'd better check this out. I felt I needed to be super cautious, because people had warned me about Rick. They'd said, "Don't get involved with him. He always has one foot out the door," but I'd gone ahead anyway. So I went over to the woman whose party it was and said, "I like David! Is he okay?" She told me, "He's terrific. He has good friendships with women and men. He's really a good person. He's looking for a good, solid relationship." I returned to David, and we spent another hour together and exchanged phone numbers.

He called the next day, but I would have called him

on the following day if he hadn't. We got together on the third day.

I was still very cautious for a long time. But we got married two years and two months later. We have a *real* relationship. It's not based on romantic fantasies or projections. It's like a relationship should be. We respect each other. We enjoy being together. We're completely honest with each other. We're both very happy.

So there's my formula. Examine your excuses one by one for not meeting people and discard them. Do something to meet people and plan ahead what that something will be. Enjoy it if you can, but don't make enjoying what you do mandatory. "Screen" a lot of people; work from abundance. Make use of the Two-Hour Date. Look for someone who wants the same thing in a relationship you do. And persevere, patiently but persistently.

By all means, keep reading your epic novels or backpacking alone or playing bridge or devoting yourself to your work. Don't ever let your quest for love take over your life to such an extent that you give up anything important to you. Go on with your friendships, your professional development, your hobbies or creative projects, for if you begin to resent your "plan" for finding love, you may begin to sabotage it unwittingly. Mate shopping does not take a lot of time if you follow my suggested formula. You should be able to fit it into your life almost without noticing that you've added something new—except that now you will be moving ahead toward a dream you have long wanted to realize.

Often after I have discussed the five-part-formula in my workshops, someone says, "But I resent that I have to go through all this. It all seems so calculating and manipulative. I feel like a predator when I behave that way."

Again, I refer to the analogy of job seeking. You *are* being calculating and manipulative. And it *doesn't* feel good some of the time. But it is necessary to produce the results you want. You may *feel* like a predator, but in fact you are just creating the opportunity for something wonderful to happen.

It's possible you would rather not wage such a deliberate campaign for yourself and just go ahead with your life and see what happens. Many people do prefer that. But if that's your choice, then you should not be so puzzled about why you are so wonderful and still single. You are letting opportunities pass you by. In the job-hunting arena, the person who gets the job is not necessarily the one with the most talent or experience. The person who gets the job is often the one who knows how to look for a job! The same thing goes for the search for an intimate partner: the ones who succeed are the ones who know what they need to do and *do it*.

Every principle has its exception. I know a woman who was watching TV in her bathrobe and rollers when the new tenant in her apartment building knocked on her door to see if he could borrow a hammer. They had a relationship for several years. But if you depend on a chance happening like that, you may be waiting for a long time.

It's normal to feel resentful at having to work so hard to achieve a loving relationship. Just don't let your resentment stop you from acting in your own best interest!

Where and How to Look: A Few Suggestions

The two methods for meeting people which succeed most often are work or work-related activities and being introduced by friends. Both of these boil down to the same thing: networking.

It is just as important to meet same-sex friends in your networking as it is to meet opposite-sex friends because same-sex friends *have* opposite-sex friends. In addition, friendship and solidarity can enhance the pleasure of the hunt and of life in general.

I encourage parties in which each invited guest has to bring along one "available" friend. Small social gatherings in homes where everyone is either a friend or a friend-of-a-friend are usually pleasant, relaxed, and quiet enough to carry on real conversations as opposed to the shouting matches you have to have in public places with loud music.

One man I know has a standing offer of a $1,000 award for the person who introduces him to his future spouse. I must admit, I have arranged some dinners for him myself!

Offering an award may be extreme, but urging your

friends to introduce you to people is, nevertheless, extremely important. It is not sufficient to mention it once. I found that when I asked my friends to sit down and think deliberately about their friends and acquaintances, they came up with ideas that would not have occurred to them in the natural course of events. Being introduced by friends is *the best way* to connect with new people. Don't overlook this method! Keep after your friends. You never know when some new eligible person will come into their lives!

Work-related conferences and meetings may offer an excellent opportunity for meeting potential partners. If your work situation doesn't offer any potential for you, perhaps you could get involved with the union or the fund-raising auxiliary or start a special-interest group of employees like a volleyball team or a political group.

The main point is that you are more likely to *do* things which lie directly in your pathway (work, friends) than you are to do things which are entirely peripheral to your established routines. So exploit your established routines as much as you can.

Conferences, conventions, retreats, workshops—especially events which are residential, that is where all participants stay overnight at the same hotel or conference center—are high on the list of match-making events.

If conventions are not a part of your vocational life (or if your work-related conventions bore you or are stressful), hook up with some interesting group that does hold conferences or conventions. Meetings away from home have a charged atmosphere, and they provide lots of time around the edges of the formal schedule to party or have informal dates.

One woman I spoke with has tried a variety of vacation styles and found that she prefers some kind of a conference, retreat, or resort to random unstructured travel. I asked her to tell me how she came to this conclusion:

I got started on my vacation system the first year after my divorce. My friend Christine was between jobs, and we planned to go camping in Hawaii for two weeks. But days before we were to leave, she was offered a job she wanted very much and was forced to cancel out on our plans.

I was painfully disappointed, having no desire whatsoever to go to Hawaii alone. But a friend strongly urged me to attend a writer's workshop at a retreat center just a two-hour drive from my front door. It didn't seem as glamorous as Hawaii, and I was skeptical. But at a loss for anything else to do, I went.

After one of the loveliest weeks of my life, I realized it had many of the components I had been looking for in the Hawaii vacation. The country setting was spectacularly beautiful and serenely quiet. The enormous ranch had a bath-warm lake, a hot tub, and miles of hiking trails. The food, all grown on the premises and lovingly prepared, was sumptuous and healthful. And best of all, there were friendly interesting people as eager for contact as I was. Every meal was a delightful social event—but I had plenty of time to myself. My opportunities for meeting "someone" came more easily than they would were I simply traveling alone.

Research the conference and retreat centers in your area—or in some exotic state or country you wish to visit. You may be amazed at the variety of program offerings available.

Of course it is important to be on the lookout at conventions and retreats for people who want only a weekend or week-long romance. Some of them may even have a spouse and family at home. Unless you, too, would enjoy such a fling, be ready to say "no," and to hold out for someone who has at least some potential for you.

Gallery openings are an often overlooked opportunity to meet people. These receptions, put on by an art gallery at the beginning of each new exhibition, every four to eight weeks, are listed in the newspaper. If you can get on the mailing list of your favorite galleries (sometimes you have to make a purchase to accomplish this), they will mail you invitations to the openings.

Gallery openings have many advantages: (a) They are short and are often scheduled between work and dinner so you can attend them even if you are very busy. You can be flexible and stay fifteen minutes or two hours. (b) The artwork provides a focus for your attention so you aren't just standing around looking nervous. Also, it gives you something to *talk about,* and provides a natural way to strike up a conversation. "What do you think of this piece?" (c) They are *free*, they provide the aesthetic pleasure of viewing the art, and they almost always include free wine and sometimes hors d'oeuvres. (d) If you are already knowledgeable about art, you will be able to keep up with the scene and meet others who are knowledgeable and interested. If you aren't, a world awaits your discovery. Your naïveté may be an asset because people love to be asked questions they can not only answer but discourse upon at length.

The List

As you make up your activities-for-meeting-people list, here are some other ideas to consider:

PERSONAL ADS

Personal ads have become entirely respectable, and every imaginable category of singles uses them. Don't forget about national publications like *The New York Review of Books* and *Mother Earth News*.

Try writing several different ads, and see what works best. Try both placing ads and answering them. And use several different publications.

One variation which a number of my workshop participants have enjoyed is for three or four men or women to stage a dinner party together and advertise for guests. Together you can screen the letters you get and choose the guests. The event itself is less charged than a one-to-one date and usually more fun.

DATING SERVICES

I'm convinced that dating services are underused. They are one of the easiest and most effective ways to meet new people because they provide a steady stream of *pre-screened*, available members of the opposite sex who are themselves interested in meeting people. When you are going for volume, dating services are a natural. If you can afford to, join several. And don't withdraw just because the first few people you meet don't interest you.

Some dating services are exploitative; they are too ex-

pensive. But many are reasonably priced. Join for a limited
period of time and then renew. (My definition of a pessi-
mist is one who pays for a lifetime membership in a dating
service.)

Bella, a forty-four-year-old computer programmer, told
me,

> Be sure to tell your readers to use dating services. I
> avoided them for a long time for a whole slew of rea-
> sons, but now I know that was a mistake. I use two
> services which allow me to say enough about what I'm
> looking for that I haven't had any encounters I would
> call unpleasant. I'm still single, but I'm more hopeful
> than ever, and I feel like the best men I've met have
> been through this service. To avoid dating services is
> to pass by an easy opportunity to meet men.

I interviewed seven women and three men who met
their current spouses through dating services and were
very enthusiastic about this method. Most of them had met
five or more people they did not continue dating. One
woman had dated seventeen men she met through several
different dating services before meeting her true love
through one of them.

SINGLES GROUPS

Some singles groups live up to all the negative stereotypes
about them, but some don't! Try a group once to see
whether it's your style. I avoided singles groups when I was
single, but after I began speaking at them I realized that
was a mistake. Believe me, *all* kinds of people participate
in them. Many organizations have activities scheduled every day of the week; some have special-interest groups. I
know several happy couples who met at singles events.

PARTIES

In your networking, always announce that you enjoy par-
ties. Try giving some of your own, too. Trivial Pursuit and
Charades are great excuses for parties if you need one.
They always provide a lot of laughs and a good time.

ADULT EDUCATION CLASSES AND UNIVERSITY EXTENSION COURSES

VOLUNTEER ACTIVITIES

HEALTH CLUBS

SUPERMARKETS

Look around and smile a lot. Don't be afraid to try the old standard, "Do you know how to select a good melon?"

Katherine, whom we met earlier, frequented supermarkets and had good success meeting people there and in bookstores and coffeehouses. When I asked her more about her technique, she told me,

> My feeling is that everybody's looking. You just have to give people an opportunity to answer back. It makes no difference what you say. But the critical thing is, you have to feel okay about feeling foolish. You may pick someone who is *not* looking, and who doesn't talk back. That happens, and you really feel stupid, but it's all part of the game plan. It's something you have to get past, being willing to feel humiliated and embarrassed. It can be intensely uncomfortable— like that cringing feeling you get when you feel the whole world is looking at you. You feel great when you get a smiling response, but you never feel good when you don't. I met people by doing this, and I think if you don't do it, you pass up a lot of opportunities.

CAFÉS, COFFEEHOUSES

Rather than reading or writing letters at home, take your book or stationery to a café and hang out for few hours. But don't bury yourself in your work; look open and available for conversation. Definitely ask other friendly-looking people—same or opposite sex—who are sitting alone, "May I join you?" or "Would you enjoy some company?" I have met some delightful men and women this way and find that, nine times out of ten, people are genuinely pleased that I asked. If they would rather remain alone, they can simply say so, and no one's the worse for it.

LAUNDROMATS

If you regularly do your laundry out, choose a laundromat with a friendly atmosphere, where people tend to joke around with each other. Do your laundry Saturday morning—not Monday at midnight when the place is empty. And then don't bury yourself in a book. Your neighborhood laundromat is full of single people who live in the same area you do. It's pretty easy to strike up a conversation with someone who looks appealing, since you are both stuck there for a couple of hours. Use this time to advantage.

BOOKSTORES AND LIBRARIES

Bookstores are an underused method of meeting people. Find a big, well-stocked one and drop in frequently. Browse in the subject area that interests you, such as sailing, cooking, child care. Also, find the bookstores in your area that hold lectures and book-signings. These are interactive, social events, often quite interesting, too.

POOL AND HOT TUB IN AN APARTMENT COMPLEX

If you don't live in an apartment complex, make friends with someone who does.

JOGGING, BIKE RIDING

Find the local lake or fire trail where lots of others jog, too.

HIKES ORGANIZED BY OUTDOOR CLUBS

DANCE CLASSES—FOLK, TAP, DISCO, BALLROOM, AEROBIC

AUCTION HOUSES

Auctions are *fun;* it is easy to be friendly with others there. Get on the mailing list of one auction house in your area.

CRAFT FAIRS, FLEA MARKETS, SWAP MEETS

At craft fairs, strike up conversations with the craftspeople behind the booths.

Remember Walter? He looked over this list and found a reason why every suggestion was a bad one. But in another workshop, a woman named Sylvia complained that she *had tried* all these methods over the years without success.

My answer to Sylvia was to persevere.

Do you know how, when you are hunting for your keys, you always find them in the last place you look? In the same way, the most effective way to meet a new lover will inevitably be the last method you try. So keep going, and you will get to that last effective method! Remember, it makes no difference what activity or method you choose. All that matters is that you choose one and *use it!*

Techniques to Get You Started

If you go to some kind of group event, it is a good idea to go by yourself or, if you go with a friend, to split up after you arrive. A person alone is more approachable than two people together. Also, you will be more highly motivated to approach others.

Starting a conversation with a stranger in a restaurant, movie line, or coffee shop, or even at a party, is not easy for anyone. But ask yourself, "Am I going to let my anxieties run my life and keep me from doing what I want to do?"

There are two facts you should remember when you are trying to work up the courage to start a conversation with a stranger:

1. You will be doing the other person a *favor* when you start a conversation. That person is probably more shy than you are. You will help other people and flatter them by initiating contact.

2. It doesn't matter what you say. You don't have to be brilliant, clever, or witty. It is hard to avoid trite questions, so be trite. Or keep a few stock openers on hand like, "How do you know [the people who are throwing this party]?" The point is simply to get a conversation started. Truly, as long as you are not offensive or intrusive, it doesn't matter how you do it.

Then you have to hope the person you approached will hold up his or her end of the conversation. Most people do, but if you have the misfortune of starting a conversation with someone who drops the ball, just bow out with the knowledge that you did the right thing.

No matter where you go, if you carry or wear or even drive something which is an obvious conversation piece, you make it very easy for other people to start a conversation with you. Conversation "inviters" can be almost anything from striking jewelry to an antique car. Pets give people a great excuse to approach you: a dog, cat, parrot, cockatiel, or even a chameleon. If you belong to a club or are active with a cause, wear a button or T-shirt. I know a woman who always carries a muff in the winter and gets endless comments on it. The more imaginative a prop you can come up with, the more conversation you will invite.

When you attend an event with the idea that you would like to make new acquaintances, communicate this with your body language. Look around. Make eye contact with people. Give the appearance of being calm, centered, and approachable. (You'd be amazed how easy it is to fake this if you put your mind to it.) Smile a lot. The people who stand out in a room are the ones who appear to be emotionally open. They have a guileless air about them; they seem to have their guard down, to have nothing to hide or fear. If you are ingenuous, naïve, or if you can emulate that quality, you will be approached by others more often.

I once counseled a woman named Kathy who claimed that she couldn't make that first connection with people at parties. Her problem surprised me, because she had quite a beautiful smile and a quick wit. I watched Kathy at a singles group and I saw that she did smile at people, but always with an air of caution and with a quick look away.

I gave Kathy an assignment to go to a local coffee shop where people often share tables, to take a magazine, and to sit near the door. She was to pretend that she was the official greeter for the restaurant, and that her job was to make other people feel welcome. She was not to initiate any conversation, however.

I went with her and chose a table from which I could watch the action unobserved. There was a big difference in Kathy. Each time people came in, she looked up, tried deliberately to catch their eyes, and gave them a big, warm smile. Sometimes she'd say "Hello." She maintained eye contact, smiling, for a few seconds. Then she simply went back to her magazine.

The message she gave was, "I'm feeling good today. Everything's fine. I don't need or want anything, but I'm in a friendly mood."

Kathy was rewarded for her effort when a single man went to the counter to order and then returned and asked Kathy whether he could join her. But she told me later she'd have felt rewarded even if he hadn't come over, because she experienced the open, innocent feeling I had been trying to convey.

Perhaps the most important overall clue to looking for love is, wherever you go and whatever you do, don't take it too seriously. Of course, looking for love is a serious matter, but you don't have to act serious. Keep your perspective and your sense of humor. Be willing to laugh at yourself. If you take it all too seriously, you won't be able to relax.

When you go out, leave your worries, self-doubts, and prejudices about "these" activities at home. It's only a few hours. Besides, you have plenty of other activities already scheduled, right? So *this one* is not critical.

You may find it helpful to do some stress reduction activities before you plunge into a "mate shopping" event. Try some deep, relaxed breathing or a short meditation, or listen to some soothing music.

When you give up the idea that there are no good ways to meet people, and start conducting an active search for your ideal mate, you will feel energized just knowing that you are systematically furthering your own goals. If you *anticipate* that some of your two-hour dates will not be completely wonderful, you will be able to take those short episodes in stride and not dwell on them. And the dates that are enjoyable will be pleasant surprises. Even if you don't relish each date, you may find that "campaigning" for yourself *is* enjoyable. You may be reminded anew that you are an interesting, appealing person and that you have much to give. View your quest as an enriching and exciting time in your life. And remember, if you do it right, it won't go on forever.

Chapter 4

The Fourth Strategy: Keep Your Standards High

When you are single, your world is full of experts who are eager to give you free advice. And one of the first things they will tell you is this:

Your standards are too high; you have to be realistic.

What you want doesn't exist. Be willing to compromise.

Don't be so fussy.

These well-wishers believe that if you will simply lower your standards, you will be successful.

But successful at what? At getting into a relationship which is less than what you wanted? What kind of success is that?

This is terrible advice. I have watched many people get into problematic relationships because they believed that what they really wanted was unrealistic. One woman actually told me, "I thought I'd better compromise because I haven't found anything better."

This belief system is insidious. By buying into the idea that we must lower our standards we perpetuate the belief that really good relationships don't exist. We all settle for less than wonderful partners and then get to look around and say, "See, I was right. There are no ideal relationships."

Such reasoning does not serve anyone. It is a pessimistic, not a realistic, worldview. It will ultimately result in a lowering of self-esteem because after you put energy into a relationship, the feeling "this is the best I could get" transforms slowly into "this is the most I deserve."

Actually, lowering your standards is impossible to do anyway. Your ideals and fantasies are what they are. It is not possible to alter them by an act of will, to simply wake up one day and say, "Well, I changed my mind. Now I don't care whether the person I date is communicative." It's like asking a leopard to change its spots. You may tell yourself you have lowered your standards, but the real ones are always there—lurking somewhere in the background.

The Importance of High Standards

Intention, desire, and belief are powerful factors in your life. If you believe you can earn $50,000 a year, if you desire this and your intention is to bring it about, you are not likely to earn $500,000 a year. What you ask for has a great deal to do with what you are likely to get. Put another way, if you don't ask for what you want, you are not likely to get it.

So, rather than lowering your standards, *you should figure out what you really want and make that your standard.* Set yourself some specific goals—high goals—for what you want in a relationship. Then believe (or act as though you believe, which may be just as effective) that you will achieve what you desire.

A diving champion mentally pictures every detail of the dive hundreds of times before actually doing it. She sets exact standards and then pushes every negative thought out of her head. "What if I don't tuck right? What if I slip on the mat?" are not a part of her mental preparation.

There's a story told of Babe Ruth when he was playing to an extremely hostile crowd. He pointed his bat to an exact spot in the grandstands, amid all the boos, and on the next pitch, landed the ball exactly where he had pointed for a home run.

I used to identify with Babe Ruth when I was looking for love. While everyone else was busy telling me my standards were too high, I was pointing my bat.

Your standards cannot be too high. The more you acknowledge your real standards, the more likely you are to achieve them.

This little quotation, attributed to Somerset Maugham, sums up the best advice I know:

It's a funny thing about life. If you refuse to accept anything but the best, you very often get it.

Getting Practical

Now, to be more specific, how does one go about setting high standards?

There are two entirely separate steps. The first is to establish your standards; the second is to apply them in the real world.

Step 1

Remember Katherine in Chapter 3? She sat down one night and wrote three pages of precisely what she was looking for in a man. I suggest that you do exactly the same thing. To find out what your real standards are, you need to unleash your dreams. Pay special attention to steps b, c, and d in this experiment.

EXPERIMENT #6

a. On paper, describe your ideal mate. List all the qualities, talents, propensities you'd like him or her to have. "Brainstorm" with yourself. Take your time and include everything. There is no need to be "realistic." Don't censor.

b. Now go back over your list and place either an "E" for essential or a "D" for desirable next to each item.

c. List all the "E" qualities on a separate page in the order of their importance to you.

d. Draw a line under the top 5 items on the "E" list.

In my workshops, participants share their lists with one another and inevitably end up adding items they hear from others but didn't think of themselves. Here is a sampling of the items which appear regularly on these lists, though I suggest you work on your own list first, before looking at these ideas.

Must like what he or she does, be good at it, be involved in it.
Must have good self-esteem, must like him- or herself.
Must have his or her own friends, good relationships with other people.

Must be enthusiastic about *me!*

Must be affectionate.

Must be thoughtful.

Must be generous.

Must care about good communication.

Must be a good listener.

Must have a sense of humor.

Must be interested in healthful eating and physical fitness.

Must be in a comfortable financial situation.

Must have young children (or, must have *no* young children).

Must *not* have a vasectomy (or, *must* have a vasectomy).

Must be attractive (tall, short, thin, blond, dark, balding or not balding, strong, etc.).

Must be (athletic, musical, a good dancer, a good skier, interested in art, pop music, classical music, cooking, hiking, etc.).

Must enjoy sex and be a good lover.

Must be flexible and able to compromise.

Must live in this area and want to stay here.

Must NOT be involved in substance abuse of any kind.

Must care about the equality of our relationship and want to give time to it.

After you have distinguished between your "desirable" and "essential" items, and selected your top five (or four or six) essentials, you have your standards. Though you may not find every quality on your "desirables" list, the top "essentials" are items on which you should never expect yourself to compromise. If you meet someone who clearly does not meet one of your top essentials, *even though you may be very attracted to the person,* you would be well advised to pass him or her by—or make it clear you are interested only in a casual affair. If you do not find your ideal mate for quite a long while, you know it means only one thing: you must persevere!

Your standards list will remain fluid and flexible. You may find yourself adding and subtracting items or changing the order, even on your "essentials" list. The standards list is designed to help you clarify your thinking and become more discriminating in your search. As you achieve clarity about what you hope to find in an intimate partner, you will know when you have *not* found him or her. And if you are dating, all your dating will not be in vain; you can view it as a way to strengthen your list. With each experience, you may become more certain about some quality you want to find or some quality you positively cannot live with.

The Standards List: A Few Particulars

There is one item which rarely shows up on any list and yet which I believe to be an essential for virtually everyone. It's this: "Desires the same type of relationship that I do."

If you meet a person who is good-looking, bright, witty, generous, communicative, loving, and self-confident, but that person wants to live alone, travel alone, and remain non-monogamous, and you want a monogamous marriage, you will have a painful relationship no matter how compatible you are in other ways. People spend some of their best years struggling through relationships that were doomed from the start because of this one area of incompatibility. If you are going to "screen for relationship-style preference first," then the relationship style you seek has to be on your essentials list.

On the other hand, some items probably should not be included on the "essentials" list if they can be avoided. For example, it may be a mistake to limit your search by categories like age, race, social class, or education level. For long-term relationships to flourish, qualities like thoughtfulness, generosity, self-assurance, physical warmth, sexiness, and the ability to listen and to express affection are more important than things like social status. Indeed, high achievers may be even less likely to possess these appealing qualities than average achievers. Of course if a certain age, economic level, education, and ethnic or religious group is essential for you and you know it, then by all means include it on your essentials list. But if you feel you can be open about some of these items, you may be surprised at what you will discover. As long as two people have compatible values and mutual respect, then there is no inherent reason why marriages with "demographic" differences can't succeed beautifully.

Thanila is a strikingly handsome woman in her early forties who is the highly respected and well-liked executive director of the YWCA in a midwestern city. After a youthful marriage, she had been single for twelve years and then married again for two when I had the delightful experience of interviewing her. It turned out she had a standards list in her mind all the while she was looking:

A well-educated man was a priority for me. I always imagined I would marry a Ph.D. As it turns out, the man I married never went to college at all! He went to the "University of the World." He's very well traveled and well read and life is a great adventure for him. He founded a Boys Club, and now he has his own landscaping business. He thinks I'm the greatest, and he's definitely the sweetest man I ever met. What more could I want? I would never advise anyone to put things like education on a standards list. For me, it limited my search. I went to Princeton alumni functions and Mensa events, and I never would have met Tommy there!

I met another woman who committed herself to a man fourteen years younger than she. I interviewed them together and could see they were delighted with each other. Jessica is a psychotherapist, forty-four, and Hank is finishing up med school at age thirty. Jessica told me,

There was never a time when I wasn't dating *a lot*, sometimes two or three men at once. I fall in love easily. I think I always wanted to find someone I could be with forever, but I didn't believe it would ever happen. I never had a "standards list." I attend so many growth groups, conferences, training events, lectures—all kinds of men show up at these and they all interested me. If I'm attracted, I'm attracted.

With Hank, things were different from the very beginning. We were amazingly right for each other. We've never declared a commitment. It just gradually became obvious we would stay together and "forsake all others," as they say. Other people bring up our age difference sometimes, but I've never felt it was a problem. We're peers in the ways that matter to me. And sometimes we find our age difference to be enriching. For example, we experienced the sixties so differently. But our relationship works, and I never worry about our age gap.

Step 2: Applying Your Standards to the Real World

What do you do with your list of desirable and essential qualities when a real, warm-blooded potential partner comes along?

Tuck it away in your dresser drawer.

The standards list is useful in the abstract: it keeps you focused on what you deserve rather than what you think you can get. And it can sometimes give you the courage to say no to someone when your "gut" is leaning in that direction anyway. But there its usefulness ends. Love has little to do with a checklist.

When you become seriously interested in someone, your "standard" becomes your intuition.

Intuition is "the direct perception of truth independent of any reasoning process." *Most of us know what our intuition is telling us, and we get into troubled relationships because we lack the courage to abide by it.* We talk ourselves out of following what we know deep inside to be true, and then months or years later say, "I knew better."

By paying attention to your intuition, you can access a reservoir of great wisdom that resides within you. This inner wisdom will always steer you in the right direction. Most of us err by following our whims or the arguments in our noisy minds rather than slowing down enough to hear the messages from our intuition.

Ben told me a story most of us can identify with. He was blissfully in love with Elizabeth, but was uneasy about one quality in her: she became strident and self-righteous at times and, especially when they argued, seemed to put him down. His nagging feelings did not go away, but he told himself "you can't have everything" and focused only on the things he enjoyed. They were married for four years before they both realized that Elizabeth actually did not respect Ben in some important ways. They tried working on the problem in counseling, but the more they talked about it, the more obvious and painful it became. Ben's strong negative intuition was telling him the truth. He didn't feel good, but he ignored this by talking himself out of it. He lowered his standards. In the end, Elizabeth and Ben broke up.

There will always be things about your new love that you would change if you had a magic wand. If these things can be classified as preferences on your part—if they seem tolerable to you—then you are not lowering your standards or compromising, and you can proceed with confidence. They may be quite major preferences. "I wish he didn't have two teenage boys." "I wish she had some money." But you should regard them as having "nuisance-value."

On the other hand, if your hesitations about the other person are "essential" items on your list, or if they are areas that you *cannot respect*, then there is reason for caution.

The difference between "nuisances" and "essential flaws" is important. It has nothing to do with the magnitude of the issue in question. Some nuisances may be colossal; and an essential item may *seem* minor.

Rather, the important question is, is the problem something you can tolerate? Does it affect your ability to respect or love your partner?

Linda had been single all her life but was always quite clear she would prefer to marry if she could find the right man. At forty-six, she was a tenured history professor and had long since owned her own home. Suddenly one evening, a friend invited her over to meet "someone," and her life was never the same again. She told me,

We were both in love within a week, and neither of us could believe our good fortune. But—believe this—he had four teenagers, and they all lived with him! The thirteen-year-old twin girls were pretty well-behaved and open to me, but his fifteen-year-old daughter and seventeen-year-old son both had difficult personalities, and they wanted no part of me. I knew my life would change radically, and that I was in for some real struggles. But I never considered letting go of Ed. Some things are just worth whatever you have to go through, and Ed was clearly worth it. We are so strong in our bond, the kids can see that, and it helps. We've gotten great support from a super family therapist. And I've learned a lot! It's been hard, but I have absolutely no reservation in saying it's been completely worth it.

Couples who love and respect each other can meet major challenges. But if an essential factor is missing for either partner, however small it might *seem*, the problem will eat away at the relationship.

I spoke with a Jewish woman who gave up a very fine relationship because her partner wasn't Jewish. She told me,

I never intended to start going with Mark. We were friends at work, and the friendship just grew. I kept telling myself it was okay because this was "just an interim relationship." But finally I couldn't deny it anymore: we were both in love. Still, I didn't let myself look honestly at what I was getting into. Then, when Mark started trying to talk me into marriage, I was desperately torn. Marrying a Jew has always been a complete *given* for me. And because I keep kosher and observe all the holidays, it was just too big a difference for me. We both realized—at about the same time—that we couldn't make it work. We didn't break up suddenly, but we let ourselves ease off slowly—but surely. I found out the hard way what *really* matters to me.

Sometimes, an "essential flaw" is hard to identify, but a restless, uneasy feeling tells you it's there. Your intuition, not your logical mind, is giving you signals.

The following experiment will help you determine whether a given person meets your standards. Remember, consult your intuition, and decide whether the things you would like to change are tolerable to you. Are they "nuisances" or "essential flaws"?

EXPERIMENT #7
Think about your partner and your relationship with him or her. List everything, big or little, that you would change if you

had a magic wand. As you do this, slow down, and pay attention. Spend some time alone, and let yourself experience what is going on inside you. List every doubt, every hesitation, everything you don't like even mildly.

Go back over each item you have listed. Place an N next to it if you view it as a nuisance, and an EF if you believe it is an essential flaw, something you cannot tolerate.

Examine every doubt and hesitation fully. Don't be afraid to look at your fears. Are the problem areas nuisances, however great? Or do they slice into the very heart of your ability to love and respect this person? Be honest with yourself. Does any part of you feel that you are settling for less than what you want?

Give yourself permission to move on from this relationship, and see how that feels to you. *Nothing is forcing you to proceed with a relationship that is not all you have been hoping for.*

If your new love passes this tough test, then you are truly maintaining high standards, and you are likely to find (or have) a very special partner and enjoy him or her for a long time.

You deserve the very best. Go for it!

This experiment is an excellent tool for tapping into your intuition. You may have to be *very* quiet in order to still the voices in your head and let your intuition speak to you.

But, remember, begin by giving yourself the opportunity to write down your standards list. Many, many singles have reported that they found the exercise very useful. Pick a sunny afternoon or a cozy evening. Curl up in a comfy chair, and give your imagination free rein. Writing down what you want makes you more conscious of it. Your standards list and your intuition—if you take the time to listen to it—will guide you in "refusing to accept anything but the best." Allow yourself to hold out for what you know is important to you. Be willing to pass up anyone who does not meet your highest standards.

Pseudo-High Standards

There is a syndrome which people often mistake for "high standards" but which has nothing to do with what we have been discussing.

John, a fifty-year-old salesman who had been involved with several different high-tech industries, played "Pseudo-High Standards." He was handsome and exceedingly warm and friendly. When I asked, he told me that he had been in eight serious relationships over the past ten years. I asked him why each relationship had ended and heard several of the stories at length. Here is a summary of his reasons for the breakups:

Number one smoked too much. Number two lived too far away. Number three just wasn't pretty enough. Number four was a mediocre conversationalist. Number five had an annoying habit of twirling her hair. Number six wasn't passionate. Number seven was too old. Number eight had fat legs.

I secretly thought John's reasons were ridiculous, but he took them completely seriously. Though he was unaware of it, his pattern became very clear to me as we talked.

John was simply deeply ambivalent about love, and whenever a woman got too close for comfort, he found something to criticize. Criticisms were a habit with him, a defense he used. They emerged automatically whenever the going got a little close. Like a protective shield, criticisms erected themselves between John and any person who threatened his private, single territory. His problem was not that his standards were too high; it was his fear of closeness.

But John's description of himself was "a person who has a bad case of high standards." He clung to the belief either that he would someday meet an incredible woman who had no flaws or that he would decide to lower his standards and be able to choose a woman who was flawed in some way.

John saw his love life as one example after another that his standards were too high. He was convinced that he had simply not met the right woman. Because he saw it all this way, he missed what was *really* keeping him from commitment, namely, his fear of closeness. Unconsciously, he didn't want to have to experience that fear, so he got all caught up in his need for "passion" or his disinclination toward fat legs.

I did suggest to John that ambivalence or fear of closeness might be an issue for him, and he promised to consider the idea and begin paying attention to it.

People who use criticism as a crutch to get out of relationships give high standards a bad name because they seem to be people whose standards are "too high." But gratuitous criticism has nothing to do with the kind of honest scrutiny which constitutes high standards, and the two should never be confused. Being overly critical is a problem. Maintaining high standards is an aid to better living.

Some people who believe they are still alone because their standards are too high are actually not looking for an intimate partner. They are looking for themselves. But they are looking in the wrong place: another person. No potential partner will ever be good enough to satisfy that search.

Maintaining High Standards in a Low-Standards World

The idea that our standards are too high is pervasive in the singles world, and I submit it is a notion which arises naturally out of the Great Emotional Depression.

I am convinced that most of us could experience more joy in our lives than we do.

Why we spend a good deal of energy censoring positive emotions and cutting ourselves off from pleasurable experiences, I am not certain. But it is my observation that we do. We behave as though too much pleasure would destroy us. We cling to the belief that genuine ecstasy should not be expected to occur with any regularity.

Pain, the other side of life, we accept as normal. "Life is tough. Then you die." Life is a series of problems and stresses. True enough. But why shouldn't we expect exactly the same measure of ecstasy and pleasure? Why shouldn't we expect deep joy and a heightened sense of aliveness to be woven in and out of our daily lives—just the way stress is?

Our expectations have an impact on what we achieve. Yet it seems as if the genuinely intimate, loving, pleasurable relationship is missing from the spectrum of relationship styles most people consider.

It is widely accepted as axiomatic that relationships are "hard work," that excitement and passion are impossible to maintain over a period of years, that everyday hassles will inevitably destroy the heightened awareness and pleasure of new love, that "dream" relationships are an unrealistic figment of Hollywood's imagination.

In a recent magazine article, a psychologist was making the point that singles have unrealistic standards and that they could find a mate if they had more positive attitudes toward more people. To illustrate her point, she quoted a fictitious single woman as saying,

"I need to respect him. And I need a man who has plenty of time to spend with me, and who will want to be a father, and who will be sensitive to my needs, and who is attractive and well dressed and interesting and successful . . ."

I was stunned to read this, because it seemed to me an entirely reasonable set of desires. If there is no man anywhere who can meet these simple criteria, then manhood is in a far worse state than I have observed. But apparently our psychologist would have this woman develop a "positive attitude" about someone who doesn't have any time to spend with her, or who doesn't want children, or who is insensitive to her needs, or who is ugly or boring or a failure. Why shouldn't she want all those qualities she listed? And why shouldn't she hold out until she finds them?

The article was an example of the low-standards mentality that pervades our age.

I met Margie at a workshop and, because I saw a big diamond on her left hand, asked if I could interview her. After the seminar, over gin and tonics, she told me,

Jack is such a honey. I love him. I have to be honest, I do have some hesitations about him—about us together. He is so heavily into race-car driving, and I can't stand the whole idea of it. . . . And I worry about the way we fight. We seem to fight a lot. And the truth is, he's not very good at talking about his feelings. But he is so thoughtful, and just a really good, kind person. He's funny, and I like his friends. And I love being with him. I figure no one's perfect. We always do get over our fights and have good times.

I remember reflecting after our interview that Margie didn't seem very excited about getting married. After hearing about her relationship, I could understand why. Margie deserved more, I felt. I wasn't sure why she was going ahead with this marriage. At some deep level, she had bought the idea that "no one's perfect" and that, therefore, you have to settle for what you can get.

Gerald, thirty-two, an accountant, was talking in a discussion group during one of my workshops:

I have met a lovely woman. We are great friends. I don't see her too often because she's very involved with her work. Besides, it probably wouldn't be too good for us to be together too much. But we have a fine time when we are together. It's okay sexually. Not great, but nice. But you can't have everything, and I respect her so much. And I know that feeling is mutual. I wouldn't be surprised if we eventually get married. This is the nicest relationship I've had for a long time.

In my interviews and workshops, I have often encountered this sense of resignation, a feeling that you have to go with what you can get; that you have to settle for less than what you would *ideally* like.

This pessimistic, Murphy's-Law-sort-of attitude about relationships is a symptom of the Great Emotional Depression. Love is low on our priority list. We build our lives to avoid intimacy but still desire romance and sex. And then we use the poor relationships that result to prove that we have unrealistic expectations about love. And we lower our standards.

But *you* don't need to sink into this quagmire yourself. Just know that you will encounter resignation, defeatist attitudes, and pessimism. To maintain high standards, you need to have a strong inner belief that you deserve what you want, that what you want is possible, and that you intend to hold out for it.

I do not mean to suggest that intimacy does not, like everything in life, involve trade-offs. There will always be some. Often making decisions about relationships is a question of weighing what the trade-offs will be. But you should expect to be able to make trade-offs in which *you gain more than you have to give up*.

So even if you are surrounded by people who are encouraging you to give in, don't.

Be sure you fully and totally respect your partner. Be sure the things you *don't* like in your partner are tolerable to you. Ask yourself how you *feel* deep down inside about being with this person, and then *honor those feelings*. Are they positive and wonderful? Or do you feel hesitations? *Pay attention.* Don't blunder through this most important of life's decisions. The secret to maintaining high standards is to keep passing up potential partners who don't meet them!

Singles have often told me that it is impossible both to maintain high standards and to be realistic. But in fact, as I have explained, *both are essential*. Many of the relationship problems of recent years are a result of our widespread abandonment of high standards!

The first four strategies we have examined are, more than anything else, about your attitude in your search for love.

- Are you ambivalent? Then, if you want results, *act as though* you want love more than anything else in the world.
- Do you get depressed by bleak-looking statistics? Ignore them. They are not about individuals—like *you*. You can do a great deal to increase your own odds of finding love.
- Do you feel defeated because you believe there are no good ways to meet people? Then find some methods with which you are comfortable, and *do* them. Actively networking is the most effective method and requires the least time and effort. Deliberately increase the flow of new people through your life.
- Do you feel resigned and pessimistic and feel you must lower your standards to get any kind of love at

all? You may misunderstand what high standards really are. Affirm your fondest hopes, and trust your intuition. If you are willing to hold out for what you truly want, you are much more likely to get it!

Now we will move on to the realities of "dating," or, to put it more bluntly, of "screening" potential intimate partners. As you plunge into dating and meeting new people, what strategies will move you toward your goal of true love and help you avoid pitfalls and sand traps along the way?

Part II

Guidelines for Kissing Frogs

Chapter 5

The Fifth Strategy: Don't Get Stuck in the Swamp

Learning to Say No

The biggest problem with going frog kissing in search of a prince (or princess) is that the terrain is swampy. As you go about looking for magic, it is far too easy to get pulled into a quicksand pit and spend a lot of time mucking around with a lot of frogs.

I met Mary Beth in her tastefully decorated Manhattan apartment. She was eager to tell me about her current relationship and was talking it through to herself as she told me about it. She was unusually attractive, thirty-two, and owned her own small dress shop.

To put it mildly, I'm nuts about Michael. He's very sensitive to me. He always knows if something's troubling me, and he'll ask. It's hard for me to talk about some things—I'm sort of a withholder—so I love it when he asks. I can always tell he cares about me. And he's affectionate. Whenever we're going to get together, I'm excited. I just love to be with him. But, you know, he's very reluctant to move ahead with the relationship. I'd marry this guy in a second. But he's not there at all. I'll give him credit: he's honest with me about it. He was seeing another woman when I met him. But I hung in there and she finally got out of the picture. I want commitment from Michael. I really do. But I can understand his situation. He's in a job transition. The company he's been with for twelve years is selling out and he's very anxious about it. He's determined to find something he'll like as much, and it's not easy. Plus, his son, who's eight, lives with him, and he's very devoted to him. He has his reasons for wanting to hold off. He knows how much I want to get married—or at least live together.

How long have you been seeing Michael? [My question]

Seven years.

Mary Beth had made a choice. She was willing to let Michael have exactly what he wanted so that she could have the privilege of tagging along behind him, sacrificing her own very deep desire for a committed, intimate relationship. Convinced that she was being "understanding," she fell for his excuses about his work and his son, facts which have nothing to do with his lack of commitment to her. There are men who would welcome a loving partner to share the stresses of parenting and career transition.

The era of long-suffering, self-deprecating, "faithful" (abused) wives and mistresses is *supposed* to be over. Yet it seemed never to have occurred to Mary Beth that she could have more control over her life. Michael may be a very fine man, but he is not the ideal mate for Mary Beth by any means. She readily admitted that she was always insecure with him, that she could never be certain that he wouldn't become interested in someone else, and that he would give her no assurances. But because she liked him and had become attached to him, she convinced herself that he was the best she could do.

I was told a very different kind of story by Phoebe, forty-one, a marketing consultant, highly respected in her field.

I divorced just about two years ago. I guess you'd say I'm pretty well over it; the divorce was a long time in coming. I haven't had any trouble meeting men. My friends seem to have taken on my cause and keep introducing me to people, and I meet men in my work. One man was really interested in me. He was rich, too. I dated him for three or four months, but I just couldn't get over certain problems I had with him. The breakup was really hard for him, but I had to do it. I just plain don't want to be in any more short-term relationships. Then I dated a man I really liked—a *lot*. He's the cousin of my best friend. He has a good track record, too; he was married for twelve years. But it became very clear, very soon, that he had big hang-ups about sex. I couldn't believe it, we were so wonderful together. Oh, it was hard to let go of him. [Phoebe became tearful.] But I wasn't going to be in a relationship with a major problem like that. I'm ready to start building my life with the person I'm going to be with for the rest of it. He loved me, too, but when it came down to it, he chose to lose me rather than to deal with our sexual problems. It was just too big a difference between us. I couldn't understand his behavior. And I didn't like it. I want to be with someone who sees life as I do, who wants what I want. He wanted to keep dating, but I told him no. I want to concentrate on finding the right person for me, not the almost-right one.

Probably the most towering mistake of all—the great big monster mistake that supercedes all the other mistakes singles make—is not knowing when and how to say no to a relationship.

Phoebe knew. But in my experience, Phoebe is unusual.

Mary Beth, on the other hand, was still single because she was not able to say no to a man who was not meeting her needs. She got stuck in the swamp.

The secret of finding love is to clarify what you want and then to *pass up everyone who does not fit the bill.* To make this plan work you have to meet many people so that you are operating from abundance, and be able to say no to all the ones who aren't right. Failing to meet enough people is guaranteed to keep you alone. On the other hand, saying yes too casually and too soon means you will end up with the first reasonably good match that comes along.

We need to examine closely, then, this matter of saying no.

The Consequences of Failing to Say No: BTNs

When you aren't able to say no at the right moment, you end up in a relationship—or a series of relationships—that are nice but not great, or great in some ways but mediocre in others. I have a name for these: I call them BTN relationships—Better Than Nothing.

Most singles have had the experience of falling in love

with the wrong person, a common topic of discussion in my workshops. Often, people attribute their propensity for being attracted to inappropriate people to a deep inner flaw that can be traced back to their childhood. Occasionally, personal pathology may be involved. But most often, falling in love with the wrong person is simply a natural, normal event. The world is brimming over with appealing, sexy, competent, attractive, wonderful men and women. Most of them aren't appropriate life-long mates *for you* for one reason or another, but that does not mean you might not be very attracted to any number of them. Falling in love with someone who is an inappropriate life-long mate is the easiest thing in the world!

The problem is not falling in love with them. The problem is *staying* in love with them! Just because there is good chemistry between the two of you, don't feel enslaved to each other. "No" is still an option.

A BTN is a "nice" relationship with the wrong person. It's a relationship that drags on and on, even though it is only partially satisfying, and the partners know it has a low probability of survival. BTNs are all those partners who don't love you back the way you want to be loved. They are the commitmentphobes you stay with anyway, the old lovers who have simply become a habit, the intimacy-avoiders who feel better than no sex at all.

If you are in a transition period and a "treading water" relationship is all you want, then a BTN *is* better than nothing. But if a life-long, intimate connection is what you seek, then BTNs are dangerous; they present a major roadblock to finding true love.

In the first place, BTNs consume time and energy that would otherwise be available for meeting new people. Night after night, you curl up next to this person you've become very used to and watch TV. If a BTN doesn't take you out of circulation altogether, at least it slows you down. For you have to save evenings to spend with your BTN, and you have to save energy to interact with him or her, however unsatisfying that may be.

Problem solving with a BTN takes more energy than usual because when the commitment between two people is limited, their willingness to make changes in order to improve the relationship will also be limited. Rather than thinking, "Barbara's probably right. I could tell her I love her more often. I know she really wants this," the thinking is more likely to be, "I resent that Barbara doesn't like me the way I am. She's awfully demanding." BTNs drain away your good, positive energy in endless, repetitive hassles. They can actually add stress to your life rather than help to reduce it.

But an even worse problem with BTNs is that they chip away, slowly but steadily, at your self-esteem and sense of well-being. They make you doubt yourself.

BTNs and Self-Esteem

Self-esteem ultimately comes from within. But it must be reinforced by positive messages from the environment and can be destroyed without them. If your primary relationship is with someone who doesn't fully appreciate and love you for exactly who you really are, but instead criticizes you or tries to change you or picks fights with you or fails to cooperate with you, then you will begin to see yourself, not as who you are, but as the other person sees you. Since you do not have the opportunity to experience yourself in any other intimate-type relationship, you will begin to accept as real the other person's view of you.

When we were discussing BTNs in a workshop one day, Dorothy couldn't wait to speak. She told us,

I actually went to therapy because I was feeling so bad about myself after three years with this guy. I can see it all clearly now that I look back on it, but I couldn't see it at all at the time. The thing was, I'm gregarious; I'm a life-of-the-party type. Well, Ike couldn't stand that part of me. He was always telling me how embarrassing I was. Like it was a fact. I got so self-conscious. I tried to tone myself down, but it was artificial. I started hating myself. I didn't want to "take up more than my share of the attention," as he put it, but I hated trying to be some wallflower. It's as if he skewered my best asset.

I see now that I was just being me. The fact that he didn't like me shouldn't have affected my self-esteem, but it did. I began to see qualities that have constituted "me" for all these years as obnoxious.

I know why I stayed with him. We're both painters and we shared the art world. We were really good when it was just the two of us. We had good times. But oh! the fights. You know, I just came to see them as normal. But they were taking such a toll on me. . . .

It was my therapist who helped me see I should get out. We were never going to last anyway. We never even lived together. And it wasn't until I got out of the relationship that I saw what a drain it was. I was half dead! I had to be to keep peace. After I left him, I felt so good! I didn't even know that I could feel that good about myself!

Although some BTNs are not as extreme as Dorothy's, nevertheless, they have similar dynamics, *and people choose to stay in them voluntarily*—because they *seem* to be better than nothing. But they aren't. Even if they have positive qualities to offset the negative ones, when you spend a lot of time with a person who does not value your positive attributes or who actually turns them into something negative, you may have a hard time keeping your self-esteem intact. If you never have a chance to experience yourself in a setting where the real you is fully appreciated, you'll lose the ability to appreciate yourself.

The very fact that you are willing to be part of a BTN relationship bespeaks a lack of self-confidence, for if you felt strongly within yourself that you deserved more, you would not easily settle for a BTN in the first place. And once you are in a BTN, only your second-best qualities get reinforced. Daily, the evidence mounts up that you make unwise choices for yourself, that you lack personal power and control over your life, that your taste in partners is not so great. These "weaknesses" would disappear if you got out of your half-good relationship. BTNs reinforce self-doubts rather than strengths. To feel powerful, in control, and good about yourself, you will have to end any relationship that is reinforcing your weaknesses rather than your strengths.

Why Do We Stay in BTNs?

BTN relationships actually waste precious time, and they are deadening. Yet virtually all of us have had the experience of staying in a relationship longer than we knew was good for us.

Why?

We stay in BTNs because we are hooked on security, and we hold on to the *illusion* of it even when we can clearly see that the relationship is degenerating. We feel safer staying in a known situation, however troubled, than venturing into an unknown situation, however freeing it might be.

We stay in BTNs because we are more concerned about meeting our short-term intimacy needs than our long-range life goals.

We stay in BTNs because we have bought the misguided idea that you can't have what you really want in a relationship, and we believe we have to compromise.

We stay in BTNs because we misinterpret our feelings. When we feel a deep longing for more intimacy or more commitment or closer sex with a partner, we think that is love. It isn't love. It's pain, pain caused by some deficiency in the relationship. But that longing makes us feel attached and makes us think we are in love.

We stay in BTNs because we find it simply too hard to get out of them. We love the other person (not a sufficient reason to stay in a partnership with big problems). We think about the pleasant aspects of the relationship and the shared history and know it will be painful to give these up. Ending a BTN can result in shattered dreams, emptiness, longing, facing uncharted waters. The problems of the BTN seem more appealing than the pain of loneliness.

I once counseled a woman in a relationship with a man who was clearly "unattainable." He told her over and over that he had no interest in commitment or monogamy, and he dated other women. I asked her to consider what she got out of staying in this "BTN." She showed me a journal entry which I'm sure many of us can relate to:

I have an investment in being embroiled over an unattainable man because

1. I get attention from my friends; I have a "problem" to talk over. I fear I couldn't get attention for positive reasons.
2. Plotting, letter writing, churning about it makes me feel alive.
3. It proves I'm right: no one will ever be there for me.
4. It keeps me from doing what I fear: moving on; taking the focus off a man and looking at myself; working on being constructive and happy.

But mostly, we stay in BTNs—love relationships with the wrong person—because we didn't say no when it would have been easy and then we lose track of the option of getting out.

No story illustrates this point better than Luis Buñuel's 1962 movie *The Exterminating Angel* about a group of wealthy people at a lavish party. When it comes time for the party to end, the guests all discover that they can't go home. No one can figure out why they can't leave, but not one of them can find a way to accomplish the task of departing from the house. Various people "try" to get out, but without success. Soon, the whole group becomes obsessed with problems that arise because they are stuck together, like finding enough food and water to stay alive.

Weeks go by. The partygoers are exhausted from their ordeal, completely oblivious to the self-imposed nature of their dilemma.

Eventually, someone decides to re-enact the moment in the original party when leave-taking might have begun. If at that point, he muses, instead of staying for one more song, someone had elected to depart, maybe they wouldn't have become so stuck.

It works!

Only by staying beyond the time when leave-taking was easy and appropriate did the guests find it impossible to leave.

The partygoers are all so grateful to be out of that wretched house, they go together to a cathedral to give thanks for their precious, new freedom. They pray and sing, but when the worship is ended, somehow they find they can't seem to get out of the cathedral. . . .

How common this scenario is in our daily lives! And especially in our amorous relationships.

As I said, almost all of us are familiar with the experience of staying in a relationship too long. We pass the moment when it would have been easy and appropriate to say no, and then we become entrenched. Obsessed with the problems related to staying in the relationship, we lose track of the option of getting out. So there we stay, stuck in a BTN, rationalizing about how much we enjoy the relationship and about how you can't have everything anyway.

Possibly for years.

When to Say No

When, then, should you say no?

The very best time to say no is the first moment you realize that the person you are with is not going to meet your needs—even though some parts of the relationship may be perfectly wonderful. That moment may come during your first two-hour date. It may come after five dates. Or it may have arrived months or even years ago and been long since left behind in the distant past. In which case, the best time to say no is now.

Perhaps the saddest epitaph of all is "I waited."

Rats make changes in their lives more easily than humans do. If you put a rat in a maze and give him cheese at the end of tunnel 3 several times, he'll keep going to tunnel 3 for cheese. Then if you remove the cheese from tunnel 3 twice, the rat will stop going to tunnel 3 and will try another one.

Not so with humans. Some humans will go back to tunnel 3 over and over and over, even though they are disappointed every time. Tunnel 3, no cheese. Tunnel 3, no cheese. "But maybe there will be cheese the next time," they say. "I like tunnel 3. It's familiar." And eventually, "I can probably learn to live without cheese anyway."

If you would prefer to be in a committed relationship, then it is critical that you keep yourself available for one. And that means saying no to ones that don't hold that potential.

Some cases are more clear-cut than others. For example, you can say no right away if you fall in love with someone who is married unless your married friend is already moving out of the married state; or unless you want to sign up for months—or years—of being the "other woman"; or unless your married friend is clearly extracurricular for you, and not someone to whom you will devote your entire self.

If you want a primary committed partner, don't stay in a relationship with someone else's spouse. Follow your head, not your heart. The person may be wonderful in every way, but if he's "taken," he's not ideal for you. Don't let yourself hang around.

Equally clear-cut: Say no if you fall for someone who is gay, if you are straight, or straight, if you are gay.

A gay man I interviewed told me, "I'm so tired of trying to be friends with straight women. They *all* figure that eventually I'll 'come around.' "

Another easy-to-spot "no" situation is anyone who is heavily involved in substance abuse. You may not discover this very early, but as soon as you suspect your friend may be an alcoholic, or a drug addict, buy yourself a book on addiction and co-addiction, or call your local Al-Anon or drug treatment center. If your friend is not ready to seek help, don't stick around and keep hoping he or she will change. Life is too short to spend any of it in the hopeless mire of addiction and co-addiction. If you stay in a relationship with an addict, you aren't a lover, you're a hostage.

But in many situations, it's not so self-evident when to say no to a relationship.

For one thing, there are times when a BTN relationship is just what you *do* want, when a BTN is in fact better than nothing. If both of you realize that a BTN is what you have, *and that's all you both want with each other,* you can have a pleasant friendship. If the two of you have similar expectations of each other, and you both know this isn't "it," you won't be trying to change each other, and you won't get involved in endless hassles about the future of your relationship. The key necessities for a BTN that *does* work are that (a) you both agree you are not each other's final choice, and (b) you are not keeping each other out of circulation—or you will be able to get back into circulation easily when you are ready. One workshop participant was delighted with his own BTN and suggested that we change the name. He said he wants to call his an "LTU"—less than ultimate!

In the end, when and whether to say no is something you have to decide for yourself. First, you have to realize that saying no is an option. That in itself is a big step that many single miss. Then, you have to decide whether no is in your own long-term best interest. It is perfectly okay to go through a period of confusion, of not knowing whether to stay or leave. Just keep listening to your intuition. Pay attention to how you feel, not what you think. Clarity about what you should do will emerge out of your confusion, and when it does, that is the time to act.

If you are in a relationship, whether new or old, and you think it may be wise for you to end it but you aren't sure, the following experiment will be useful. Remember, sometimes you have the option, not of ending the relationship, but of deciding mutually to "de-escalate" it, to agree to remain friends. This is possible only if both parties see it as *the best* option.

EXPERIMENT #8

If you are trying to evaluate a specific relationship, whether new or of long duration, one or more of the following may be useful for you:

1. How does your partner measure up to the top five items on your essentials list? (See Experiment #6.)
2. Write down your long-range life goals. If you could have *everything* you want, what would you most like your life to look like in five years? In ten? In twenty? Will staying with this partner help you to achieve these goals? Will staying with this partner keep you from achieving these goals? (If you aren't at all certain what your long-range goals are, think about your immediate goals, your present life. Is this partner helping or hindering you from having the life you want now?)
3. List all the qualities you like about your partner. Now list all your areas of dissatisfaction with him or her. Now, on both lists, put a 5 next to your extreme likes and dislikes, a 3 next to your medium-level likes and dislikes, and a 1 next to your mild likes and dislikes. Finally, rewrite the lists in order with 5s on the top and 1s on the bottom.
   Which list is longer?
   Which total score is higher?

How likely is it that your areas of dissatisfaction will change?

4. Do you spend more time experiencing pleasure from your relationship, or pain, frustration, and stress?

5. On a sheet of paper, complete this sentence in as many different ways as are accurate:
   I am staying in this relationship because _____.

6. Write down any reason or reasons why your partner might be the "wrong" person for you.

7. Get out your "experiments" notebook when you have forty-five minutes or so, and try this "journal writing" exercise. Imagine that you have traveled many hundreds of miles to visit an oracle you know to be full of truth and wisdom. You approach her in her temple and ask her what you should consider in making a decision about this relationship—and what you should do about it. Now, become that oracle yourself, and write down your reply.

Let me now share with you the responses of some men and women who have done this experiment in my workshops:

PAULA [in a letter to me two years after she had taken my workshop]: My long-range goals were to be married and have a family (plus other career and travel goals). At the time I was with a man who had children already and was dead set against having any more. But I was not at all ready to leave him. It was a wonderful relationship, and ending it was not even a remote possibility for me. But I was really hit in the face by this experiment. I started bringing the subject of children up with him more often. *Very* slowly, we started pulling it out from under the rug where we had swept it. Finally, after almost two years, I could no longer escape that I had to do something about this. It's a long, sad story, but we ended up having a trial separation. It was agony, but I actually dated two men in the first three weeks. Then, my lover called me back and said he realized he was making a dreadful mistake, and that he would consent to children. Now, suddenly, I'm married and pregnant, and I'm in heaven!

That experiment was a real jolt for me. I hated it at the time. But it was an important turning point for me. I probably could have gone on for years not looking at my conflict—until it was too late.

JEROME [during a workshop]: I'm stunned by the list of things I like and don't like. I didn't realize it, and I hate to admit it, but I think I'm staying in this relationship for sex—and putting up with a lot else. And I don't think it's worth it.

CLAIRE: I have a long list of qualities I like and a short list of qualities I don't like about my partner. But it seems that the dislikes outweigh the likes because they're more important. And I think I might be staying in this relationship to please my friend who fixed us up. Not a great reason! Also, I realize I'm afraid I won't be able to meet anyone else. I think I'm going to re-evaluate my relationship with Fred.

DEENA: I loved consulting the oracle! The message I got from her was wait and watch. I realize I just don't know this man well enough yet. But I think the watch part is critical. The relationship is moving slowly, and I like that, but I can't *just* wait. I have to pay attention too and not just drift into it if it isn't right. That's what I did the last time.

The Chief Obstacle to Saying No: It's Too Hard

Saying no is definitely difficult. I have no argument with this. But that is not a reason *not* to do it if it is in your best interest.

I am not unsympathetic to how difficult saying no is. I know as well as anyone that it can be awkward, guilt-inducing, tormenting, frightening, and sometimes excruciatingly painful. Saying no can seem so Herculean a task that it *feels* impossible—just as leaving the party, in Buñuel's film, became impossible.

Still, sometimes it is by far the lesser of two painful

choices. Avoiding the immediate pain of saying no should not be your top priority if you have had a few dates with a very attractive person who is wrong for you, or if you are in a BTN and you want to get on with your life.

Writing this chapter has made me recall a man I said no to over twenty years ago, and I still feel twinges of the agony I went through. He was the minister of a church about two hundred miles from my college campus whom I met when I went home with my roommate for a weekend. Completely taken with me, he drove two hundred miles to see me every Sunday after church. He saw me as the perfect minister's wife, a role I had no interest in whatsoever. I was very fond of him, but hadn't nearly the level of interest in him that he had in me. So I wrote him a long letter saying in the sweetest way I could that I didn't want to see him again. He called, begging me to change my mind, to give him another chance. That phone call was torture for me. I liked him a great deal, and continuing to see him would have been so easy. But I knew it was the wrong thing to do. He was so devastated, I could hear his heart shattering two hundred miles away. I felt terrible about how I had hurt him, and couldn't stop worrying about him and tormenting myself for weeks.

Another time, I was the one with the broken heart, but I was still the one who said no.

I had the misfortune to fall in love with a gay man; I'll call him Theo. We met at a conference, and I was smitten the moment I saw him. I actively pursued him. When he told me he was gay, I was crushed—but not deterred. We formed quite a lovely, warm, close friendship, seeing each other frequently for dinner, and joining in several activities together. Seeing him was always a special treat for me.

Then one night we took a long moonlight walk. Atop a hill looking out over the San Francisco Bay, he told me that he felt he wanted to become closer to me and to express his feelings physically, but that he was absolutely certain he did not want to become sexual with me. I was incredulous and had not the least hesitation, whereupon he took me in his arms and gave me one of the most ecstatic, gentle kisses of my entire life. Then—he took me home with him. We slept together—on opposite sides of the bed!

We continued our intensified relationship for exactly one month. I was insane with love for him. But I soon realized that there would never be any sex—or any full commitment. I became fully conscious that the pain of my unrequited desire was greater than the pleasure of being with him. Yet I couldn't even conceive of not seeing him anymore; our friendship had become incredibly close. What was I to do?

I beat my breast and gnashed my teeth and sobbed and analyzed myself and wore out my friends' good will, but in the end I had to pick up the phone and tell him I didn't want to see him again. He understood. My unbearable pain over this no didn't ebb for more than a year.

So don't tell *me* that no is too hard to say.

It's hard. But when you decide you have to say no to preserve your own life, you can find a way to say it. A difficult no is preferable in the long run to a painful or mediocre relationship or a BTN that is getting you nowhere.

Even when no doesn't break your heart—or someone else's—it can still be awkward, embarrassing, and scary.

Saying no requires trusting yourself, your intelligence, your faith in the future. In fact, trusting is the only way to overcome the difficulty of saying no. You have to do what you determine is best, and then believe totally that you did the right thing. You have to trust that events will continue to unfold in a positive way for you. Often, you can't anticipate what form that positive unfolding will take. But you can't let go of something without knowing what will take its place *unless* you trust that something better lies ahead for you. Without this trust, no becomes not only difficult, but pointless.

Try this experiment to discover what your own objections are to saying no. It is important to do this *before* you move on to practical strategies. For only if you are aware of your excuses can you begin to overcome them. As long as you remain unconscious of the reasons why no is difficult for you, the reasons will sabotage you, and all the practical strategies in the world won't help.

EXPERIMENT #9

Think about a time when you might have said no but didn't. With that incident in mind, choose the appropriate endings for this sentence.

Saying no is hard for me because

- I'm afraid I will hurt the other person.
- I feel guilty.
- I want to find a way that won't cause the other person pain.
- It's easier to say, "I'll call you," and then just not call.
- Basically, I'm a coward. I just want to avoid what's difficult.
- I'm afraid the other person will talk me out of it.
- I believe I should be honest and it's just too hard to say "I don't like your fat legs."
- I've tried but the words just get stuck in my throat. I can't get them out.
- I generally want to be liked, and I can't stand the thought that this person might be angry at me.
- I'm afraid of a lonely future.
- I'm just too hung up on this person, too attracted. I know I should say no, but I *can't*.
- Other. (Spend some time with yourself, and write down as many reasons as are accurate for you.)

Practical Strategies for Saying No

Let's assume you have determined that a no is called for. How do you bring it off?

We shall begin with guidelines for saying no in the early stages of a relationship, when you have seen a person once or a few times and you do not wish to pursue the relationship at all.

1. If you can, say something positive before or after you say no. Make it a genuine compliment. "You are a great conversationalist." "I really enjoy your sense of humor." "Thanks a lot for turning me on to this movie. I would hate to have missed it." Bad news is always easier to take if there is some good news along with it.

2. State your position simply. Avoid getting into the realm of honest critical feedback, especially if this is a

person you are not planning to see again. An honest dialogue about difficult interpersonal subjects is time- and energy-consuming, and is just not a possibility with everyone. Such frankness can be reserved for ongoing relationships. You may carry on at length *with a friend* about how your last date talked too much or had this or that bad habit, but when you are telling that last date that you don't want to see him or her again, don't volunteer your honest opinions.

3. You are not responsible for giving a reason for saying no. In some circumstances, you may decide you want to, but it is not necessary, especially if you do not know the person very well. You should be polite, respectful, and kind, but you do not need to go on at great length, for you do not owe an explanation for your decision.

4. Your no should be clear and effective. Don't be vague and leave your partner guessing.

5. It is crucial to understand that—as long as you are kind and respectful—*you are not responsible for how the other person responds to your no.* You may want to repeat this to yourself one hundred times until it really sinks in. You are not causing the other person to feel bad. You have to do what is right for you. And the other person will respond. If your no is painful, you can express your genuine concern. "I'm really sorry this is painful for you." But you should never try to "fix" the other person's pain or blame yourself for it. You cannot be both the disease and the doctor! The most you can do is to be decisive about your own decision and understanding about the other person's disappointment.

6. For relatively casual no's, *standard formulas are an enormous help. Memorize some.* Say them over and over so you have them handy when you need one. A few samples:

"Thank you for asking but I think I'd rather not."

"I had a good time with you last weekend, but I'm not in a place right now to pursue this relationship."

"I prefer not to continue dating, but I want you to know how much I have enjoyed [your sense of humor, your dancing skills]." (Be specific.)

Never say, "I'll call you" unless you mean it. By now, we should all be mature enough to avoid this trite, cowardly, dishonest cop-out. "Maybe we'll see each other again sometime" is just as easy to spit out if you need a parting line, and far more respectful and honest.

The guidelines for saying no to a BTN that you have been a part of for some time are similar to those above except that you may want to say more about your decision.

1. Consider writing a letter to your soon-to-be-ex-partner as your initial step, simply because it may be easier than breaking the news in a conversation. This is not always appropriate, but it may ease the burden. You may wish to have your lover read the letter in your presence, or to set up a time when he or she can respond.

2. Whether you are writing or talking, make "I" statements and avoid "you" statements. That is, say things like, "I feel frustrated with our lack of commitment." "I like sex more often than we have it." "I feel sad too much of the time." Do *not* say, "You won't make a commitment." "You aren't interested in sex often enough." "You make me feel sad." Do not blame or judge your partner. Talk only about your own feelings and your own decision.

3. Keep your no simple. Do not get involved in long analyses. Do not review bygone events. Stay in the present, and talk about your feelings. You will find you can say virtually everything you need to say if you stick to this formula: "I feel _____." For example, "I feel restless." "I feel unloved." "I feel frustrated." "I feel ready to move on." Such statements are the simplest way to present the truth, and your partner cannot argue with them.

4. Do mention the things you like about your partner before or after you talk about the problems you are having.

5. You are not responsible for explaining your decision *to your partner's satisfaction*. Your partner does not have to understand you or agree with you. Simply repeat your "I feel _____" statements.

6. Make your no clear and effective. Don't be vague.

7. You are not responsible for how your lover responds to your no! (See guideline #5 above.)

EXPERIMENT #10

The best way to learn how to say no is to practice. And practice really does make a difference. The next time you get together with a friend spend a half hour role playing no's with each other. It's best if you can think of an actual situation in which you had to say no—or should have said no—or still might say no. But in lieu of that, make up situations. Do some in which you practice standard formulas, and some that are more complex.

One of the advantages of role playing is that you get to experience being in the other person's shoes as well. When you are in the role of being told no, you may discover ways you like—or do not like—being treated.

You can always take a few moments to practice saying no by yourself, too. Repeat your favorite formulas occasionally to keep them fresh in your mind. And try rehearsing an impending no in front of the mirror.

Just keeping firmly in mind that *no is always an option* may begin to make a difference in your love life.

One of the secrets to success in looking for love, then, is to avoid BTN relationships by saying no at the right time.

Saying no to a relationship that is *partly* wonderful is difficult. The fear of being alone again, of facing major changes in your life can be immobilizing and can keep you in a relationship that has major problems for a long time. It may even be too scary to say no to someone you just met and don't care to see again.

But the price you pay for avoiding saying no is enormous: at best, tedious evenings with boring people; at worst, months or years of BTN relationships.

Consider the advantages of saying no to the wrong relationship—or the half-right relationship. You may have a painful transition time, but you will also begin to experience the inner power that results from truly taking care of yourself. Your self-esteem is sure to go up! You may feel better about yourself than you have for a very long time. If you don't want to be alone (although you may discover you like it more than you thought you would), you will be free to start a systematic search for the right person. And, if you are deliberate and tenacious in your search, you won't be alone for long.

Saying no can be freeing and empowering. It means you are not a slave to whatever you happen to blunder into.

You deserve more than a BTN relationship! And you can have it. But you have to make it happen yourself.

One big reason these are troubled times for relationships is that so many people settle for so much less than they truly deserve—because they lose track of no as an option, or they just can't bring themselves to say it.

So keep working on saying no. By the time you find someone to say yes to, you will be an expert.

Chapter 6

The Sixth Strategy: Watch for Frogs in Royal Clothing

Distinguishing Between Pseudo-Intimacy and the Real Thing

One vital element of the magic you seek is closeness.

A craving for close human contact is a natural response to the impersonal, urban environments—often far removed from family—and the alienating workplaces where many singles find themselves.

Genuinely satisfying closeness can be achieved only over a period of time, through shared experiences and honest conversation. Intimacy is the experience of stripping away your outer, more public ways of being and of sharing your inner life with another person. But in our busy, achievement-oriented lives, we are often unwilling to commit the time and energy required to enter into this process of becoming genuinely close with someone.

So we have developed "pseudo-intimacies," experiences that *look* and *feel* like genuine intimacy but in fact have little to do with it.

Pseudo-intimate experiences are extremely common, especially in the single subculture—and I do not mean to condemn them altogether. Indeed, I shall point out the positive aspects of each one I describe. The problems arise when we *mistake* these games for genuine intimacy. The "games" have a place, but they will never satisfy the deep longing for genuine closeness that creeps over involuntary singles from time to time. Pseudo-intimacy can be a trap. Unless you are fully aware of the "game" quality of it, pseudo-intimacy may cause you a long and painful delay in your search for love. That is why we shall stop to examine it here.

Genuine intimacy is the process of being close with another person. Couples who are intimate come out from behind their "masks" when they are with each other. They have moved beyond fear and anxiety about each other. They have nothing left to suspect or to withhold.

Pseudo-intimacy is intimate-type gestures and actions without any content beneath the dewy eyes and soft caresses. Just as a two-dimensional, black-and-white silhouette *suggests* a real person, so pseudo-intimacy is a shadow of what is possible in relationships.

In an intimate partnership, you are generally focused on the object of your affections. In pseudo-intimate exchanges, you tend to focus more on your *own* pleasure. Indeed, one of the outstanding characteristics of pseudo-intimacy is that the "intimate partner" *role* may be played by almost anyone who is handy! Pseudo-intimates do not love each other; they use each other as a means to experience intensity and passion.

Let us look at the main forms in which pseudo-intimacy appears: the Closeness Game, infatuation, and sex.

The Closeness Game

You've been laughing together and teasing each other all evening and flirting across the table. Now you find yourselves in front of a warm fire on huge, comfy pillows sipping wine. You discover you like the same kind of music, you've both been to Mexico, and you both like to ski. Or, if you know each other a little better, you may catch each other up on recent events or talk a little politics. Eventually you stop talking and just touch and hold each other. If you are both accomplished at playing this game, you look at one another and whisper thoughtful and affectionate comments to each other. And then you move easily into some degree of sexual activity as you continue to caress each other with your voices and your eyes. A few years ago, the scene would almost certainly have ended with lovemaking, but now you probably stop short of that, having tactfully—or tacitly—agreed to keep this encounter "safe."

The next night—or weekend—you repeat the entire ritual with a different person.

EXPERIMENT #11
Think about specific incidents when you have

- behaved in a more close, romantic way than was appropriate for the level of intimacy you actually had. Did you realize at the time or only later that you were "acting," at least a little?
- had several dates in a row and on, say, the third one, found yourself gently repeating the same affectionate phrase for the third time to the third different person.
- felt, right after your date and you parted, "Whew! Now I can be me again." The feeling comes as a surprise. But when the door closes behind your date, your face relaxes, and you are suddenly aware of having put out an enormous effort to sustain your little act with the person.

Why do we play the Closeness Game? What causes us to engage in this curious drama in which our inner experiences are incongruent with our outer behavior?

To begin with, it's pleasurable. Why *not* play a game that titillates our egos and bodies all at the same time?

Second, the game may be as close as some people ever get to genuine intimacy, and it is far better than nothing at all.

Third, we have become conditioned to play this game by seeing so much of it in movies and on TV. Close *behavior* is the easiest way a movie has of portraying closeness itself. I remember once rolling around on the couch with an old boyfriend and thinking, "This could be a scene out of a Neil Simon movie." Truly, after a lifetime of watching closeness gambits on the tube, it would be surprising if we didn't mimic them. The actors make it look so easy!

It seems to me that since the sexual revolution of the sixties, our repertoire of behaviors has become limited. When there was such a thing as "courtship," I suspect that at the various stages of it, behavior corresponded more directly with the level of intimacy that had actually been established. But now, a relationship can move from formal to friendly to sexual in the course of one evening. All the subtleties in between have been lost entirely. A person wanting to move ahead with a relationship feels he or she has no choice but to send sexually oriented messages, even if they are—in some sense—premature.

We play the Closeness Game out of habit. Because it is quicker and easier than the real thing, we have all conspired to allow this game to fill our longings for close, warm human connection. We are aware of the benefits of the game—and almost entirely unaware of its drawbacks. Let's review both.

To be said *for* the Closeness Game: Closeness Games can be pleasurable and provide good entertainment. They can give the players excellent practice with intimacy skills, flirting, and sexual techniques. The sexual revolution left a legacy of "how to's" and the notion that we all need to perfect our "skills"; to the extent that this is now true, the Closeness Game can serve as "training." We can expand our sexual identities by learning and experimenting with different partners. Finally, the Closeness Game has become a kind of ritual that can ease the initial stages of a relationship and lead to genuine intimacy little by little.

But dangers are inherent in this game: the worst problem is that the Closeness Game may deceive its players, bringing pain instead of pleasure. The game looks and feels like genuine intimacy but leaves you feeling empty in the end. When played on drugs or alcohol, it can create an even more vivid illusion of sensuous, warm, erotic, and joyful communion.

One woman said,

> When I am playing the game on an especially pleasurable occasion, I think, "How I long to feel this way with someone with whom I am actually intimate!" Sometimes the "Game" just makes me all the more lonely for the real thing in the end—after the immediate pleasure is gone.

Of course, these pleasurable episodes can be harmless *unless* they lead to serious involvement based on the play-acting of the Closeness Game, and nothing more.

A second danger is that the Closeness Game gives rise to frustrating communication problems, for our language does not differentiate between the game and the real thing.

Allison had been in a relationship with Frank for over a year, and she wanted to feel more connected to him. She would say things to him like, "I want to be close," or "Please talk to me more."

But Frank was baffled. "How much closer can we be?" he would say. "We make love a lot. We eat out all the time. We love to snuggle up and watch TV. I actually think I'm quite romantic! What more can I do?"

"I like all that," Allison would respond, frustrated. "But I still don't feel close."

Allison didn't want more of the *trappings of closeness*. What she sought was conversations with Frank about his feelings. She wanted Frank to trust her enough to let her see what he feared or felt insecure about.

The Closeness Games Frank played were all part of his act. Allison longed for Frank to relax with her and tell her what he really felt about her, not just give her compliments that they both knew were part of a good romantic act.

But because neither Frank nor Allison understood the distinction between the game and genuine closeness, they had a terrible time communicating. They were using the same word, "close," to indicate two entirely different types of behavior.

"I would like to be more close and intimate," Allison would say, meaning genuine closeness.

"I am being close," Frank would say, meaning the Closeness Game.

How could they proceed? They didn't even realize they were talking about two different things!

When the Closeness Game is played frequently with lots of different partners, a third problem arises which I call the "wolf, wolf syndrome."

I used to fear that I was "using up" all my love language playing the game, and that I would be without ways to express myself when I was finally, truly in love. I felt like the boy who called "Wolf! Wolf!" when there *was* no wolf and worried that, when I finally did want to convey sincerity, I would be unable to do so convincingly. Affectionate language and behavior used so glibly during various Closeness Games simply lose their impact on an authentic occasion.

The fourth problem I call the "hors d'oeuvres-only syndrome": A taste of warmth and sexual closeness stimulates one's appetite, and, when the feast is not forthcoming, it simply increases one's longing for the real thing. To switch metaphors, a woman told me,

> I keep my hopes for a real relationship sleeping like a bear in a cave. When my fantasies are in hibernation, they don't bother me, and I feel terrific about my life. But if someone shakes the hopes gently awake, they come leaping out of the cave and take up a lot of my energy. I focus on what I'm missing. It takes work to put the hopes to sleep again. So I become annoyed when someone wants a little closeness and that's all. I am better off alone than with a half relationship!

A final, significant problem with the Closeness Game is that it cannot last. This is no problem when it is played on one-night stands or summer romances. But if you try to build a relationship on nothing more than the game, you will either grow dissatisfied and become distant from your partner or settle into a mutually deadening relationship and wonder why it doesn't work anymore.

I often ask my workshop participants if they think emotional pleasure and sexual excitement can be sustained over many years of a relationship. The majority of people I have polled believe they cannot!

In fact, a genuinely intimate partnership becomes deeper, closer, and more pleasurable as the years go by. The belief that sexual excitement and emotional pleasure always die an early death is a direct result of the inability to distinguish between genuine intimacy and the Closeness Game. Genuine intimacy improves with age. The Closeness Game becomes boring soon after it begins.

Before we discuss what to *do* about the Closeness Game, let us look at two other forms of pseudo-intimacy: infatuation and sex.

Infatuation

Infatuation, also known as falling in love, is defined by the dictionary as foolish, extravagant, all-absorbing passion; irrational love or desire; blind love. Those of us who have been "in love" know that the experience can be wildly exciting.

Both biologists and psychologists (to say nothing of poets and songwriters) have studied the phenomenon of infatuation in an attempt to explain the intensity and mysteriousness of it all. Biochemists hypothesize that an amphetamine-like substance, phenylethylamine, is released by the brain of an infatuated person, causing a natural drug-induced high. When the infatuation ends, the thwarted lover's brain stops production of the "upper," and the resulting pain, which can be agonizing, is like—or may actually be—drug withdrawal. (It turns out that chocolate contains phenylethylamine. Could this be the reason unrequited love often gets drowned in boxes of chocolate?)

Psychologists suggest that infatuation has its origins deep in the subconscious psyches of the lovers. For example, a woman may fall in love with a man who resembles her father in a subconscious attempt to win her father's withheld approval. Or a woman may project her own inner male qualities onto a man in her attempt to unearth these qualities within herself. In both cases, the woman may be powerfully drawn to the man, but she will be subconsciously wanting from him what he can't possibly produce (her father's love, her own self-sufficiency). Meantime, the man may have his own subconscious reasons for falling in love with her. For example, older married men become infatuated with their young secretaries as a way to thwart subconscious fears of impotence.

Infatuation, while it may feel intensely intimate and may look even more like intimacy than does the Closeness Game, is not intimacy. And it, too, has its pros and cons.

Pros: It can be extremely enjoyable while it lasts and may result in pleasing side effects like weight loss or renewed energy for other projects. It gives you an appetite for intimacy and may give you practice in intimacy skills. And, if you have been fortunate enough to fall in love with a more or less suitable partner, infatuation may be a beginning to a relationship of genuine intimacy.

But the drawbacks to becoming infatuated are impressive. First, this kind of love is blind. It puts you into such a rose-colored universe that cruel teasing may be seen as warmth, your lover's simple amateur paintings may be seen as masterpieces, the Closeness Game may be seen as true love, and thoughtless behavior may be overlooked completely. After hours of delightful conversation, two people in love will conclude that their value systems match like pieces of a jigsaw puzzle. Only months later will they discover that he is a loner and she likes togetherness, or that he doesn't want children and she does. Infatuated lovers hear what they want to hear and see what they want to see until eventually they discover, in the words of the late California folksinger Kate Wolfe, that "the picture on the cover doesn't match the one inside."

This brings us to the second problem: Infatuation never lasts, and the crash can be painful. The rose-colored universe will fade away as the partners begin to see each other as they really are. If the relationship ends, both partners will be in a lot of pain for they will have lost not only each other but a dream that was very dear to them. If the relationship does not end, the fading of infatuation can also be painful and difficult. The partners may blame each other for a change they fear and cannot explain. They must both be willing to readjust to a relationship based on reality.

Though most of us dream of falling in love, infatuation is not the only route to intimacy. Leisurely beginnings can be equally pleasurable, are safer, and can ultimately lead to periods of ecstasy that resemble infatuation in intensity and pleasure but are rooted in reality.

Sex

Most people equate sex and intimacy. When they hear "intimacy," they think "sex," and vice versa.

I suspect that more misunderstanding and heartbreak result from the assumption that intimacy and sex are synonymous than from any other mistake described in this book.

Sex and intimacy are discrete, separate experiences. They sometimes occur together, but each can and often does occur without the other. Two non-sexually involved women spending the evening together over a leisurely meal may be self-revealing, emotional, and trusting—that is, they may be intimate. By contrast, a sexually involved couple may make love every night with mutual enjoyment; yet if they are not being emotionally and verbally honest with each other, gradually building trust, and sharing their "inner lives" with each other, then they are not intimate.

Ironically, sex can be the very device that hinders the development of intimacy. For example, if a person begins to feel "too close," is uncomfortable with the amount or type of information that is being exchanged, or is beginning to feel "bored" (usually a disguise for fear) with what the other is revealing, he or she can initiate sexual activity, thereby eliminating further intimacy at that time. Because both people will assume that sex is furthering intimate contact, the receiving partner will think it unloving not to respond. Yet he or she will justifiably feel cut off, frustrated, and confused.

It has been my experience that the desire for sex and for intimacy is still sometimes divided along gender lines. One couple expressed this classic dilemma:

HE: I feel like I have to take her to dinner and have "long talks" in order to get her to have sex with me.
SHE: I feel like I have to go to bed with him in order to get him to talk with me at all.

He endures closeness when what he really wants is sex; she endures sex when what she really wants is closeness.

When this problem arises within a couple, it may be a symptom of complicated underlying power dynamics in their relationship. If so, they may need some in-depth exploration to sort it out. However, with regard to the isolated issue of sex versus talk, they must realize three things:

- Sex and intimacy are *two separate needs*. Usually, each partner thinks that his or her activity should be sufficient for the other person. If they wish to satisfy both people, they must have *both* activities.

- Each of them has a legitimate request.
- As long as they plan to have intimate conversation *and* sex, the activities can occur in any order. Men often feel more relaxed and ready for conversation after making love, but women often feel more like making love after close verbal contact. So they will need to see each other's point of view and be willing to do some of each.

In one workshop, we spent an hour dealing with an experience the women agreed was common for them all. It illustrates again problems that can arise when sex and intimacy are not understood as separate. One woman put it this way:

If I am open and warm and "just me" with a man, he assumes that I want to go to bed with him. When I say no, he says I am giving mixed messages. I feel like I either have to be cold and distant all the time or else sleep with every man I smile at or talk to!

This woman was trying to be genuine, to offer, tentatively, the possibility of intimacy, of honest emotional exchange. But because the man did not make a distinction between intimacy and sex, he assumed her intentions were sexual.

A surprisingly common experience among the women I interviewed is that of crying unexplainably immediately after making love. Women report feeling deeply lonely— even "homesick." Sometimes the level of self-disclosure between the partners is so low that the woman is able to conceal her tears from the man. When these women get some distance from their experience, they explain it by saying, essentially, that they wanted intimacy and all they got was sex.

DAWN: Making love without real affection just makes me want affection all the more. But it is not forthcoming. He wouldn't even look at me. It's just painful.

ELAINE: Even though I, too, wanted to make love, I

found that afterwards I had an awful sense of
having been used. I felt like all he wanted was
his own pleasure. That's all he communicated.
We weren't close during sex—or after. I felt
very distant from him.

Sex can be an exquisitely intimate experience for a couple who have a close, ongoing relationship. Actually, it may
be more accurate to say that sex is an expression of their
intimacy. But most often for singles, sex is a pseudo-intimate experience—the external behavior of intimacy without the intimate content.

The alarming advent of AIDS has made a dramatic impact on the use of sex as a form of pseudo-intimacy. To
begin with, it has created more than a health crisis: Since
we had become dependent on sexual behavior to produce
the illusion of closeness and now sex is less of an option, we
are left with the fear that we must give up closeness itself.

In fact, however, closeness *is* still available to us. Although the AIDS epidemic is a catastrophic development,
it may have the side effect of forcing us to return to the
more subtle realms of honest communication and tender
affection. We may now be thrown back upon our creative
resources to find new ways to relate closely, to explore the
realms of genuine intimacy. In any case, as we sharply
curtail our sexual behavior, we will no doubt become more
keenly aware of the distinction (as well as the relationship)
between intimacy and sex, and realize that each is a valid,
enjoyable experience. With "fast sex" no longer an option,
we will seek to know and trust and care about our partners
more before establishing physical intimacy.

I do not wish to suggest that sex without intimacy is
"wrong." Erotic activities between consenting adults became a kind of norm in the post-Pill era and can be pleasurable and entertaining. Though sex for sex's sake has greatly
diminished in the post-AIDS era, still casual, non-intimate
sex is an activity some individuals enjoy.

I do want to emphasize, however, that sex within the
context of a relationship that is already intimate or is becoming so is an entirely different experience—more a
form of communication than of entertainment. The real
tragedy of sex without intimacy is that many people settle
for it because they think that's all there is. As theologian

Thomas Oden, author of *Game Free: The Meaning of Intimacy,* says,

> The temptation to reduce interpersonal encounters to sexual encounters has . . . yielded untold misery in our culture. . . . Sex without interpersonal intimacy is like a diploma without an education. Intimacy is closer than sex.

What to Do About Pseudo-Intimacy

Actually, there's nothing to "do." Just becoming aware of the distinctions between pseudo-intimacy and the real thing allows you to make choices. There is surely no reason to avoid close, warm, pleasurable experiences with people even though you have no intention of becoming intimate with them. Just go into such situations with your eyes open. Remember the benefits of pseudo-intimacy—fun, good practice—and enjoy playing the games. Pseudo-intimate games are very often played in the early stages of relationships that do become intimate. Just be careful that you don't start feeling burned out or jaded. Don't mistake sexual compatibility and proficiency for compatibility and proficiency in other areas. Be aware that if sexual intimacy becomes established as the primary mode of communication before other modes develop, the latter may be forever stunted, and the former may never develop beyond superficial, habitual levels.

If you start to get serious about someone, get out my definition of intimacy given at the beginning of this chapter, and see how your relationship measures up. How do you assess the potential for increasing honest communication, emotional availability, trust, respect?

Know that you cannot build a solid, lifelong commitment on the slippery foundation of pseudo-intimate games.

EXPERIMENT #12
Choose one relationship you want to evaluate, and answer these questions with "always," "often," "sometimes," or "never":
. . . .

_____ My partner seems passionate when we make love, and then remains in close contact with me afterward.

_____ I know what my partner is feeling.

_____ My partner and I talk about how we feel about each other.

_____ I have a good sense of what my partner's worst fears are.

_____ I know what my partner's fondest dreams are.

_____ I do little chores or favors for my partner.

_____ I make an effort to please my partner when we make love.

_____ I find it easy to forgive my partner's shortcomings.

_____ I could take a week-long trip with my partner and not be bored.

_____ My partner and I are good friends.

_____ My partner and I can discuss religion and politics without putting each other down.

_____ My partner and I are well aware of each others' plans and hopes for the future.

_____ Our plans and hopes for the future are compatible.

_____ My partner is not selfish, but is concerned about the welfare and needs of both of us.

_____ My partner does little chores or favors for me.

_____ My partner makes an effort to please me when we make love.

_____ When my partner is feeling anxious or depressed, he/she discusses this with me.

_____ When my partner is feeling especially happy, he/she shares this with me.

_____ I enjoy spending time with my partner under many different circumstances.

_____ I believe what my partner is telling me.

_____ I feel giving toward my partner.

_____ My partner is generous and giving toward me.

_____ My partner and I handle our disagreements with mutual respect.

Based loosely on the results of workshop participants, if you scored 10 or more "always" or "often," you are in the process of building genuine intimacy (which is always an ongoing process).

If you scored 10 or more "sometimes" or "never," you may want to look closely at whether what you have going with your partner is some kind of a charade.

Understanding the distinction between pseudo-intimate games and real intimacy is the best defense against getting deeply involved with a person who cannot open up to you, become vulnerable, and share closely in the way a lifetime of living together demands.

Pseudo-intimacy is relatively easy to come by, and most of us have enjoyed it at one time or another. Just remember your goal of an abiding closeness with another person, and don't linger for a long time with a partner who can never provide this. True love is fun, but it is not a game.

Chapter 7

The Seventh Strategy: Beware of the Temporary Prince or Princess

Avoiding Commitmentphobes

Commitmentphobia has reached epidemic proportions during the Great Emotional Depression. Never before have so many people fallen completely in love only to find themselves heartbroken after a short but intensive romance with a person who simply could not make a commitment. Yet in spite of all the publicity it receives, many singles still seem unable to identify commitmentphobia when they see it in another person and to avoid the painful cycle to which it inevitably leads.

In virtually every workshop I have conducted, someone relates a tragic tale about an encounter with a commitmentphobe. And every time a new article appears on the subject, singles everywhere Xerox it excitedly as though it offered a brand new insight. They distribute it to all their friends, and they send anonymous copies to offending former lovers, fervently hoping that it will help them to see the light and reform. They write letters to editors about how they now feel understood and vindicated.

The problem is that these same singles will, with much heartache, extricate themselves from their current commitmentphobic relationship—and turn right around and get entangled in another one!

Here are some of the other names for "commitmentphobia," a term introduced by Helen Singer Kaplan:

The Dance-Away Lover (Daniel Goldstine, *et al.*)
The Go-Away/Come-Closer Disease (Ken Kesey)

The Playboy Syndrome—Flight from Commitment
    (Barbara Ehrenreich)
Puer Aeternus (Marie-Louise von Franz)
The Peter Pan Syndrome (Dan Kiley)
Men Who Can't Love (Steven Carter)

Although other writers seem to feel that most commitmentphobes are men, I have seen many commitmentphobic women and do not agree that men have a
corner on this affliction.

So—once again now—what is commitmentphobia? How
can we identify it early? And what should we do when we
find it?

Commitmentphobia is a pathological aversion to commitment *combined with* an insatiable desire for affirmation by the opposite sex. Commitmentphobes are torn
between a craving for intimacy and a fear of it. They fear
both abandonment *and* engulfment. Both their obsession
to become closer and their aversion to closeness are more
extreme than the ordinary passions and fears most of us
experience with regard to commitment and intimacy.

Commitmentphobes are usually exceptionally good at
being intimate. They are loving, open, self-disclosing, and
intense. They can look you in the eye and tell you you are
the answer to their dreams. They, too, just like you, crave a
deep connection that has the feeling of being unique in the
universe. One commitmentphobe I know of told three
different women, "We must have been married in a previous life."

But just when your lover becomes closest to you—or
when you begin making noises about living together or
traveling together—the commitmentphobe will find a way
to create distance. And you will start feeling pain!

The distinguishing characteristic of commitmentphobes
is that they give out both messages *all the time:* "Come
closer, go away. Don't abandon me. Don't engulf me."
They are masters at the highly developed art of giving
mixed messages.

The reason we have such difficulty identifying commitmentphobes is that we hear and see selectively in the early
stages of a potentially intimate relationship. Caught up in
the excitement of finally finding someone who seems capa-

ble of closeness, we don't *want* to notice any distancing clues, so even if they are there, we ignore them.

Though I have heard dozens of sad stories about commitmentphobes, the most dramatic example was this one:

Rebecca, a thirty-two-year-old therapist, had for six weeks been seeing a man who seemed to her the closest she had ever come to a potential lifelong partner. Travel commitments made before they met kept John away from time to time. But they made plans for her to visit him during his sojourn in Hawaii. After he had been there two weeks, she got a beautiful card from him declaring his devotion to her and giving her detailed arrival instructions. Tucked inside the card was a second folded letter. It was dated three days after the card and began, "Dear Rebecca, This is a sad letter for me to write, but I feel now that I don't want you to come . . ."

Why didn't he send the letter by itself?

He had to send *both* the letter and the card because he always had to give both messages: "Come closer—go away. I enjoy all this closeness and I need to know I'm good at it, but don't tie me down. I need to be close with other people besides you, too. I love you, but I have to keep big parts of myself private. I want you to love me, and let go of me. Come closer—go away."

In *Sometimes a Great Notion,* Ken Kesey talks about the "go-away-closer disease: Starving for contact and calling it poison when it is offered . . . making sure no one gets too close, too intimate, too involved . . . yet unhappy in isolation."

Psychologist Daniel Goldstine describes what he calls the "dance-away lover" and points out that he often uses criticism as his excuse for avoiding closeness. According to Goldstine, the dance-away lover is the charming romantic who loves to date but is preoccupied with his fear of being trapped. He is critical toward all the women he meets, and as soon as he begins to get close to one, he simply invokes these criticisms and dances away, leaving a cloud of dust—and a broken heart. Secure in his belief that he just hasn't met the right woman yet, he clings to the illusion that he really does want to settle down. His life is governed by his fear of intimacy, but it is well disguised—to himself, if not to the women he dates.

During one of my workshops, Bonnie, a forty-year-old

graphic designer, made one of the clearest commit-mentphobic statements I have ever heard:

> I am more interested in honesty than commitment. I want quality now. I don't care about tomorrow. The whole idea of commitment clutters a relationship. As soon as someone starts to worry about commitment, people get scared. They get cautious. They start focusing on each other's faults, like, "Could I really learn to live with this person's sloppiness?" They don't talk freely and openly anymore. I can be very honest with someone I know I'll never see again. But the more involved I'm going to be, the more cautious I have to be.

The "intimacy" Bonnie is describing is very limited compared with genuine intimacy. It gives an idea of what the real thing is like, but it's not the same.

Now that we understand what commitmentphobia is, the big question is how can you identify commit-mentphobes, and how can you avoid them?

1. *Pay Attention to Any Hints of Commitmentphobia.* Since commitmentphobes are always giving out both messages, the distancing clues *will* be there, even early on.

Being on the receiving end of mixed messages will make you feel as though you are going crazy! As one woman said, "It is the ecstasy and the agony! First we have a blissful day together. Then he doesn't even return my calls!" As we all learned in Psychology 101, the pattern that makes rats the craziest is intermittent reinforcement. If you start feeling crazy, remember the rats! Are you getting intermittent reinforcement? If you find you are obsessing endlessly in conversations with friends about what to do next, whether to call or not, whether your new lover will think you are too eager, etc., *ad nauseum,* notice how you feel. Are you enjoying this?

A person's relationship history reveals a lot. Has he or she been in a series of short relationships? Why and how have recent relationships ended? What does the person say that he or she wants for the future? And how does the person treat you?

Don't ignore the first three times your partner forgets to call or changes an arrangement you've made. Is this a mixed message? Don't ignore the first time you notice you are feeling hurt about something. Is it an isolated incident? Or is it becoming a pattern?

Any serious new relationship will require adapting. Commitmentphobes are usually unwilling to change their routines in even the smallest way to accommodate a new relationship in their lives. Are you doing all the adjusting and compromising?

All these things are clues; watch for them. Always pay attention to how you are feeling.

2. *Act Quickly Once You Make the Diagnosis.* This will, of course, be difficult. However, if, when you pay attention to your intuition you know that this person is going to cause you pain, and especially if he or she is already hurting you, your heartache will ultimately be less if you have the courage to get out quickly.

A relationship with a commitmentphobe is like a splinter: it's painful if you leave it and painful if you take it out. If you leave it in, it will swell and get worse over time. It may even get infected and become a real mess. If you take it out, the pain will be more intense, but it will be over more quickly, and healing will be able to take place.

If you don't act quickly once you recognize you are with a commitmentphobe, your "splinter" will swell. You will hang around for months of being on the receiving end of mixed messages: months of feeling powerless, out of control, and angry—months of longing for something you can't have. You may easily slip into becoming a "woman (or man) who loves too much!" *Think.* Is this what you want for yourself? If not, act *now.*

Whenever the pain of a relationship exceeds the pleasure, it is time to move on. Taking the initiative to leave is the lesser of the two painful alternatives. It is the one that will lead you to the relationship of your dreams sooner. Make yourself let go, move on, and steer clear of commitmentphobes in the future. Remember, the only thing more painful than learning from experience is *not* learning from experience.

3. *Don't Try to Change Commitmentphobes Through Discussion.* Commitmentphobes may spend a lot of time rationalizing their behavior. Some believe that they want to be married and go on at length about the unsuitability of

specific partners—including you. Others are certain they never want to marry.

"Marriage is equal to deadness," one man told me. "If you want stability, pick dull people. If you want excitement, don't get married."

Another man said, "You shouldn't bring the same expectations to romance that you bring to a marriage. You don't get married for excitement, and I want my life to be exciting."

A heterosexual woman told me, "I've decided I want my deep, long-lasting relationships to be with women. With men, I want short romances. The way society is today, that's the safest and best thing to do."

Commitmentphobes typically defend their behavior, not with statements about their own preferences (which may be honest evaluations), but with general statements about how the world is. You may be tempted to answer back with speeches about the much deeper excitement possible in long-term relationships. You will find yourself discussing life in philosophical generalizations.

Discussing life may feel to you like a way of hanging on to the last shred of hope. But you will only give commitmentphobes the opportunity to reinforce their rationalizations if you argue with them. It is a mistake to try to convince commitmentphobes that their vision is limited, that their fears are in charge of their lives, or that another point of view exists. We all need our belief systems to support our behavior; only when behavior or experience changes will beliefs change. Young, attractive, financially stable commitmentphobes may not be unhappy. Unless for some reason they become unhappy, their belief systems will serve them well. *Don't ever try to change a commitmentphobe.* Just chalk your experience up to education and move on!

4. *Don't Let a Commitmentphobe Convince You That You Are the One with the Problem.* If you are in love with someone who is afraid of commitment, he or she might try to persuade you that you are neurotic, that you are too "needy" and you demand too much.

Don't fall for it. The desire to be in a committed, intimate relationship is healthy and natural. You have a right to be with a person who views your desire for connection as an asset and who has a desire similar to yours to form a lasting bond.

Women especially often end up blaming themselves for problems that arise when they want to become closer and men distance themselves. "I expect too much. I'm moving too fast," they tell themselves.

Commitmentphobia is the problem, not the desire for closeness. A woman has a problem only if she remains in a relationship when her deepest desires continue to be unfulfilled.

Don't blame yourself when your affections push him away. Rather, recognize that you are with a commitmentphobe, and back off yourself—way off. Go searching for someone who wants your affections as much as you want to express them.

5. *Don't Worry About* Why *Commitmentphobes Are the Way They Are.* Who knows why some people fear commitment or why commitmentphobia is now at an all-time high? A person's commitmentphobia may be the result of socialization, family history, the social upheavals of recent years, fears, or the dearth of good role models. But getting caught up in theories about why things are as they are is ultimately futile with regard to changing them. These conversations about "why Doug didn't call me back" or "what Jim is trying to tell me" or "why Donna seems to be backing off" may be stimulating and cathartic, but if you have the illusion that through these conversations you will eventually *understand* Doug or Jim or Donna and that by understanding you will be able to change anything, you are doing yourself a disservice. When you are faced with a commitmentphobe, focus on what you *feel* and what you are going *to do.* Let "why" wait for an idle summer day when you have nothing else to do and your life is not depending on the outcome.

6. *Don't "Enable" Commitmentphobes.* The concept of "enabling" comes from alcohol counseling. Whenever there is an alcoholic, there is also a co-alcoholic who *unwittingly* enables the alcoholic to continue drinking. For example, if a man is an alcoholic, his wife may call his office and say he has the flu or take him home from a party early before he becomes an embarrassment. By protecting him from the consequences of his behavior, she positively rein-

forces his habit. She makes it easier for him to go on drinking. At the same time she may be pleading for him to stop.

In this same way, people who continue to date commitmentphobes positively reinforce their behavior.

Remember the women in *Lysistrata* who refused sex to all men until they agreed to stop fighting wars? If only we could somehow join together and agree to stop dating commitmentphobes, maybe they would begin to feel the negative consequences of their unwillingness to become close! As long as there is always another ingenuous lover for each commitmentphobe to love for three months and then leave, commitmentphobes will have no reason to reevaluate their lifestyle. Like co-alcoholics, while on the one hand we rail against the offenders and plead with them to change their ways, on the other hand we continue to reinforce their behavior by dating them and responding enthusiastically to their Closeness Games.

Turning down commitmentphobes or extricating yourself from them is usually not easy. But if a genuinely close, mutual relationship is what you seek, it may be the wisest decision in the long run.

One woman told a workshop this story about a commitmentphobe:

I had just moved to a small town to take a job as a professor at a liberal arts college. Before I even arrived, I had been hearing about Woody, an extremely eligible, handsome bachelor who taught in my department. He was obviously well loved, and everyone was eager to marry him off since his divorce five years ago. I seemed to many the ideal candidate for a fairy-tale romance.

When I finally met him, I was thrilled. He seemed *really nice.* Our flirting seemed to me to be going well. Finally, we arranged a date for dinner and a play the college was giving. At 4:00 that afternoon, he called to say something had come up and that he would be able to have a quick dinner but not go to the play. I was crushed, and I pressed him for his excuse. It turned out he had a meeting with a student, which seemed to me not at all pressing. Hadn't he been looking forward to this evening as much as I had? How could he do this?

There followed two months of dates a lot like the first one. We had perfectly glorious times together. I was smitten! But our dates continued to be few and far between. And Woody seemed content to go on that way forever. I wanted to see him every day!

One day the realization finally surfaced that the only thing for me to do was to get out. This man's priorities were well established, and they were incompatible with mine. But I was so in love! I tortured myself with indecision. But it was clear that the pain was already greater than the pleasure and I saw no way this would change. I actually picked up the phone, called him, and told him that I didn't want to see him for a while—a long while. His protest was mild.

The next weeks were difficult to be sure. I couldn't stop thinking about him. But after a month, I was almost normal again, and there followed one of the best years of my life—getting acquainted with many new friends and thoroughly enjoying my work. I am grateful every day that I didn't waste that year chasing him around, waiting to be squeezed into his life. But I still think that phone call was one of the hardest assignments I have ever given myself.

Compare this experience to that of Judyth, a thirty-eight-year-old banker who is very pleased with her four-year-old relationship. I asked her to describe the initial phases of it. This is what it can be like to connect with a person who is not a commitmentphobe:

Marty told me very early—by the end of the first month—not only that he was genuinely taken with me, but that he wanted to be both married and monogamous. One of the sources of such great pleasure and excitement between us was that we knew we were in complete agreement on these issues. We both longed for an abiding closeness. After spending hours describing to men what I was seeking and then having to defend and justify it, I had a feeling of deep connection with Marty because I did not have to explain what I wanted. I felt I was dealing with an equal, an emotional peer. I had been close to other men, but I had always missed that feeling of total mutuality that I had with Marty. I found out that there is no such thing as one-sided intimacy. If one of you is *there* for the relationship and the other is spaced out somewhere, you don't have intimacy. Only when I finally experienced this total mutuality with Marty did I realize the difference. And he was having the same experience I was.

Commitmentphobes are a disaster if you know you want a committed, intimate relationship. Keep your antennae out, and if you sense one coming your way, maybe you should consider wearing a little sign around your neck—something like songwriter Hilman Hall's memorable words: "Pass me by if you're only passin' through!"

Postscript to Commitmentphobes

Whenever I lecture to audiences about *avoiding* commitmentphobes, someone inevitably raises a timid hand and asks, "What if you think you *are* one?"

First, realize that not all fear of commitment fits the syndrome I have just described. Just because you have been alone for a time, you are not automatically a commitmentphobe. Maybe you just haven't met the right person yet. Maybe you are choosing to remain single for reasons other than fear of commitment.

Do you have a strong craving for closeness *and* a strong aversion to it? Do you "seduce and abandon" often and with great intensity? Do you have a history of many short-term relationships? When your hesitations about a potential partner arise, do you feel secretly relieved inside that you have found some flaws? Is being critical of lovers a habit with you?

If you answer no to these questions and you feel sincere about your desire for commitment, you are probably not a commitmentphobe. You may be ambivalent, and you may find closeness to be anxiety-producing. Both of these are manageable problems *if* you genuinely want to work through them. Take a look at Chapter 9 where I discuss the more normal, everyday fears many people have about becoming close with another person.

If you answered yes to my test questions, and you recognized yourself in this chapter, then you need to ask yourself whether you want to "cure" your commitmentphobia, or learn to live with it. If you want to "cure" it, I refer you to Chapter 10 of this book, my suggestions about how to begin to correct your "mistakes," your self-defeating behavior.

But maybe you are a commitmentphobe who is content with your lifestyle and has no interest in hooking up with anyone on a permanent basis. Then my only suggestion to you is that you be honest with the people you date—early in the relationship. Don't watch a person fall in love with you knowing all along that you aren't the permanent type. As soon as you can gracefully bring up the subject, let your date know that you have no interest in a long-term commitment. Look specifically for partners who enjoy the same lifestyle you have, and who feel certain that they, too, do not wish to become committed to one person.

Long-Term Commitmentphobia

Many singles who would like to be married end up in long-term relationships with commitmentphobes. Their anti-commitment partners may even be nine-tenths involved in the relationship, but seem compelled to keep one-tenth of themselves out the door.

Andrea, an advertising executive in her mid-thirties, told us her story at a workshop.

> I've been living with Robbie for six years and I want to get married. But Robbie just plain *won't*. We talk about it; and he always sounds as if he's on the verge of giving in, but by now I know he never will. It's not that he's against the institution of marriage. It's that he doesn't want to make a final commitment to me. We are *so much* a couple; it's really crazy he has this holdout. He *says* he doesn't want to stay with me out of a sense of duty or because he made a vow. He wants to feel each day that he is staying with me because he wants to. This is supposed to make me feel good. But all I hear is that someday he may decide he *doesn't* want to be with me.
>
> The thing I hate most is that I know his position on

this affects the *quality* of our closeness. I mean, we go for months without talking about it. Whenever we do, it's really unpleasant. But even when we don't discuss it, I feel as though I have to protect myself, and I withhold from him. I know I do. I'm insecure. I don't believe he loves me. But most of the time he acts like he does, and he *says* he does, and I fall totally for it. But his not being willing to make a commitment to me makes me feel powerless and insecure.

I've been through it with myself a million times in the past six years. I have two choices: accept the situation or leave. I have no real question about what to do: he's too special a guy to leave. If I left, it would feel like curing my toothache by cutting off my head!

Unfortunately, the best cure for Andrea's all-too-common problem is prevention. If she could have "cured her toothache" much earlier, by recognizing long ago that Robbie was a commitmentphobic type and saying no then, it might not have felt so much like cutting off her head.

Now, her dilemma is an exasperating one. If Robbie will not make a commitment to her, the possibility that he may someday leave is real indeed. He is saying one or more of the following things to Andrea:

- "I have hesitations about spending my life with you."
- "I don't love you enough."
- "I am afraid of cutting off all my other options."
- "I'm afraid I'll change my mind later."
- "I don't want to be tied down."

If these statements are true for Robbie, neither he nor Andrea can pretend they aren't.

Andrea was absolutely on target in pointing out that commitment or the lack of it affects the *quality* of a relationship, not just the potential duration of it. The holding back, the insecurity, the powerlessness, the pressure one or the other partner feels just won't go away. Such a relationship is totally different from one in which the mutual love is wholehearted, enthusiastic, and unrestrained.

Hesitations, doubts, and fears impede the flow between two people. It is dangerous for Andrea to become completely vulnerable and honest with Robbie if she always knows that at some point he might disappear. If the love he puts out to her is like a desert oasis that turns out to be a mirage, vanishing as she draws near, how can she give him her heart as she would like to?

People in love relationships where there is no commitment have to spend part of their energy protecting themselves from hurt and preparing for the part of their lives that will not include the other partner. There can be no complete letting go into a full intimate bond. Lack of commitment is withholding, and withholding is antithetical to intimacy.

Relationships that are without the cement of commitment suffer from a sad irony: The lack of commitment causes stress, problems, and dishonesty, and then the stress, problems, and dishonesty reduce the likelihood of commitment. It is a vicious circle in which many spend their whole lives. This ironic pattern is true on a cultural level as well: Few people are willing to make serious commitments because they see that relationships are in such bad shape, but relationships are in bad shape precisely because there is such a widespread aversion to commitment.

So what should Andrea do?

She has to decide whether she wants to continue to live with insecurity, powerlessness, and buried anger, or whether she deserves to have someone love her wholeheartedly and completely.

Andrea will have to make this decision by herself. Robbie will be of no help to her, since he has a vested interest in the status quo. He is getting everything he wants; he gets to be with Andrea and keep his options open. Why should he change? (This is not a judgment or criticism of Robbie. It's just the fact Andrea has to face.)

The decision should take a lot of Andrea's attention, possibly a period of months.

As a part of making the decision, she may want to have some very specific conversations with Robbie, *not with the goal of trying to change him,* but with the goal of getting him to clarify his position. She should make her decision based on the most accurate data she can get. She may wish to enlist the support of a third party for such a conversation, a couple counselor, for example, just to ensure clear, honest communication.

Andrea should find out from Robbie exactly what he is saying to her with his unwillingness to commit. Exactly what are his hesitations? Insofar as Robbie knows this, Andrea has a right to know it, too. Is he commitmentphobic? That is, does he play come closer, go away? Does he both crave closeness and fear it? Or is he actually ambivalent with regard to Andrea herself? If so, how and why?

This is valuable—although not necessarily pleasant—information for both Robbie and Andrea to clarify. Precise data *may* open up new options for both or either of them.

Andrea told us that she deliberately avoids bringing up the subject of the future of her relationship, because she is afraid that if Robbie feels pressured, he will leave sooner. Robbie and Andrea have tacitly agreed to a system in which Andrea has no way to talk about her problem with the relationship. She's in a "double bind": If she doesn't bring up her problem, it remains. If she does bring it up, it may get worse.

What kind of a relationship is this? Not a close, open, flowing, mutually growth-producing one! Why is Andrea so eager to stay in it? What is she getting from it?

Many people stay in relationships with commitment-phobes because of their own low self-esteem. At some level, they believe they don't deserve to be loved and that this half-hearted love is the best they can do. They feel they should be grateful for it.

Or, they deny the evidence before them, and keep hoping that the commitmentphobe will change.

In the first year or two of a relationship, it may still be true that one partner is slowly becoming more and more certain of his or her commitment, and that mutual commitment will be forthcoming. But this process doesn't take six years. In my own observations of couples, I have never seen a long-term commitmentphobe make a dramatic change *within the same relationship.* I know of several couples who married after years of living together only to split up within the next several years. The commitmentphobe's doubts and hesitations did not suddenly evaporate, but, in a spirit of good will or out of desperation, he or she "gave in." Both partners were denying reality. But they knew something had to change, and they used marriage as a way to move off dead center, to find a way out of their deadlock. Other couples buy a house together or have a baby. They do eventually achieve the movement they seek, though sometimes at great cost to themselves and their families.

After all is said and done, Andrea was right when she said she has two choices: stay or leave. (She also has the option of getting more clarity from her partner about exactly what his position is.)

Only she can make the decision.

Chapters 10 and 12 contain more information that will be useful to the Andreas who are reading this book—information about self-examination, self-esteem, and choices.

Commitmentphobia is a hazard of modern times. *Watch out for it!* If you are alert, you will be able to detect it early in a relationship and avoid the heartache that inevitably results if you stick around for too long, trying to change the commitmentphobe, blaming yourself, feeling powerless, angry, and—ultimately—alone. Don't let a commitmentphobe bog you down. Know that your desire for a loving bond with a person who loves you back is an entirely valid desire and an achievable goal. Persevere!

Chapter 8

The Eighth Strategy: Don't Try to Make the Prince or Princess Love You

How to Handle an Intimacy Gap

Jonathan was one of the sweetest men I interviewed. He was an internist, forty-one and very gentle. Jonathan told me,

Arlene and I get along so well. Truly I love her. But she just won't get close. She says she's "not sentimental" and "not romantic." But she never tells me how she feels about me. She won't discuss our relationship. When I try to tell her how I feel, she brushes it off—usually with a joke. I know she's happy in our relationship, but she always finds a way to keep a little distance between us.

A thirty-eight-year-old woman, Ginny, had a similar problem with the man she dated. A beautician and personal style consultant, Ginny told me,

In the eight years since my divorce, I've dated a lot. I've had four relationships that I thought had potential. But the issue always seems to be the same: when I feel close and I start to talk about it or act it out, men don't like it. One guy I was with always teased me and laughed about it. He told me I should "lighten up," that I had no sense of humor. It was always my problem! Another guy would get angry and tell me to knock it off. For a while when this happens, I always figure there's something wrong with *me*. But when I get any distance from it, I know that what I want is entirely reasonable. I mean, what's the difference between love that never gets expressed or experienced and no love at all?!

I would have introduced Jonathan and Ginny to each other, but they lived 3,000 miles apart! They were both experiencing what I call an "intimacy gap." One partner is more interested in expressing and experiencing genuine intimacy than the other.

If any of the following sentences applies to you, you may be experiencing an intimacy gap with a person you are dating. These sentences express *your perception.* Your partner may not see it this way at all and may not agree with you. You don't have to ascertain whether what you experience is an objective reality, only whether it is your subjective experience. With regard to any relationship you have been in or are now in, does it *seem to you* that

- you love your partner more than your partner loves you?
- you express love, affirmation, and affection for your partner more than your partner expresses the same for you?
- just when you feel extremely intimate, especially intense and close to your partner, your partner creates diversion, is unavailable or unwilling to acknowledge or to stay with the intense pleasure you feel?
- your partner never says "I love you" (or similar expressions of endearment) unless you say it first?
- your partner does not like to discuss your relationship?
- you never have prolonged periods of physical affection that are purely affectionate and not designed to lead to intercourse?

There is no such thing as one-sided intimacy. In genuinely intimate exchanges, both partners are full, equal participants. This does not mean that each partner must both talk and listen, necessarily. For example, a therapeutic relationship in which the client talks and the therapist listens and responds may be quite intimate. The therapist is not sharing, but is fully "there" for the relationship. He or she is attentive, focused, compassionate, and participating totally in the interaction.

Intimacy is about *connecting* with another person. The thrill, the joy, the pleasure of intimacy is precisely sharing that moment of connection—or that lifetime of connection —with another human being. In an intimate exchange, the connection is honest, real, and therefore deep.

If you desire this kind of connection with another person, and you find that the other person is unavailable for it —because of fear, social conditioning, hesitations about you, low self-esteem, or whatever reason—you are bound to feel frustrated.

A relationship in which the desire for intimacy is one-sided is a BTN! What you want is a partner whose desire and ability for intimacy is equal to yours.

This type of BTN is slightly different from a BTN with a commitmentphobe. Commitmentphobes are often very good at intimacy, but only because they keep their exit door open. It is not intimacy, but intimacy *combined with commitment* that they fear.

So what can you do if you are in a relationship with a pseudo-intimate, a commitmentphobe, a person with whom you experience an intimacy gap, or any other BTN in which the relationship itself is somehow unbalanced?

Before we look at what *will* work in unbalanced relationships, we must examine the methods that most of us have, at one time or another, tried without success. These are "mistakes" we are sorely tempted to make, because we want what we want so badly. Become familiar with these methods. Learn to recognize when you are on the verge of using one of them—because you can save your energy. They have never worked in the past, and they never will in the future. The better you get at any of these techniques, the worse you will become mired in your swamp.

1. *Asking for It.* Sorry. I know that in all your assertiveness classes you have learned to ask for what you want. "If you don't ask, you won't get it." But asking for intimacy from one who is afraid of it will only frighten the person more. You are in an intolerable double bind. If you ask for intimacy, you trigger your partner's fear, and he or she may push you away; if you don't ask for intimacy, you will let your partner's fear govern your relationship. Your part-

ner will simply continue to be distant. You won't get intimacy if you ask for it, and you won't get it if you don't.

If you are dealing with a "pleaser," you may get, in response to your request, a good intimacy act. The pleaser will remember to tell you "I love you," kiss you good-bye, and hug you the way you like to be hugged. Pleasers disguise their fear by behaving according to what they think people want. You may be confused because you will not feel satisfied, but you won't know what else to ask for. You will seem ungrateful and insatiable if you say, "But it's not coming from your heart." You will be right, but you will find it hard to talk about because you will be tapping into your partner's fear.

The second tactic that won't work when you want intimacy but are dealing with a fearful person is

2. *Not Asking for It.* We have all reached the point where we say, "I'll just back off for a while. I'm not giving my lover the space to take initiative. I'll stop pestering and stop saying 'I love you' all the time. Maybe then this recluse will start to miss it and will start being more affectionate and demonstrative."

If your lover is afraid of intimacy, you'll wait forever.

3. *Playing Hard to Get.* This is a variation of the above. In the early stages of a relationship, there is something to it. If you become a bit aloof, feign a lack of interest, you become more desirable. But it is people's ego that is titillated when you shun them, not their heart. When you give up your aloof act and seem interested, their egos are satisfied and they have no more need of you. It is not the pleasure of intimacy they are seeking, but the success of winning you over. Since they are afraid of intimacy, they will not get close, no matter how desirable a creature you are.

4. *Emotional Blackmail.* You blackmail a person when your message is "I love you so much. You ought to love me back! Look at all I do for you. Look at the wonderful ways I show my love. I'll keep loving you so much you'll *have* to love me back."

You might succeed in making your lover feel guilty and you will surely get to feel virtuous yourself—even long-suffering if you like to play the victim. But you will be furthering the gap between you. Your inadvertent message to your partner is "You are a bad person. You are an inadequate partner." Thus, while trying to show your love you will in effect be putting your lover down. And your partner will sense this and feel criticized and badgered.

It is a great pleasure to be generous, thoughtful, and loving to one you love. But to avoid emotional blackmail, you must be crystal clear that you are not doing anything *in order to get something back*.

Dianna once gave a huge surprise birthday party for Donald, a man she had been seeing for some time. She knew he was fond of her, but he seemed "hard to pin down." The party was a success, and he told her during it that he was very moved by her generosity. Dianna was stunned when he didn't call for three days and then told her he wanted to start dating around.

"I thought surely that party would remove his last doubts. How could he dump me after all that work I went to?"

She expected love as return for her own loving thoughtfulness, and she felt cheated and betrayed. But Donald had never agreed to a fair exchange. Anyone afraid of intimacy is bound to run when he sees that kind of devotion.

You can't make someone love you.

5. *Lecturing.* The lecture goes like this: "Intimacy is wonderful and you will be happier if you try it. I want you to change—*not for me*—but because I see that you will be happier if you open up and relax. Listen to me. I know what's good for you."

Unless you are well beyond wanting to be intimate with this person yourself, you can't be sincere about your selflessness, and the recipient of your lecture knows it. People who have not come to an independent decision that intimacy is something they want will simply not take your generous advice. Besides, it is difficult to take help from one who sets him- or herself up as more knowledgeable. Help is help only if it is perceived as help! You can't get a person to cooperate with you by making him or her wrong and yourself right.

6. *Punishing.* Punishing someone who has hurt you by withholding is a delicious temptation. You may lie awake plotting your revenge, figuring a way for the offender to get the message once and for all. You may withhold sex, embarrass the person in front of a friend, forget to run an errand, or just burn the toast. Fantasizing the revenge is

harmless enough. But carrying it out will only exacerbate the hostilities. Indirect aggressive behavior is immature and always counterproductive. Anger is best expressed directly or not at all.

7. *Denying Your Needs.* A lover who fears closeness will eventually convince you that he or she is right. When you talk with your partner over and over about what you want and you seem unable to make yourself understood, you begin to doubt yourself. The experience is like looking at a very dim star. When you look directly at it, it seems to disappear. Only when you look slightly to the side of it does it reappear. In a similar way, when you talk directly about intimacy to one who has never experienced it, you will find yourself thinking, "What I want is unrealistic. I'm too influenced by movies. After all, we have a great relationship in many ways. I'm too needy. My lover is right. It's my problem." The star you saw so clearly disappears.

I was once with a man who told me I had a "propensity for intensity." I bought into his idea that this was my "problem." The phrase became a joke between us and got invoked every time I started to express my feelings for him. I started feeling I was neurotic, and he got to avoid becoming close with me.

But when you view the star not directly but with peripheral vision, it will reappear. For me this happens when I talk with women who know exactly what I mean. We don't have to describe intimacy. We can just talk about "it." We know positively that we are not unreasonable for wanting what we want. The star becomes clear.

If you never get validation of your own needs, you will eventually set up your own little "things-are-fine-as-they-are" disguise. You will simply put your needs on a back burner or deny them altogether. This is how many relationships become stalemated into routines that lack spark. You will never achieve the intimacy you seek by belittling your desires.

Another problem with the "denying your needs" gambit is that your needs won't stay buried forever. Something eventually jolts you into feeling them again. You may experience envy at witnessing a relationship that seems genuinely intimate. You may have an affair that awakens you to how little intimacy you are getting in your present relationship. Or you may start talking with other people about what you are missing and have that powerful experience of being understood.

Burying the desire for intimacy is the choice many do make. In some ways the strategy may "work." It removes a major hassle from the relationship so that other aspects of it may flourish. But it is not a technique that will lead you to richly rewarding experiences of genuine sharing.

These are the strategies that won't work.

But the predicament remains. Most of us have been in the bind of either wanting more closeness from someone, or feeling pressured to "be close" when we aren't sure exactly what this means and haven't any idea how to bring it about.

So what *will* work?

It's a challenge.

Differing levels of desire for intimacy is a major source of incompatibility in couples. No matter on which side of the dilemma you sit, this disparity can be a continuing source of anxiety and conflict. The best of all possible solutions to intimacy problems is to avoid getting enmeshed in them in the first place. If the scenarios in this chapter were familiar to you, then recognize that a desire and ability for intimacy that closely matches your own is an "essential" item for you, a standard you are not willing to compromise. If you become aware of an intimacy gap while you are in the early stages of exploring with another person, consider ending the relationship before your intimacy issues lead to even greater problems.

Of course, genuine intimacy unfolds slowly and deepens with months and even years of shared experiences. And some people require more time to begin revealing themselves than others. Nevertheless, if you pay attention to the messages you are getting early in a relationship, you will be able to tell what your partner's propensities are. If you pick up differences in your intimate communication and behavior, *pay attention* to this. Don't ignore it, and don't assume you can change it by asking for it, not asking for it, playing hard to get, using emotional blackmail, lecturing, punishing, or denying your needs.

But suppose you are already well into a relationship with an intimacy gap. Or suppose you like a person well enough to pursue him or her even though you recognize that you have some conflicts about intimacy. Is there anything that will work in these situations?

Yes.

If you are both highly motivated to work on meeting each other's needs, you can undertake activities to improve this area of your life together. Specially structured conversations, "active" listening, intimacy games, couple counseling, and increased awareness about intimacy can make a difference for couples interested in deepening their intimacy together. A description of these techniques belongs in a book for couples, however, not in this book for singles. If you are still single, you still have the freedom to choose a partner for yourself who is as interested in developing intimacy as you are.

Let me give you an opportunity now to reflect upon times in your own life when you have experienced an intimacy gap with a partner. Have you ever used any of the techniques that don't work? Exactly what did you want from your partner that was not forthcoming? What happened when you tried talking about your problem?

EXPERIMENT #13

1. Think of a relationship, past or present, in which you have experienced an intimacy gap. What techniques did you employ in response to your frustration? For each technique listed below, recall a specific incident that was an example of you using the technique. Make a few notes to remind you of the incident.

   - Asking for intimacy
   - Not asking for it
   - Playing hard to get
   - Emotional blackmail
   - Lecturing
   - Punishing
   - Denying your needs

   Look back over the list and ask yourself whether any of these techniques resulted in more closeness between you and your partner.

2. Write a letter to the person with whom you feel or felt an intimacy gap. As best you can, tell that partner what you feel (or felt) toward him or her. Describe the intimacy gap

you experience(d). When do you (or did you) experience it? Exactly what do you feel when it happens?

If you could have anything you want, what would you like from your partner? Mention everything. Don't censor. Tell your partner how the intimacy gap you feel manifests itself and what the term "intimacy gap" means to you.

The point of this exercise is not to give your partner the letter (although you might decide you want to do that), but to help you clarify what your own experience is and what you want from a relationship.

In summary, then, if you desire more intimacy in your life, you need to

- recognize when you are trying to "make somebody love you," using the methods that never work, and give up the effort;
- give less of your energy to relationships in which you experience an intimacy gap; and
- focus on finding other people who are as interested in and available for intimacy as you are.

Intimacy and Autonomy: Finding a Balance

One of the reasons intimacy has become so elusive in the last two decades is that self-sufficiency has become a high priority for singles, and self-sufficiency is *incorrectly* viewed as incompatible with intimacy.

What the healthy individual seeks is a *balance* between autonomy and intimacy, between individuation and connection. Too much or too little of either quality can create an unbalanced life: independent but alone, or connected but overly dependent.

Many singles these days have developed their ability to be independent and self-sufficient to a very high degree. But they have done it at the expense of their ability to connect with another person. Self-sufficiency is not a challenge for the average single person anymore. Connection is. Singles today are so busy proving how self-sufficient they are, they have forgotten that autonomy is only half of the equation that constitutes a balanced life. The other half —being intimate—has been neglected.

The intimacy gap has become a cultural reality as well as an issue in many individual lives. In the next decades, one of our cultural tasks will be to restore the role of intimate human relationships to its proper place in our hierarchy of cultural values.

But since the primary way in which cultural transformation takes place is through the gradual build-up of individual transformations, begin with yourself. What is the balance of self-sufficiency and intimate human connections in your own life?

No single person *needs* to have an intimate partner in order to have a full life. But be careful of being *too proud* of how independent and self-sufficient you have become. Maybe the real challenge for you is to be able to relinquish some of your independence, to become (perish the thought) *dependent* on another person. *Intimacy is not possible without a certain amount of healthy, mutual dependence.* By its very definition, intimacy involves becoming vulnerable to another human being—at least to some extent.

Many singles who are extremely self-sufficient and independent fear becoming dependent and vulnerable within an intimate relationship. Some elect never to become intimate for this reason. But it is because many singles would like to overcome their aversion to dependency and vulnerability that we must move on to the next chapter and consider this toughest problem of all: fear of intimacy.

Chapter 9

The Ninth Strategy: What to Do When You Find Your Prince or Princess, But You're Afraid of the Castle

Learning to Say Yes

Finding the person you want to say yes to is a challenge, as we have seen. But actually saying yes is, for some, the most formidable challenge of all, because it means facing and overcoming fear.

In the end, fear is what keeps many singles alone. Fear of rejection. Fear of closeness. Fear of dependence. Fear of losing oneself. Fear of failure. The comfortable single life may be lonely at times, but it is safe. If you keep just the right amount of distance, you won't have to risk being rejected—or being loved. You won't have to risk becoming so close with someone that you will have to reveal closely held secrets or discover secrets you didn't even know you had. You won't have to risk pain.

Plain old fear keeps many singles from saying yes. They plan to say yes someday, but they will always have an excuse not to—because they haven't faced the fears that are keeping them alone.

Two psychologists I know invented a new word: flove. They say that in many clients they see, love and fear are closely connected. Every time a person falls in love, fear comes up. And every time a person experiences fear, love is somewhere in the background. So these days, we don't fall in love, we fall in flove!

The problem is not that we are afraid, for fear is natural and normal. The problem is that we let fear control our lives. Learning to say yes means not eliminating our fears, but being willing to act in spite of our fears. You can say yes when you take fear out of the driver's seat in your life and stick it in the trunk!

The story is told of a nine-year-old boy who was about to walk across a bed of hot coals as a demonstration of courage. A reporter asked him, "Are you afraid?" "Yes!" replied the boy. "Then why are you going to do this?" inquired the reporter. The boy looked incredulously at her and replied, "I'm not going to let fear stop me from doing what I want to do!"

Perhaps it would be wise to memorize this young man's statement, and then say it to yourself every time your fears are trying to stop you from approaching a person at a café, or calling a potential date on the phone, or placing a personal ad, or going to a singles' event.

But of course, overcoming fear isn't that simple. The complication is that fear is difficult to experience, let alone to overcome, because it is almost always disguised as something else.

Fear and Its Disguises

Fear is a natural instinct designed to protect us: Someone aims a stone at me, so I quickly put my arms over my face.

Fear instincts protect our bodies, *and* they also protect our egos. If I sense the world is throwing stones at my ego, I will erect an invisible wall to keep people from crushing me. I will put on a disguise to keep the stones from reaching the real, fragile me.

We all experience assaults on our egos as small children. So we put our arms over our faces, figuratively speaking. The "arms" take the form of behavior that is designed to protect us from experiencing pain or fear. Then this behavior, this disguise, becomes a habit. It keeps the world from seeing our fragile inner selves. *But* it cuts us off from ourselves, too. And rather than solving problems, the protective disguise creates problems of its own, for usually the cover-up is more harmful than the original flaw.

Each of us has deep fears: I'm not okay as I am. I'm not lovable. I'm not capable. I'll be abandoned. To hide these fears, we develop defenses, for we believe it is safer to maintain a disguise than to expose a self that we imagine to be inadequate or ugly.

Remember, a "disguise" (or call it a wall, a game, a role, a mask, a persona, a defense, or a facade) is simply *behavior designed to protect us from having to experience pain or fear.* Examples:

Julie feels inadequate in her job. But this is too painful for her to experience fully, so instead she blames her boss and her working conditions. The blame is her disguise, her defensive behavior. It protects her from the painful feeling of inadequacy, and it keeps others from seeing her alleged deficiencies. And Julie believes in her defense. She believes her boss is to blame. She has probably convinced many of those around her as well.

Arthur's lover, Joy, is seeing another man. The pain of losing Joy is too much for Arthur to bear, so some part of him denies that he is losing her. Arthur's denial mask, his "everything-is-fine" game, protects him from having to feel pain.

As psychologists tell us, defenses that we maintain as adults sometimes begin very early in our lives. When Annie was growing up, her father was a traveling salesman, and her mother also had a career and was almost never home. Annie took over major household responsibilities, caring for the younger children, cooking, cleaning, and doing laundry. But what was even tougher, Annie's parents were both cold, businesslike people. They never thanked Annie for all her efforts. They often criticized her, but rarely gave her praise and almost never hugged or kissed her. When she was a baby, they used to let her cry because they believed she needed to be self-sufficient.

Annie longed for expressions of love from her parents. Her pain over their indifference to her was almost unbearable. Her heart ached; her body cried out to be hugged.

So what did Annie do to protect herself? She performed an extremely common psychological maneuver: Rather than having to feel the terrible pain of her parents' lack of love, she *subconsciously* tricked herself into believing that she did not want or need their love. She covered up her real longing with a mask of self-sufficiency. She pretended that she was perfectly okay all by herself. This was much easier and more sensible for her than feeling pain and longing all the time.

The pain was not gone; if Annie could reach deep enough and be honest enough, she would feel it. But the pain was well hidden—even to Annie—under her driven, "neurotic" need to be self-sufficient, to be free of the need for love.

Defenses like Julie's, Arthur's, and Annie's are *healthy responses*. They are the human organism's way of protecting itself from hostile elements in its environment, just as the chameleon changes colors. But three major problems may follow after the construction of a defense.

How Our Defenses Defeat Us

The first problem is that most defenses outlive their usefulness. Julie's continuing blame of others will make it impossible for her to see her own role in her problems and she may never be able to help herself to change. Arthur must eventually accept that Joy has another love, or he will be unable to take a course of action that will serve his best interests. If Annie continues as an adult to believe she does not need love, she will be unable to form a loving bond with a man.

The second problem with defenses is that they deceive their creators in the end. We are unaware of the walls behind which we live, yet they keep us in an emotional prison.

To return to our example above, Annie genuinely believes that she is a loner, and that she doesn't need or want love. She made this up long ago to protect herself when her parents ignored her. But now, she believes it is true. Everyone else becomes convinced, too, and treats her accordingly. Annie does have a certain feeling of unrest. She does continue to date and to crave sexual experiences that never turn out to be quite satisfying. But she does not experience any fear, and she does not risk the pain of being ignored, for her "self-sufficient" wall protects her against any chance of it. The disguise is "working." What Annie can't see is how it is cheating her. She can no longer experience her need for love *or* her fear that she won't get it. She believes her wall of self-sufficiency and it is making it impossible for her to be intimate.

Psychologist John Powell, in his book *Why Am I Afraid to Tell You Who I Am?*, writes,

> None of us wants to be a fraud or to live a lie: none of us wants to be a sham, a phony, but the fears that we experience and the risks that honest self-communication would involve seem so intense to us that seeking refuge in our roles, masks, and games becomes an almost natural reflex action.
>
> After a while, it may even be quite difficult for us to distinguish between what we really are, at any given moment in our development as persons, and what we pose as being.
>
> It is such a universally human problem that we might justifiably call it "the human condition."

Annie's life took a wrong turn long ago, and she has been racing along the wrong road ever since. She can't see that it is a dead end. All of her attention and energy are directed toward the maintenance of her wall, her pretending that she doesn't need love. She has forgotten that little self that wanted love, and has become identified with her loner image.

The third problem with disguises is that they distort our vision. Everything we see or hear is filtered through the mask and thus reinforces the world as viewed through the mask. In our example, Annie sees everyone through her loner disguise and so becomes convinced that no one is warm and loving. She is experiencing what the great poet Shelley recognized when he said, "the eye sees what it brings to the seeing."

Even though our protective behaviors outlive their usefulness and distort our vision both of ourselves and of the world, nevertheless we cling tenaciously to them. So to move through our fears toward saying yes to love, we must become familiar with the disguises we and others wear in order to hide our fears.

Disguises come in a huge variety of sizes, shapes, and colors. In fact, though some are similar, every person's disguise is unique. But defensive behavior does fall into categories. Some common disguises are:

snobbishness	alcoholism	isolation	anxiety
ambition	machoism	illness	guilt
workaholism	clowning	blame	inferiority complex
paternalism	prejudice	projection	boredom
pride	hostility	wanderlust	control

Involuntary singles who are actively seeking an intimate partner need to be well acquainted with the fear/disguise syndrome and to watch for it both in themselves and in the people they date. Most of us feel afraid and insecure from time to time. And we respond instinctively to hide the fear from others—and from ourselves. All too often, our relationships consist of one "mask" relating to another. The longer the two "masks" date, the more terrified they are that the other will see the disguise for what it is and try to remove it.

Suppose, for example, Phil discovers that June is not always the cheerful person he first fell in love with, but that, in fact, underneath her smiles, she is depressed. June hates her "moodiness" and does not want anyone to see it, so when Phil sees June depressed, June becomes terrified. She is more afraid of exposing her true depressive self than she is of being alone, so she withdraws from Phil and protects her cheerful image. On the other hand, Phil may find it extremely difficult to reveal deep feelings. When he thinks June is beginning to see how deeply he feels for her, *he* backs off. He, too, is more terrified of exposing his true, feeling self than of being alone. As long as their masks are in place, June and Phil can have a good relationship. But the experience of being seen without their masks is so frightening for both of them that when the masks begin to slip off, they find a way to end their relationship.

In her beautifully decorated New York apartment, I spoke with Nelda, an art gallery manager, fifty-two, now married to her second husband for twelve years. Here is the story of her first marriage, which is an example of what we've been discussing:

It took me years to get a perspective on all this, but I'll tell what I see as I look back on it now.

When I married Rod at age twenty-two in a long white dress with four bridesmaids and an hour-long service that we wrote ourselves, it was going to be the perfect marriage. Period. So anything that started to seem like a problem, I ignored. I more than ignored: I fiercely denied! For example, our sex life got very routine very soon, but I told my women friends our sex life was fabulous. I guess I believed it. Also, Rod liked his privacy and could get downright rude to people who inadvertently invaded it. Rod could be watching TV and I could ask him what he wanted to drink with dinner and get my head bitten off. But I would always defend Rod. He could do no wrong. I wanted the whole world to see what a great husband I had.

Rod's thing was that he was completely rational. It was as if he had no feelings. He knew he was supposed to have feelings so he would behave as though he did. I mean, he gave great hugs, but it was because his "computer" told him, "hugs are good. Give hugs."

We didn't see this at all at the time, but I think what happened is, Rod got tired of my lies, my denials. He started asking for some honesty from me. He couldn't stand that I *never* got angry. I got *terrified*. I couldn't even begin to look at anything that seemed like a "problem." If we had a fight, even a disagreement, it would shatter my whole story—which was my whole *life*—that I had a perfect marriage.

At the same time, I started asking Rod for some real *feelings*. Well, that terrified *him!* I mean that was really threatening, because he was afraid he didn't have any, or that if he did, they would be dreadful, not nice.

Once that marriage started to end, it ended *fast*. Rod seemed to have no hesitation: If his choice was having to look at his feelings, he'd rather get out. When he started talking divorce, can you imagine what that did to my "perfect marriage" story? When he moved out, I lost a lot more than a husband. I lost my whole "perfect" life! It was horrible. Of course, I went into therapy, and over a period of years I was able to see that there was a reason for my desperation to see my life as "perfect," namely, I had a lot of self-hate I didn't want to look at. The huge breakthrough for me in therapy was admitting that there was *anything* about myself that I didn't like. And once I did that, it was like the floodgates opening. Whew! It was painful. But the end result now, years later, is that I don't have to lie anymore. What a relief! I'm not perfect anymore. But I'm genuine! I'm honest. I'm just me, for better or for worse. I can see how much energy it took to hold up that stupid image. And I was the only one who believed it anyway. If there's one thing you say in your book, tell people to figure out what they are trying to pretend and then to figure out why they think they have to pretend it. I'll tell you, it really changed my life.

Rod went into therapy, too, by the way. He found out it's not all that horrible to feel things, and he's getting pretty good at it. After we both got into new marriages, we were able to become good friends, and I think if there were any way we could have made our changes within our relationship, we could have been really good together. But as it is, we are both much more mature people for our new relationships—and we're both very happy now. [She chuckled.] Now I really *do* have the perfect marriage!

Nelda and Rod were an example of two people who had not looked at their fears and insecurities and so were a case of one mask relating to another. Variations of their story are *extremely common.* The specific fears and masks differ greatly. And many people never get as far as marriage. *Mask maintenance is one of the major "mistakes" singles make that keep them single.* To get close to somebody, you have to be willing to let down your mask *with that person.* That's what getting close is. Being intimate requires sharing your fears and insecurities with the person you love. (Sharing your inner joys, hopes, and pleasures is part of it, too, but that's the easier part.) Many singles would rather keep their masks in place than let anyone see their inner selves. So when closeness starts to happen, they back off. After all these years, they are still single, and that's why!

Letting your fears control your life, or "mask maintenance," is the hardest mistake to correct. Discovering what your mask is and what fears it is covering up requires motivation and tenacity.

Only you know whether you have sufficient motivation to undertake looking at your mask and your fears. Do you believe that fear is keeping you single? Does closeness feel

frightening to you? If you think about it, can you see that
you have a public self and a more honest inner self that no
one ever sees, maybe not even you?

Angelica is a thirty-nine-year-old manager who attended one of my workshops. She works in the personnel
department of a large corporation.

I was the ultimate mask maintainer. I was a corporate
bigwig twenty-four hours a day. I was my proper, well-
behaved, modulated, reasonable, play-by-the-rules,
dress-for-success self at the grocery store, with my
best friend, at the health club—even with my sister
and my parents. I had to wear the right jogging
clothes. I had to date the right men. The real me was
buried under a mask that was made out of cast iron
and concrete.

What changed for me was, I took a sabbatical year—
which turned into three years—to see whether I
wanted to become a therapist. I started going to Gestalt workshops and something started to give inside
me. I felt emotions. I screamed, I cried, I got furious, I
danced all night to bongo drums. When I would walk
back into the corporate environment, I could feel myself closing down. It felt awful.

When the corporate "me" met men, it was all part
of the act. I was the perfect corporate woman: assert-
ive, capable, successful, tough. On dates, I was busy
trying to show this. All my relationships were competitive. We were each trying to prove to the other what a
good catch we were. Several relationships ended because I knew there was no closeness there, but I hadn't
the least idea how to go about getting it.

It took a different setting altogether for the real me
to begin to emerge. The whole experience was totally
stunning and amazing to me. I liked it, but it was so
new, so different. After a while, I had to start looking
at some very painful things, too. But I wouldn't go
back for anything. I had lost *me!* And now I've found
me.

I'm starting to understand what real closeness is
about, too. I'm in the first relationship in my life I've
ever felt really good about. And Denny is *not* your
basic corporate type. He's a carpenter, a ski instructor,

an environmental activist, a gardener. And he loves the real me, not the corporate me. The corporate me, he tolerates. Actually, we laugh about her together. It's a game that has to be played. But I feel okay about her now, because I can let go of her.

Of course, I'm telling you this after several years. I didn't discover my real self overnight. I had to commit myself to it. That's why my sabbatical ended up being three years instead of one. Becoming more real, more honest, was pretty much a full-time job for me.

Angelica reminded me of a quotation by the nineteenth-century theologian Søren Kierkegaard:

The greatest danger, that of losing one's own self, can pass off as quietly as if it were nothing.

Every other loss—that of an arm, a leg, a wife, five dollars—is sure to be noticed.

Michael Lerner, director of the Institute for Labor and Mental Health in Oakland, California, and editor of *Tikkun* magazine, believes that the values of the workplace contribute to "mask maintenance." If the "feminine mystique" was that homemaking was a source of joy and fulfillment for women, the "masculine mystique" is that the world of work will provide men with validation and will make them feel good about themselves. In an interview, Michael told me,

Some men do not experience work as fulfilling and validating, so they seek an escape in their personal life. But that escape is always clouded with their feeling terrible about themselves, which they have to hide from their women. So they enter into a relationship starting out with the sense they can't be fully honest because they can't acknowledge that they are failures in the world of work. The world of work is structured in such a way that it is impossible for all men to be successes. Not everyone can rise to the top of a company or department. Most men can't. But men interpret this in individual terms. This is the key emotional contradiction that leads men to be inaccessible at home: they can't be honest about their failures in the world of work. How can they be honest with women when what they really believe about themselves is that they are failures? So they adopt a pose: I'm together and my life is together and things are working. This is the fundamental lie that then makes it impossible to let a woman in too close—because she might discover the lie.

Of course, women are now getting caught up in exactly the same contradiction: They'll be betraying the women's movement if they admit that their highly competitive jobs are creating a great deal of stress for them.

The first step toward correcting this "mistake" of being too invested in our masks, our images, is to recognize it. So we shall begin by looking at a sampling of defensive behavior or masks that can be seen frequently among singles who are afraid to get close. As you read through these examples, think about whether they might apply to yourself or to someone you know.

1. The Workaholism Mask

Workaholics avoid intimacy by keeping themselves constantly busy and by being exceptionally responsible. Feelings are not their long suit, and they avoid them. They are threatened by their partner's desire for tenderness. They would rather show their love by thoughtfully opening the garage door, or bringing home big paychecks and lavish gifts. The workaholic's defense is well regarded by the outside world. It keeps the fearful person safely distant from other people, especially those who love him or her most.

2. The Denial Mask

Some people simply never look at their own problems with intimacy at all. One woman I interviewed told me this story:

I went with Jerry for three years. We were great friends and compatible in many ways. Our big problem came when I felt warm and close to him. He would distance himself and I would cry. After it became clear we wouldn't make it, he told me, "I really do want an intimate relationship. I want to marry— somebody." Yet the only thing he didn't like about me was that I wanted to be intimate! He couldn't see this contradiction. He clung to the illusion that it would just happen to him—even if he did nothing to work on his aversion to intimacy.

3. The Sex Mask

People sometimes go after sex when what they really want is caring and closeness. Sexual prowess, flirting, or seducing is acceptable behavior, and they know how to do this, but they don't know how to express a need for real intimacy.

Singles who have relied on sex as a way to relate to members of the opposite sex have been especially affected by the AIDS epidemic. With casual sexual encounters greatly reduced, they must either become more solitary, come up with a new "mask," or look for someone with whom they feel safe enough to try coming out from behind the mask.

4. The Peacock Mask

A woman I interviewed, Sarah, said this:

Of course men want closeness, but they sure go about it in a funny way. They think if they polish up their Porsche to a high enough gloss, you'll come around. And if it isn't a Porsche, it's a Ph.D., a fine wine, or the number of times they have been arrested for a worthy cause.

Many people relate to others by trying to be impressive. They surround themselves with tangible evidences of their self-worth, or they talk about their achievements.

The defense is designed to make you feel you are with someone special. But Sarah continued,

> What I want in a friend is someone who takes a genuine interest in me. I'm actually attracted by all the achievements, but not if that's all there is. I feel I have a thick wall to break through if I want any tenderness or love.

The classic peacock man will see his partner as part of the evidence of his self-worth and will dress her in fine clothes and expensive jewelry. As one man I spoke with pointed out, when a man does anything to put his woman on a pedestal and idealize her, he is diminishing his chances of intimacy with her.

This "peacock syndrome" often appears in less extreme versions. By focusing attention on our possessions or our achievements, we are able to hide self-doubts and keep others from getting close enough to see them.

5. The Attention-Seeking Mask

Highly visible public figures, life-of-the-party types, loquacious group members, comics, and storytellers are people who thrive on attention. Everyone needs a certain amount of attention to survive, but people who use attention as a defense are so busy getting it, they have no time to sit back in the quiet shadows and get to know themselves—or another person. They are indiscriminate about where they get attention; they just want a lot of it. It's enjoyable for them and it allows them to avoid intimacy.

Attention seeking is one of the more pleasant defenses because skilled attention seekers are entertaining, likable people. But when you get attention seekers alone in a dimly lit room, they still expect you to be their audience, to laugh at their jokes, and to ask them questions about their work. They are poor listeners. Worse, they won't separate you out as a unique human being; they see all people as potential sources of attention, and as long as they are getting plenty of it, they never need to be afraid: You *can't* get close to them.

6. The "Let's Have Some Fun" Mask

Fun is the product of specific activities designed to produce it: parties, bars, dinners out, movies, vacations, games, etc. Fun is often used as a defense against inner feelings of emptiness, boredom, terror, insecurity, or even self-hatred.

A woman feels lonely. She goes to a bar in the hope that fun will be the antidote. But her denial of her inner feelings is antithetical to the aliveness she seeks. Ironically, her search for "fun" may actually undermine her capacity to feel good. She would achieve genuine fun sooner if she were willing to explore her feelings of emptiness rather than trying to deny them. If she escapes her depressive mood, it will continue. But if she looks at it directly, by talking about it, for example, she will be more likely to transform it.

7. The Boredom Mask

Boredom is easier to feel than fear. If you can convince yourself that you are bored, you can escape painful or difficult feelings. Sometimes boredom, though it may seem very real at the time, is actually a mask, covering up fears or insecurities.

Listen to Ron's story:

> My girlfriend and I went to a weekend workshop on relationships. It was excellent and was getting at some of the really important issues between us. By Saturday night, she was so bored, she decided to leave. I was stunned. It was one of the best events I'd ever been to. Only much later did I realize that she just couldn't handle what she was hearing. She didn't want to face those issues. She was terrified, not bored! But I'm sure she herself believed that she was bored.

8. The Rationality Mask

In the super-rational person, feelings and emotions have atrophied through lack of use. Rational people are rewarded for their cool control, their brilliance, and their ability to think things through. They will excuse a feeling in themselves or anyone else only if it is logical, for they are, above all else, reasonable. Since feelings are sometimes unreasonable and since they may cause these people to lose rational control, when one emerges they quickly suppress it.

The human organism is capable of experiencing a wide range of emotions.

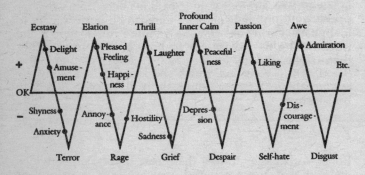

However, the rational person's emotional range is severely limited by fear.

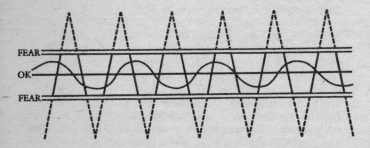

Because rational people encounter fear as soon as they begin to feel very emotional in either direction, they spend their entire lives hovering around "okay." They never feel terribly depressed or terribly ecstatic. They decide (subconsciously) it is far safer to operate from their head than from their heart, so they never get to feel much of anything.

When a rational man falls in love, his partner keeps saying, "Tell me you love me. Not when I ask for it, but when you feel it. I want you to feel passionate about me, to look at me and feel, 'How lucky I am, how lovely you are!' " He can't produce this for her, though he may try, because he doesn't know how to feel. He knows in his head that he loves her, and he knows she knows it, too, so he can't understand why she wants to hear it all the time.

Working out problems with rational people is exasperating. They will always be asking you to explain why you feel as you do and when you can't, they will try to convince you that you ought not to feel that way. You never get to the solution stage because they can't see the problem.

Rational people won't be caught dead in a therapy or counseling situation. They are always certain they can solve their problems on their own. Besides, they realize they might have to feel something in a setting like that, and above all else, they don't want to—or are afraid to— feel.

9. The "Arms Race" Mask

When we practice masking the truth as individuals, it becomes easy to justify behaving similarly on a collective level. The arms race is a societal version of personal walls or defenses. It is our national "defense system," and functions in exactly the same way that defenses work on a personal level. The arms race provides an example (albeit somewhat oversimplified) of the parallels between personal and social psychology.

We fear "enemies," so we pour most of our energy and money into weapons that we believe will protect us. The more we focus on the defense system, the more we fear being attacked; then we feel justified in strengthening our defenses all the more.

Like the adult still defending against childhood dangers that are no longer a threat, we as a nation are in the habit of military defense. To support our habit, we overlook that we have entered an age in which weapons are so dangerous that war has become absurd. We ignore dramatic peace gestures our "enemy" is making toward us. We disregard models for cooperative planning toward third-world development that show great promise over military fights for control of developing nations. We disregard evidence that a budget directed toward health, education, and other social programs would produce more employment and meet people's needs far better than a budget devoted to war.

All we, as a nation, know is that we are terrified of our "enemy" and that out of this terror, we must continue to expand our "defense system."

Individuals react exactly the same way. The more they focus on their defense system, the more they feel they need it, and the less attention they pay to their real selves, the fragile, neglected, frightened person under the disguise. In the same way, as a nation, we give little of our attention (money) to staggering domestic problems.

The story is told of a man who sprinkled very fine gold dust on his lawn every day to keep away the man-eating tigers. He had to make many personal sacrifices to obtain the gold dust, and at times he could not even afford groceries, but he could not be dissuaded from his daily habit because, of course, it worked.

This is the same reasoning we use to perpetuate our national defense system and our personal defenses. We continue our military build-up, and the Russians have not attacked us yet, so the military build-up must be working. Obviously, we must continue it, even if it means we must make domestic sacrifices.

Whether your own personal defense is workaholism, denial, attention seeking, talking too much, or being a wallflower, somewhere inside you believe that your survival depends on keeping this defense operating. We are all like the man who sprinkles gold dust on his lawn. Many of the assaults we fear are imagined, but our defenses are a habit. We are compelled to maintain them—even at great personal cost.

The Essence of Intimacy

This sampling of common defensive behaviors illustrates how defenses may be at work in your life or the life of someone you know. While a defense protects you from having to expose your vulnerable ego and your inner fears, at the same time it "protects" you from intimacy. *What intimacy is about is precisely stripping away your outer, more public ways of being and relating to another person with your inner, more genuine self.* It is because we all have such well-functioning defenses that intimate relationships become so important. For if you never become intimate, you never have the opportunity to become acquainted with the self behind the facade. We are taken in by our own defenses, and we are comfortable avoiding our fears—until someone else cares enough about us to look beneath the veneer into our more genuine selves. Love is about knowing and accepting *all* of another person, not just that person's public facade. This is why love—or psychotherapy or a close friendship—can be transforming: you may actually be a different person in the context of an intimate connection. And that intimate connection may be the only way for you to become acquainted with the inner, more real you. If you deny your fears, you reinforce them. Then your fears keep you isolated, and the more isolated you become, the more afraid you become. As Marilyn Ferguson says in her book *The Aquarian Conspiracy,*

> Denial, however human and natural a response, exacts a terrible price. It is as if we have settled for living in the anterooms of our lives.

The *only* way to break this lonely cycle is to *connect with someone.* You have to connect, not superficially, but at a genuine level. You have to be willing to let someone see the real you beneath the disguise. Otherwise, you'll spend years in the anteroom of your life.

What to Do About Fear

So what can you do if you recognize that fear is standing in your way? What if you see that you have habitual defensive behaviors that keep you distant from others?

A thirty-eight-year-old man told me quite a dramatic story. We'll call him Bruce. He is an affable, warm man with a twinkle in his eye, a successful professional. He has never been married, and he lived with a woman only once, briefly, while in his twenties. But he is very much interested in women, and he dates a lot.

Bruce attended a workshop in which the participants were invited to examine and work with their fears. During the day, they took many experimental risks, saw examples of fear operating in their lives, and actually experienced overcoming their fears in certain situations.

Several weeks after this workshop, Bruce was invited to a Thanksgiving dinner with eight or ten others. They spent most of the day together, preparing and eating the meal and relaxing afterward. Bruce was quite attracted to one of the women there, Martha. He made some contact with Martha during the day, but with no conclusive results.

Over the next several days, Bruce realized he was thinking a lot about this woman. He told me,

Before I attended the workshop, it is inconceivable that I would have called her. I might have considered it, but my excuses would have been far too convincing to have ever pulled it off. But I realized that it was only fear that was keeping me from acting. And I now realized that I didn't want fear to run my life. So, I went over to the phone and dialed her number. She was there. We chatted for a few minutes about the dinner, and then I asked her for a date. She seemed pleased. She said her next several weeks were very busy and that she would call me back.

After I hung up the phone, I realized two things: one is that it didn't really matter whether she called back or not; and the other is that I felt better than I had ever felt in my life!

I believed Bruce completely when he told me this story. The incident may seem minor, but for Bruce, it was an epiphany. This was the first time he had recognized *fear* and deliberately overcome it. It was a genuine breakthrough for him.

What changed for Bruce after his workshop experience? Did this one experience magically wipe out all trace of fear in him? Is it that he faced such a major fear that now all other fears seemed minor?

No. Bruce still experienced fear when he thought about

calling Martha. Courage is not the absence of fear; courage is the ability to act when you do feel fear.

The only thing that changed for Bruce is that he now realized he had a choice about what he would do when he felt fear. Before the workshop, his fears controlled him so thoroughly but so subtly that he did not realize he could do anything about them.

Fear always disguises itself, remember? So before, Bruce would probably have told himself that he didn't care enough to call anyway, or he would have intended to call but put it off so long that it finally seemed inappropriate. But after the workshop, he realized that he was simply afraid, and that he did not need to go along with those excuses. Once he paid attention to his fear, he discovered he could do the things he feared anyway—if he chose to!

And this is the first step for each of us: to identify our fears and pay attention to them. As long as fear lies below the level of your awareness, it will control you. It will always disguise itself and provide you with convincing excuses.

Step One: Get Acquainted with Your Fears and Your Disguises

You don't have to attend a workshop to become aware of the power of fear in your life.

One way to begin is to look at the way you disguise fear. In biology, we learn that every organism has a fear response. A deer stands very still. A chameleon changes colors to blend in with its environment. A skunk sprays; a cat arches its back and hisses.

When you are faced with an intimidating situation, how does your organism respond? Do you laugh it away? Do you find a way to get super busy? Do you procrastinate and hope it will go away? Do you rationalize and get caught up in your excuses? Does your highly efficient, in-control adult take over and just "handle" everything?

EXPERIMENT #14
1. Think of three situations you have been in recently in which you stopped yourself from getting what you wanted.

How did you stop yourself? What excuses or defensive behavior did you use?

For example, maybe you wanted to ask someone to dance at a party, but instead you started telling the person some irrelevant story. Or, maybe you wanted to ask someone over for dinner, but instead you got involved with your work and decided you didn't have time. Or maybe you wanted to attend a singles event, but you told yourself you were just too tired.

2. Make a list of adjectives that characterize you. For example,

intelligent	controlling
funny	charming
intense	lazy
close to my	
family	

Now go back over the list. With regard to each item, consider whether it *might* be behavior that you use as a disguise when you feel fear. For example,

Intelligent—I explain things to people a lot. That way we don't have to get personal.

Funny—When I get close to difficult feelings, I crack jokes. Or when someone gives me a compliment, rather than taking it in, I brush it off with humor.

Intense—When someone tries to tease me in a loving way, I get all serious. I can't "flirt" back. Or, I often want to talk *about* things and analyze them rather than just experience them. I could "lighten up."

Close to my family—I make plans with my mother rather than going out where I might meet other singles. Or I avoid closeness with the excuse that my parents wouldn't approve of this person.

Controlling—My dates have to do things my way, or I let them know and create distance. For instance, if my date is late, or does or doesn't pay as I think is right, or if my date doesn't tell me what I want to hear, I make an issue of it.

Charming—I don't let go of my charming act, even in the privacy of our bedroom. I'm afraid I won't be liked if I'm not charming.

Lazy—I haven't done anything to meet new people for months. I tell myself I'm lazy. But maybe I'm scared.

It is crucial to understand that disguises are not *bad*. Don't put yourself down because you recognized your fear or your cover-up behavior. Remember, disguises are the organism's natural defense system. Also, *a person's disguise for fear usually looks very much like the real person underneath.* If you tend to laugh away fears, you are probably a genuinely funny person and a delight to be around. You don't need to throw away your sense of humor; only become aware of the times you use it to mask fear. If you become a workaholic when you confront something scary, you probably are a reliable, conscientious worker. This is an asset—except when it becomes automatic, when you no longer have a choice over how you behave.

Once you have identified what you feel may be defensive or disguise behaviors on your part, start paying attention when these behaviors emerge. When you catch yourself "doing your number," what are you trying to avoid? What would you rather not look at or feel?

Another way to become aware of your fears is simply to look at them directly.

EXPERIMENT #15

Complete this sentence as many different ways as is appropriate:

   With regard to relationships, I fear _____.

I suggest you make your own list before you look at this representative selection of responses from workshop participants:

"With regard to relationships, I fear . . ."

- I'm going to get left out; I'll never find the right person.
- I'll be rejected.
- I'll get well into a relationship and then discover I don't want to be there.
- I'll lose my independence and freedom. I don't want to be tied down.
- I'm afraid to commit myself because someone better might come along.

- I'm afraid to make the initial moves. I'm terrified of flirting or asking for a date.
- I don't want to be vulnerable to anyone else. I don't want to give anyone else the ability to hurt me.
- I'm not sure why, but when I feel I'm getting too close, I just pull back. I don't know what I'm afraid of. I long for closeness, and then when I get it, I feel dreadfully uncomfortable.
- I'm way too needy. I'm afraid I'll drown anyone who tries to love me. I've got to keep my neediness under control.
- I'm afraid the other person might find out about the parts of myself I don't like and then reject me because of them.
- I'm afraid of what I might find out about myself in a relationship. I know I've got a lot of defenses and I don't want anyone tampering with them.
- I was close to my first wife and she left me. I don't want to risk that pain again.
- I'm afraid I'll lose control.
- I'm afraid I'll lose myself. I have a vision of this big ocean with an undertow that will just swallow me up.
- I'm afraid I won't have time for a relationship. Love would interfere with my work.
- I don't want to be responsible for anyone else.
- I'm afraid of social settings. I don't know how to play. I take the whole thing too seriously.
- I come from a terrible family and I don't know anyone who has a good relationship. To me, relationships mean trouble.

Becoming aware of your fears is an ongoing process; an exercise like the above experiment is just a beginning. The process is not necessarily pleasant because it usually involves feeling vulnerable and letting others see your vulnerability. But you can't get beyond your fear by going around it; you have to go *through* it. If fear is keeping you from intimacy, then getting acquainted with your fears could be the most important thing you ever do.

Step Two: Acceptance

So let us assume you recognize how fear is stopping you. This is the first and by far the most important step. Now what?

Begin by accepting your fears and your disguises. Don't fight them. Your fears are your old friends. They've been with you for a long time. Fear is not pleasant, but it is natural, and you won't make it go away by wishing it weren't there. Instead, try to get better acquainted with the you who feels fear.

The only way to get better acquainted with the fearful you is to stop and take notice at those times when you feel fear. It won't do very much good to think about your fear in the abstract.

So the next time you feel fear, see if you can stop and pay attention to it. Your fear will manifest itself somewhere in your body. Where do you experience it? Are your knees weak? Do you have "butterflies" in your stomach? Do you feel tearful? Do your palms sweat? Does blood rush to your head? Does your "heart skip a beat"? Does your chest feel empty? Does your mouth feel dry?

What cover-up behavior is emerging? What are you tempted to do instead of the thing you fear?

Can you actually stay with your fear for a few moments? Just let it be there and notice what it feels like. Say to yourself, "Oh! Now I'm feeling afraid." Stop and relax for a moment. Take a few deep breaths and see what it feels like to feel afraid.

Try this technique from the practice of yoga: Students of yoga are encouraged to get into a stretch position so that they are definitely feeling some stretch—maybe even a little pain—but not so they are traumatizing the muscle. Then they are encouraged to hold the position. They discover that after some seconds, as they relax into the position, they can easily stretch the muscle a bit more.

Try the same method with fear. Let yourself experience a little fear. It won't be pleasant. But try to relax into it. Trust that you will automatically protect yourself from anything you can't handle. When you have pushed yourself a little bit, let go. Back off. The next time that situation arises you may be able to tolerate a little bit more fear.

Once, in one of my groups, there was a woman named Marcy who had many fears. At first, it was hard for us to see them because she was a very facile, entertaining speaker. She would talk on and on *about* her fears, always throwing in humor to keep us entertained. After a while, we realized we were doing Marcy no favor by being a good audience. By laughing at her stories, we were supporting her mask, not her real self.

As an experiment, and with her consent, we agreed not to laugh at her humor for a while. When she began a story, we would listen only long enough to understand her problem. Then we would invite her to stop talking, to close her eyes, and to focus her attention on what was going on inside her. This was difficult for her, and often she would start talking again, engaging us rather than paying attention to her feelings. Each time we would gently invite her to try to stay with what she was experiencing and resist the urge to tell us more "about" it.

One time, another group member got angry with Marcy over a difficult interaction they had. The anger frightened Marcy, and we saw a golden opportunity to help her confront her fear.

"We are all here with you," I told her. "It's okay to be afraid. Tell us how you feel."

"I'm afraid!" Marcy cried. "I'm really afraid."

We had worked with Marcy enough to know that fear situations reminded her of times when she was afraid as a very small child. On this occasion, Marcy looked about two years old. Her eyes were wide, her body tense.

I went over to Marcy and touched her. "Don't avoid those fearful feelings. Talk about them."

"I'm afraid I'll be left alone," Marcy said in a shaky voice. "When my mother got angry with me, she left me by myself."

After a few minutes, Marcy began to cry. One of the women held her, and finally she was able to talk about her experience.

"It's amazing to me that I could be that afraid and not be left alone. Here you all still are. I feel incredibly comforted, incredibly safe."

Of course, Marcy knew intellectually that we wouldn't leave her if she showed us her fear, but she had to experience it before she could understand it emotionally as well.

After that, Marcy was able to reveal her fear to us more easily and more often. Her fear became more familiar to her and had less of a hold on her life. Gradually, she was able to begin doing things that were scary for her, in spite of her fear. The main thing was, she had to *experience* her fear first, and not keeping running away from it.

Not everyone's fear is as intense as Marcy's was. You may be able to experience your fear on your own, just by being willing to pay attention to it every time it emerges. Next time, don't let yourself escape into your "mask" behavior. Try saying to yourself, "I'm afraid." Pay attention to your fearful feelings for a few moments. The more you do this, the more control you will gain over your fear, and the less it will be able to stop you from getting what you want in love—and in life.

Step Three: Talk About Your Fears

A very important step in getting control over your fears is to talk about them.

In my women's group, we used to say, "If it has a charge on it, talk about it." That is, if you feel agitated about something, mention it! It is easy to avoid talking about the things about which we have the most feelings. But labeling something and talking about it *can transform it.* On the other hand, failing to talk about it can bury it deeper within your psyche where it becomes less accessible, yet has a tighter hold on you.

First find a trusted friend, preferably someone who won't give a lot of advice but who will encourage you to talk. (In fact, you can tell your friend that's what you would like.) No one can predict what you will discover as you try to put into words what you are feeling. It may not be easy at first. And it is not important for you to make sense or to reach any conclusions. You are simply increasing your awareness about your fear and making it more accessible to yourself.

When you feel ready, try talking about your fear with the person with whom your fear comes up. Be careful to make clear that you do not expect him or her to "fix" it or to change in any way. You just want to talk about what is going on for you.

Talking about your fears, especially to the one with whom you are experiencing fear, is not easy. But that is no reason not to do it. It requires courage and practice. You must be patient with yourself and willing to flounder at first. But above all, you have to believe that talking about your fears will enable you to gain control over them. Until you have begun to experience this, you just have to accept the idea on faith—or on the basis of hundreds of other people's experiences with it.

Talking about your fears may be difficult for a variety of reasons. You may be unclear about what you really want to say. You may be experiencing such a rush of feelings that they obstruct your ability to express yourself clearly. You may fear that your partner will feel hurt or resentful or angry. You may simply feel such anxiety that you will want to avoid the whole discussion.

When any of these obstacles arises, the best approach is to mention the obstacles, to say what is going on for you. For example, statements like the following will both ease your anxiety and prepare your listener to be open and sympathetic toward you.

> I feel that there's something I want to talk about with you, but I'm not clear about exactly what it is. I think if I begin to talk about it, it will begin to come clearer. Could you just be patient with me while I work at it?

> I'm having a lot of feelings right now. I'd like to try to talk about them, but I may not be very clear. Is that okay? Will you just bear with me?

> I have some feelings I'd like to talk about. But I'm afraid you're going to be angry (or hurt). Please realize that I'm not asking you to do anything. I just need to talk about what is going on with me.

Statements like these are a way of bringing yourself into the present moment by talking about your "process" rather than your "content." When they work, they will create an emotional openness that should make your conversation easier. Both partners will be fully present, fully attentive, and fully focused on the immediate interaction between you.

When you are talking about fear, the distinction between "process" and "content" will be useful. Content is *what* you want to say; process is *how* you say it or how you feel when you say it. Process has to do with what is going on for you *right now;* it is about the interaction taking place at that moment. For example,

Process ⟶ This is hard for me to tell you. I feel hesitant, but I want to say it anyway.

Content — I find myself liking you a great deal. But I also feel some fear about our relationship. I don't know whether I'm afraid it won't work out or afraid it will. But I know I feel better about you than I've felt about anyone for a long time. You're very special to me.

Process ⟶ Don't feel you have to say anything right now. I feel better already, just having said that.

Telling the truth—especially about something as difficult to talk about as fear—requires practice. But beginning to discover and to talk about what is true for you regarding your fears is a critical step in increasing your awareness of your fears and gaining control over them.

Usually toward the end of my workshops, I provide an opportunity for people to say what the workshop has meant to them. During one such period, a man said,

I experienced something quite dramatic today. It may sound simple, but it feels very profound to me. I found out it is okay to say, "I feel afraid. I'm scared." I have always thought that saying this would make me feel like a real wimp. It had the opposite effect; it has made me feel stronger.

This man had learned a simple but elusive truth.

Many people—especially, in our society, men—believe that vulnerability is bad. They will pay almost any price to avoid being vulnerable—that is, open to being hurt, open to being seen as afraid.

Vulnerability is not bad. Vulnerability is *good.* When you can expose the reality (which everyone knows anyway)

that you are afraid, you become free, for you are no longer enslaved to hiding your fear. To be vulnerable is to let another person see you as you really are. Only then is it possible for another person to love you as you really are.

The truth (for example, inner fear) is almost always difficult; that's why you spend so much energy masking it. Thus, revealing the truth makes you feel vulnerable. But revealing the truth sets you free. Vulnerability, then, is a necessary step on the way to self-love, intimacy, and deep inner peace. What a world this would be if we all understood that vulnerability is something to work toward, not to avoid!

A Few Helpful Hints About Fear

A psychologist once measured the levels of fear in paratroopers during a practice mission. It turned out that the highest level of fear occurred just *before* the jump. Once the jumpers were out the door, their fear levels dropped dramatically.

Just sitting and thinking about something can feel far worse than actually doing the dreaded activity. If you can make yourself take the first step and get into action, you may find your anxiety level will be greatly reduced.

One man I spoke with told me that what kept him from acting was that he would always imagine the worst possible outcome of his action. For example, when he wanted to call a woman, he imagined that she would be rude to him, or cool, and say she had no interest in seeing him. Why would he call her if that's what he imagined would happen? But now he says, "I still imagine the worst, but I *expect the best!* It makes a big difference!"

Gestalt therapist Fritz Perls said that fear is excitement without breathing. When he worked with people who were fearful, he would suggest that they sit still and pay attention to their fear while breathing deeply and easily. Sometimes people would discover that what seemed frightening also seemed exciting.

It is true that the body distinguishes little between fear and excitement physiologically. In both cases, the palms sweat, the heart beats rapidly, the breathing gets shallow and quick. Both fear and excitement are simply energy flowing through the body. It is only in our minds that we interpret the sensations as "fear" or "excitement." Some people find these sensations to be so unpleasant that they withdraw or run away. They wall themselves off, but then their self-inflicted isolation reinforces their fears!

Next time you feel afraid, try Fritz Perls's method. Rather than cutting off your flow of energy by withdrawing, increase it by breathing deeply. Try saying to yourself, "I feel excited." See whether it feels true. Maybe you can transform your fear into a pleasant sensation—or at a least a mixture of excitement and fear.

Another thought that may help you to pay attention to your fear and stay with it rather than running from it is this: Freud believed that every fear has hidden within it a wish. For example, a lonely man who has lived alone for years looks under his bed to be sure no one is there. Deep inside, he hopes someone will be there! Are you afraid someone will get so close to you, he or she will discover the *real* you? Maybe deep inside you want this to happen.

Look at the list of fears you made for Experiment #15. Is there a wish hidden in any of your fears? To look at just a few possibilities,

- I'm afraid I'll lose my freedom. (Is there a part of you that would like to have a feeling of obligation to someone you love; someone who loves you?)
- I'm afraid of what I might find out about *myself* in a relationship. (Would part of you like to know more about your inner self? Would you like to find out what you are so busy hiding from yourself?)
- I'm afraid I'll lose myself, lose control. (Do you have a secret longing under your fear to be swept off your feet? To let go of your careful control and be caught up in a sea of unpredictable passion?)

If you feel that fear is keeping you from saying yes to love—and if you want to experience love—then choose one of the suggestions in this chapter and begin to work with it. Also, Chapters 10 and 12, which follow, contain more suggestions about dealing with the fears that keep you from saying yes to love. The wonderful irony about paying attention to your fear is that the more you do it, the safer you begin to feel. Fears you know well are far less scary than fears that are deeply buried.

Fear of Rejection

The fear which most singles mention first as the most obvious and most frequent one they face is the fear of rejection. So let's take a moment to look at ways of handling this particular problem by using a metaphor from which you will be able to draw parallels to your personal life.

I learned a great deal about rejection being married to a ceramic artist. My husband, Mayer, and I used to send slides to galleries with a request that they consider carrying his work. For every ten letters we sent out, nine would come back with comments like, "The work is very nice but it doesn't fit in with our gallery aesthetic." Or, "We are not accepting any new artists at this time."

It hurt. My first reaction was, "His work must not be all that good. How could nine out of ten galleries be wrong?" But Mayer, who had been playing this game for years before I met him, had quite a different attitude. I watched him in amazement. He would say to me, "Don't worry about it. These galleries have their reasons. Ninety percent of the American public has bad taste; they don't know good work when they see it. We are looking for an elite audience. My work is very strong and I'll find the right galleries to carry it."

He was unperturbed by the rejections. In fact, he seemed to go at his work with all the more fervor, confident of how strong it really was. He was frustrated at not finding galleries that recognized his quality. But he knew this was not a reflection on his work.

Over a period of time as we traveled, I was able to visit several of the galleries in question. It turned out that some of them didn't carry much clay at all. Some of them carried nothing in the price range of Mayer's work. Many of them carried work that seemed mediocre by our standards. And some of them already had more artists than they could handle. One gallery owner told me she didn't like to carry work that was fragile! So Mayer had been right: Their rejections had nothing to do with the quality of his work!

By persevering, we found galleries that were appropriate for Mayer's work and did extremely well with it. Eventually, we were in the position of turning galleries down rather than the reverse.

Most of us, upon being rejected, do exactly what I first did: "There must be something wrong with me. I'm too boring. I'm too needy. I'm not sexy enough. I'm too aggressive," etc. But the only sensible response to being rejected is the same one Mayer had. *The person who rejects you is making a statement about himself or herself—not about you.* You are a great person, but 90 percent of the American public has bad taste. You are looking for an elite group: someone who recognizes real quality *and* can handle it! If other people don't have the good sense to love you, *they* have a problem, not you. And if you could ever get to know these people better, you would almost certainly discover—as I did with the galleries—that you didn't have such a good match anyway.

As I look back over the painful rejections I had to endure during my single years, I can see that, in one case, I was older than the man; we wanted different things from life at that point, and he recognized that. In another case, the man I loved was gay, and though we were fond of each other, he could not alter himself to meet our needs. Nor could I! In another case, my desire for intimacy was just plain unappealing to a man. I felt very bad about it, but if that was his choice, that was his choice. It did not mean I was wrong.

"What about timing?" a workshop participant asked me. "What if you meet the right person but at the wrong time in his or her life?"

Meeting the right person at the wrong time is exactly the same as meeting the wrong person. It's sad, but there is nothing to do about it except to move on. What you seek is the right person at the right time, and wishing things were just a little different from the way they are will not change them.

All this does not mean that rejection is not painful; it usually is. Rejection is especially pain-filled if you had any good "chemistry" going between you. In such a case, rejection can cause physical and mental anguish similar to the pain of drug withdrawal.

However, rejection does not have to affect your self-esteem. What most people do with rejection is turn it against themselves: "I'm a nothing person. If I can only change this or that about myself, maybe the next person won't reject me." It is as though every time a gallery rejected Mayer's work, he went back to the work and said, "Maybe I should make it bigger, or do it in blues rather than reds. Maybe I should make platters instead of vases." Don't keep re-examining your product every time you get rejected! Don't take a stranger's opinion when you have had twenty or thirty years to perfect yourself. The problem is not that you are a bad piece of pottery; the problem is finding the perfect setting for the unique work of art you are.

The most important thing to remember, then, when you are rejected, is, "This person is making a statement about him- or herself, not about me. I am who I am, and this person either can't see it or just doesn't like my style."

After you have been rejected, make yourself dwell not upon the things you liked in the relationship, but upon the ways in which you did not fit. And persevere. What you are looking for is someone who wants to be with you, not someone who—for whatever reason—doesn't.

I finally developed a whole new attitude about rejection letters. I said to myself, "If we need ninety rejection letters for every ten acceptance letters, then we should welcome rejection letters! We should collect them as fast as we can. The sooner we get ninety rejection letters, the sooner we get ten good galleries." In the same way, if you assume you will have to kiss a number of frogs before you find your intimate partner, the faster you collect rejections, the sooner you will meet your true love.

Another negative side effect of rejection is that each rejection exacerbates your fear of rejection and makes it harder for you to face the cruel world one more time.

But fear of rejection does not deserve a special place of honor in the repertoire of fears that affect our lives. Fear of rejection is just fear. It is more concrete than other fears, and is nice because it is so justifiable, so reasonable. But in the end it is just another fear to either honor—or move beyond. The choice is simple: Are you going to tell your fear of rejection that it *cannot* run your life? Or are you going to build an altar to your fear of rejection and spend a lot of time worshipping it?

Saying Yes to Love

For many people saying yes to love may be virtually the same thing as saying yes to life.

A love relationship with one special person is not the only way to experience the kind of intimacy I have been describing; unattached singles may reveal their genuine selves to their friends, their children, their therapist. But unfortunately, many unattached singles *are* without any intimacy at all in their lives. (This is of course true of many married people as well.) Nowhere, with no one, do they have the opportunity to experience their fears and the deep reaches of their inner selves. They have become their disguises. They are imprisoned behind their walls, afraid, but more afraid than anything of feeling their fears. Because they must keep hiding from themselves, the deepest joys of life elude them.

Saying yes to love is saying yes to adventure, to risk, to experiencing life on many levels. It is saying yes to a life that is more than work, play, sleep, eat. In short, it is saying yes to yourself, your whole self.

Saying yes to love is saying yes to continuity, to staying with one person long enough to allow the subtlest levels of yourself to emerge. It is affirming that only by choosing to experience the difficult and painful parts of life will you be able to experience life's richest rewards.

If you seek love, you have to be willing to accept the whole package, the work and the struggles as well as the joys. Of course, it is the difficult aspects of love that you fear, not the fun. But perhaps the saddest choice of all is to seek *only* the pleasure and fun of love and to escape as soon as fear or vulnerability arise. Such a life is like eating only sugar all day long with its sweet taste but its complete lack of nutrition.

Remember, the question is, are you going to let fear keep you from experiencing life at its fullest? Are you going to stay in Candyland where life is sweet and easy but not very satisfying? Or are you going to pull together every ounce of courage and say *yes* to love, to journeying through life with another person, to opening yourself to deep intimacy and the pain, the joy, and the fullness it will surely bring you?

The choice is yours, and the time to make it is now.

Part III

Keeping It
All Together
While You Look

Chapter 10

The Tenth Strategy: Increasing Your Self-Awareness and Self-Esteem

One big question underlies all we have discussed so far and remains unanswered: Why haven't we been applying these strategies all along?

Why do we lower our true standards and settle for less than we want? Why do we convince ourselves there are no ways to meet people? Why do we hang around in BTN relationships for months on end? Why do we have so much trouble saying no? Why do we let fear control our lives so that we can never let go and say *yes?*

According to Jewish folklore, most of us are driven by dybbuks we hardly know. A dybbuk is the soul of a dead person that enters the body of a living person and controls him or her. It's a kind of metaphor for the reasons we engage in self-defeating behavior.

We are complex psychological beings. We carry around the "souls"—or at least the behavior and beliefs—of our parents, our grandparents, and who knows what other people who influenced us in our early years. When you scold your child, you hear your mother's voice. When you criticize your lover, you sound like your dad criticizing your mother. Dybbuks—beliefs and behavior of others, now deeply etched into our beings. They control us. They *are* us. They make correcting apparently simple mistakes *very* difficult.

What sort of person are you—you, who want to be in a relationship with someone else? What do you have to offer another person? What are your liabilities as a partner? Are you controlled by certain beliefs or behavior that make it hard for you to settle down—or for someone else to settle down with you?

In other words, some people are single because they make mistakes in running their love lives: They give in to ambivalence or lower their standards or stay in a BTN relationship too long. But other people are alone because they aren't very good love partners. They may be too self-centered or too domineering or too depressive. Some people are cold and unloving or very tied to their parents or reclusive. Many people these days are narcissistic and can't enlarge their world enough to include the welfare of another human being. These people may *think* they are wonderful, but from the point of view of another person, they *aren't*.

So in order to make your survey of the reasons you may still be single really complete, you have to take a realistic look at yourself. Correcting major personality deficits is beyond the scope of this book. But most of us ordinary, wonderful people can benefit by looking at how we might make ourselves even more desirable (or less undesirable) as partners. What are your dybbuks? Put another way, how are you getting in your own way of making love work for you?

That is what we shall examine in this chapter.

First, you stand in your own way when you fight against yourself, rather than moving with yourself.

I like to use the metaphor of western fist-fighting versus martial arts. In westerns, when Gus aimed his fist at Joe, Joe put his own arm up to block the blow. The impact on his arm hurt. Then Joe would hit back. Gus would block Joe's fist, and the fight would escalate. If Joe were using martial arts, however, Gus would punch, and Joe, rather than resisting the attack, would grab Gus's fist and just keep pulling it in the direction it was moving anyway. He would pull the fist, pull Gus off balance, and possibly even flip him over onto his back. There would be a minimum of injury, and the fight would be over.

These days, our adversaries are mostly internal.

Suppose you realize that every time you get into a relationship, you become critical of your partner, and you decide you want to stop this pattern. If you just force yourself to stop, you will be like the western fight. The dybbuk inside you that needs to criticize will come back with a vengeance. Then you'll try all the harder to stop it, and your criticizing will escalate. Now, besides being critical, you will feel bad about yourself for not being able to stop, and your self-esteem will plummet.

What you resist persists. Indeed, your dybbuk will persist with added energy, precisely because you are trying to kill it. The dybbuks inside you *believe they are serving you.* They are interested in survival—theirs and yours. Deep in your subconscious mind, your criticizing dybbuk believes that if you somehow kill it and stop criticizing, *you will die.* Your dybbuk is protecting you from some alleged disaster. That is why it criticizes so convincingly.

But suppose you use a martial arts approach. Rather than resisting your critical self, you move with it. You watch yourself being critical. You notice how you feel inside when you are critical. You start thinking about why you are so critical, who else in your family is critical, what might happen if you weren't critical.

Rather than hating and resisting your critical dybbuk, you accept it. You view it as a friend who has been with you for many years, serving you, protecting you. You recognize aspects of your critical self that you like and value, as well as parts that you loathe and feel you could give up now. You make friends with this dybbuk, and you and the friendly little monster agree to work *together* toward a balance that will serve you better.

There is a word which describes this martial-arts approach to yourself. It is "self-acceptance."

Few people are perfectly self-accepting. But if you understand what self-acceptance is and you are on the path toward self-acceptance, your chances of succeeding with the program outlined in this book will be far greater. If you want to change a personality trait that you feel makes you less desirable as a partner, you will see in this chapter that change and self-acceptance are closely related. And, if you are self-accepting, when you do find a relationship, it will have a far greater chance of success. For all these reasons, we shall discuss self-acceptance here at length.

We can best understand self-acceptance by looking first at four "steps" along the pathway to it. The steps are not chronological, for each is going on all the time. Yet there is a sense in which one step must precede the next. The steps are all *very* closely related; indeed, they overlap quite a bit.

But I have divided them into separate steps because I believe it will be easier to discuss certain concepts by doing so. Let us look, then, at

1. Self-awareness
2. Self-love
3. Change
4. Self-esteem
5. Self-acceptance

Step One: Self-Awareness

You can't accept your whole self if you aren't aware of your whole self. Most people know only about half of who they really are.

Let me illustrate with a personal example. When I first joined a women's group, after some trust had developed, a woman asked me why I felt I had to smile all the time. She said it made her uncomfortable and that she found it hard to take me seriously. I asked several other people if they had noticed this, and they all quickly agreed. I had been utterly unaware of my constant smile. But then I began paying attention to it. Soon after that, I was telling my group about an incident with my husband that had hurt me very much, and I suddenly noticed I was grinning. Then I noticed that I felt nervous, embarrassed, and that I wasn't actually telling the whole story. I relaxed my face and was surprised at how much calmer I felt and how much easier it was to tell my story. The women reported that they could believe me more easily.

That little piece of self-awareness helped me to become more genuine, more honest. Yet before the incident, I didn't realize there was this "something" that I wasn't aware of.

My women's group continued to work with me on my smiliness. When I smiled inappropriately, they would mention it, not in a critical way, but as a supportive reminder. And we talked more about it. I discovered it was a mask I wore because I was terrified that people would not like me unless I was warm and sweet and bubbly. How ironic! The very thing I was doing to make people like me actually put them off.

I could have gone through my whole life smiling inappropriately. I would have missed experiencing the calmness of talking more directly and honestly to people. I would never have understood why some people were put off by me, and I probably would have blamed them and resented them. Worst of all, I may never have realized that I don't have to "make" people like me. Imagine how deeply pleasurable and peaceful a feeling I had the first times I let go of my smily routine—and people seemed to like me just fine anyway!

All these things I would have missed if I had never become acquainted with my smiliness—but I wouldn't have known that I was missing something! I just would have gone through life vaguely concerned that I wasn't really well liked and not knowing why. And I wouldn't have known what was standing in my way of feeling good about myself.

Self-awareness is *optional.* Many people go through life with a limited amount of it. But expanded self-awareness enriches life!

It took me a long time to let go of my compulsive smiling. Giving it up was a difficult struggle because it was a lifelong habit, and because I was so afraid when I ventured out without it. But I forced myself to experiment and finally learned that people could get closer to me and liked me better when I let go of my bubbly act. The alternative was not, as I had imagined, that I had to go around as a morose zombie. I learned that the real me is very energetic and enthusiastic, and I didn't have to let go of that. As is often the case with defenses, they closely resemble the real person. The difference may seem subtle to an outsider, but it was a life-changing difference to me. And it came about because of a new piece of self-awareness.

Self-awareness is the first critical step on the way to self-acceptance. You can't accept your whole self unless you know your whole self.

So how do you go about expanding your self-awareness? It all boils down to two things: getting input, and paying attention.

GETTING INPUT

Except to a limited extent, you cannot expand your self-awareness just by an act of will, because by yourself, you have no way to discover what you are not aware of! You need someone or something to direct your attention to what you are missing.

Sources of input are limitless. One obvious resource is people who know you well. Other people can easily see behavior that is so habitual to you or so long-denied by you that you will miss it even when they point it out. When my smiling behavior was first mentioned, I was *stunned* to learn that *all* of the women in the group saw it. Then I began to remember comments I had heard in the past: (To my mother) "My, you certainly have a bubbly daughter." (To my husband) "I don't think I could live around such high energy all the time," or "Is she really that happy all the time? She doesn't seem real." (How accurate that person was!) These people were all seeing something in me that I didn't see.

Other people *do* see you more clearly than you see yourself. Think about your own friends, co-workers, or relatives. Does one talk too much? Does one interrupt a lot? Does one put people down all the time? Does one fail to look you in the eyes during a conversation? Does one laugh loudly whenever he feels uncomfortable? These people *don't see these things about themselves*. But you can see them clearly. Now don't you wonder what they may see in you that they never mention?

You can get a lot of information about yourself from the people around you.

But how? In our day-to-day lives, this is not the sort of information we generally share with each other.

One possibility is to ask for it.

EXPERIMENT #16

Think of a friend, relative, or co-worker whom you trust. It should be someone you like and with whom you do not feel competitive.

Create a relaxed setting with an open-ended closing time. Perhaps you could invite the person over for dinner.

Your friend may want to both ask and answer questions or only answer them for you. In any case, whoever has asked a question and is listening to an answer *must agree not to comment on the answer.* As the listener, you may ask questions of clarification only. Your goal is to get information about yourself, not to *do* anything about it. (We'll talk about what to do with it later.)

Select one or two of the following questions to ask your friend:

1. If you could change one thing about me, what would it be?
2. Please jot down and then tell me five things you like about me and two things you don't like about me.
3. Is there anything you see in me that you think I don't see in myself?
4. If you had one piece of advice to give me about how I live my life, what would it be?

Where else can you turn to get more information about yourself?

Movies, TV, dramas, novels, biographies, self-help books. Whenever you have a strong reaction to something you read or see, ask yourself what it might have touched off *in you.* Why do some parts of a book make you angry or sad, while other parts don't? How are the characters in a movie similar to you?

The same also goes for real-life dramas taking place all around you. When you have a strong reaction to anything, don't assume it has to do only with the other people involved. Ask yourself what your reaction tells you *about yourself.*

One of the best ways to expand your self-knowledge is to ask yourself questions. You may have a great deal more information within you than you have ever stopped to look at.

The following questions are really several experiments, not one, but I shall group them together because they are all ways of getting more information about yourself. You will probably not want to do them all at one sitting. Take your time with them. They may bring up some unpleasant feelings, but that's okay. Expanding your self-awareness is often somewhat painful, for you are attempting to unearth parts of yourself that you buried precisely because they were painful or difficult for you.

We will discuss in a moment what you *do* with new self-knowledge once you acquire it. Don't worry about that now. Just begin to consider and experiment with ways of becoming aware of different aspects of yourself.

EXPERIMENT #17

In your journal or notebook, respond to the following questions. Remember to take your time with them.

1. What are the positive qualities or attributes that you bring to a potential intimate partner? What do you have to offer to a person in an intimate relationship?
2. What are your liabilities as a potential partner?
3. What obstacles do you put in your own way that are keeping you from finding and connecting with another person?
4. Are there things about you that other people do not like? What are these things?
5. Look at your list from #4. How do you feel about these qualities in yourself? Do you like them, dislike them, or feel neutral about them?
6. What about you satisfies you?
7. What about you does not satisfy you?

The first part of expanding your self-awareness is getting input, information about yourself. But whatever your sources of information about yourself, none of them will work unless you do the second part of expanding your self-awareness.

PAYING ATTENTION

Normally, as we go about our lives, we pay attention to only a small fraction of what is going on around us and within us. We can't pay attention to everything all at once, but we can pay attention to a great deal more than we do.

I was smiling all the time, but I wasn't paying attention to it. Once it was pointed out to me and I did start to notice it, a lot happened. What a loss for me if I had never paid attention to my smile!

The same world we are used to can look dramatically

different when viewed through different "spectacles," that is, with new awareness. For example, suppose you read an article by a researcher who has discovered that men tend to interrupt more often than women. Suddenly, you may notice every time a man interrupts. Or suppose a friend tells you that she feels you gripe a lot. Suddenly, you, too, may begin to notice how often you complain about things.

There's a story told of a man who sold his brother a mule with the promise that it was a superior animal, never given to bouts of stubbornness. The brother was delighted, took the lead rope, and started off toward home. The mule wouldn't budge. The man tugged and pulled and swatted the mule, but the mule was oblivious. Finally, the man went back to his brother with angry complaints.

"I thought you said this was not a stubborn mule!"

"Oh, it's not," said the first brother. He grabbed an enormous two-by-four, raised it high and brought it down full force on the mule's head. Then he picked up the lead rope and off they went. He called back to his bewildered brother, "You just have to get his attention first."

Most of us could benefit from a good swat with a two-by-four. There is a great deal going on within us, and we generally pay attention to just a fraction of it.

The reason expanded awareness is critical is that *the more you are aware of, the more choices you have.*

If I had never become aware of my excessive smiling, I could never have chosen to stop doing it. In my early childhood, I probably got positively reinforced for being "happy" and "enthusiastic," so way back then I programmed myself to keep that act going. It became *unconscious.* I was behaving automatically, as though I were on automatic pilot—with the switch rusted to "on." My first task was to get off of automatic pilot and back to making fully conscious choices.

People who elect to remain "unconscious," who never make any effort to expand their awareness, are not very free. They are enslaved to their own programming. They never ask themselves why they think or believe or behave as they do. They never consider alternatives because they aren't aware of alternatives. They don't make choices about their lives; they just live them.

Once you embark upon a path of expanded self-awareness, you will probably get drawn in to wanting more. The path of self-knowledge goes deeper and deeper within you. You can choose to stop at any point, and you may, for I reiterate that expanded self-awareness can be painful. But if you are willing to experience some pain, stay with it, and go a little deeper, the rewards can be very great indeed.

Suppose you begin to expand your self-awareness and you discover that you interrupt people far more than you realized. The next thing you will want to ask yourself is why you do this. Pay attention to how you feel when you catch yourself interrupting. You may have to admit that you are more interested in getting attention than you are in giving it to someone else. Why? Because although you appear to be confident with all your verbal abilities, in fact you are very afraid of being left out, and you want more than anything to be a part of things. Why? Because you had a hard time getting attention from your family as you were growing up. This was painful for you as a small child and as a teenager, so you became strongly motivated to engage in behavior that would force others to notice and respond to you.

Now comes the exciting part. As you begin to experiment with interrupting less, you discover that people like you *better* and you are *more* a part of things. It turns out you don't have to work so hard to be liked. And you will discover what a pleasure it is to listen to others, to give *them* attention. You begin to connect with people more quickly and more genuinely. Gradually, you can let go of your fear of being left out.

I am describing in a few sentences a process that happens gradually over a period of months or even years. Awareness and behavior change slowly by means of small, seemingly insignificant events. Over and over, you may notice, after the fact, that you have interrupted. Then you may start catching yourself as you are doing it—or even before. You may start noticing when other people interrupt each other. But eventually you will reach a point where you look back and say, "Boy! I really used to be obnoxious!" You will be able to feel a very big difference in yourself—the absence of your frantic effort to get your share of the attention. You will have increased your self-esteem, not only because you gave up an annoying habit, but because you found out that the real you, underneath all the interrupting, is very likable.

One more word about self-awareness: We have talked mostly about expanding your awareness about your own *behavior*. But that is just one aspect of all the things you are probably ignoring now.

If you choose to, you can become more aware of what you are feeling, what emotions you are experiencing. You can see more of what you look at, taste more of what you eat, listen to more of what you hear, fully experience more of what you touch. You can become aware of how your thought processes work and how your thoughts assist or hinder you. You can become aware of your values and how they affect your life. You can become aware of your fears and whether or not you are in control of them.

All that is required is that you keep asking for input, getting information about yourself from whatever sources, and then keep paying attention.

In Aldous Huxley's vision of utopia, described in his book *Island,* magpies are constantly flying about the island crying out, "Attention. Attention," simply reminding everyone to wake up and be fully alive, and not to miss anything.

We would all do well to have little magpies flying around in our brains reminding us to pay attention. "What are you feeling?" they would say. "Are you doing what you want to be doing? Notice this. Notice that. Wake up. Pay attention."

Self-awareness is a skill that increases with practice and becomes easier over time.

Here is an exercise to help you begin to notice and to change your patterns of awareness. You will find it useful whether you are a beginner at the awareness game, a veteran, or somewhere in between. It is a pleasurable, relaxing exercise. I hope you enjoy it.

EXPERIMENT #18

a. You may want to have a friend sit with you for this exercise, just to be there and listen. But if you are alone, speak to yourself, softly, but out loud. Do the exercise the first few times with your eyes closed. Later, be sure to try it with your eyes open.

Sit or lie down and get comfortable. If you are sitting, sit up straight.

Now begin saying to yourself, "I am aware of ____." Just

keep saying it over and over, filling in the blank with whatever is appropriate at the moment. For example, "I am
aware of the car going by. I am aware of my toes being cold.
I am aware of my leg muscle being tense. I am aware of the
rice simmering on the stove. I am aware of my nose itching.
I am aware of feeling silly. I am aware of my back resting on
this chair. I am aware I'm thinking about my date tonight. I
am aware of the quiet in this room. I am aware I just moved
my feet," etc.

Keep going for a while, say, five or even ten minutes.

Repeat this exercise once a day or twice a week—whatever fits for you. *But do it at least fifteen times.* See what
happens. Notice how your awareness begins to change. How
do you feel after the exercise? You may feel more "tuned in"
to yourself. You may view the world around you with new
eyes.

b. See if you can deliberately give attention to what you are
experiencing in your body several times a day. Stop for a
second and say, "I am feeling ____ in my ____ ." The first
blank is a *feeling* and the second blank is a *part of your
body.* ("I am feeling tension in my jaw," or "I am feeling
hungry in my stomach," or "I am feeling warmth in my
chest.")

Step Two: Self-Love

So what do you *do* with your newly expanded self-awareness? What do you *do* with the new "you" you have discovered?

As much as you can, you become like a compassionate,
loving parent to yourself and give yourself unconditional,
tender love.

Let's return to our hypothetical "you" who interrupts.

As you pay more attention to your interrupting, it may
begin to drive you nuts. But trying not to interrupt will be
even worse. You may start to hate yourself. You'll experience fear as you try to venture forth without a habit which
has served you for many years.

But through it all, keep saying to yourself, like the most
loving mother in the world, "I know it's hard. But you're
doing just great. Keep it up. You are courageous. You are
wise to even tackle this big problem. It doesn't matter if

you backslide. Interrupting is part of who you are! No matter what you do, I love you."

Many people have a mistaken notion about self-love; they believe that people who are self-loving have simply gotten rid of all their dybbuks, their fears, their faults, their insecurities. They love themselves because they are such good people.

Wrong.

People who are self-loving have simply learned how to take the bad with the good. Self-love is not about loving the parts of yourself that are easy to love. That's no challenge. Self-love is about loving *all* of yourself including the parts you don't like or don't want to look at. Self-loving people have become well acquainted with their weaknesses and fears; they realize that's who they are, and they have learned to love the entire package.

This doesn't mean you can't change things you don't like about yourself. Change is the next step we shall discuss. But even if you hope to change something, you can be loving toward yourself in the meantime.

Self-love is not easy to come by. For many people, it is a lifelong struggle. But achieving it is possible, and striving for it is the only sensible choice.

You are who you are. You have done what you have done. Nothing can change that, so why fight it? Generally, it makes better sense to ride the horse in the direction it is going.

I took a friend of mine out to lunch for her fortieth birthday. "So how does it feel to turn forty?" I asked her.

"I really like it," she told me. "I finally feel that I'll take what I've got and be happy with it. If I haven't accomplished all my self-improvement goals by now, I figure I probably never will, and that's just fine. I'm going to quit pestering myself to get better organized and write more letters, and bake for the kids more, and all that stuff. I'm not perfect. I'm not even where I thought I'd be at forty. But I'm very content. Somehow turning forty seems to give me permission to let go of the struggles and enjoy myself."

That's self-love.

At one of my workshops, I invited participants to choose an issue or problem in their lives and spend a few minutes meditating on it. One woman asked herself, "How can I

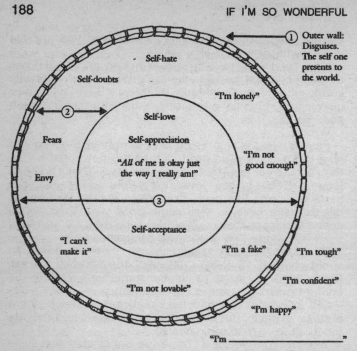

① Outer wall:
Disguises.
The self one
presents to
the world.

Self-hate

Self-doubts

"I'm lonely"

②

Self-love

Fears

Self-appreciation

"I'm not
good enough"

"All of me is okay just
the way I really am!"

Envy

③

Self-acceptance

"I can't
make it"

"I'm a fake"

"I'm tough"

"I'm confident"

"I'm not lovable"

"I'm happy"

"I'm _____"

stop being so hard on myself and finding so much fault with myself?" She told us that during her meditation, the image of an ornately carved and beautifully painted totem pole emerged in her mind, and she had no idea what it meant. To me it was a perfect answer to her question, and I told her what the symbol meant to me.

"The totem pole is all the different parts of you. You have many 'faces.' Sometimes you are kind, sometimes impatient, sometimes energetic, sometimes lazy, sometimes proud of yourself, sometimes ashamed. The totem pole is reminding you that all of you is lovable, not just the 'good' faces, but all of the faces. The entire totem pole is beautiful —just as it is. Your subconscious self is just patiently waiting for you to realize this."

Genuine unequivocal self-love is harder for some to achieve than for others, because the parenting we received as young children makes such a major, lasting impact on our propensity for self-love. Children who are abused or neglected may carry a belief into adult life that they are "bad," unworthy of love. Children who were affirmed and loved have an easier time experiencing themselves as lovable. Nevertheless, no matter what your background is, you can experience self-love. You can be patient with yourself as you struggle to change things you don't like. Tell yourself that you are doing the best you can, and that is all you can ask of yourself.

Let me describe the journey to self-love using this picture as a map of the self.

1. The outer layer is your public self, the self you present to the world. For people who have never gone on a journey of inner discovery, it is the only self they know. The outer circle is the regular, everyday "you" including all your "defensive" or "mask" behaviors that we discussed in the last chapter. It is the professional "you," the competent "you," the adult "you."

When you begin to expand your self-awareness, it is the outer circle that you become more aware of first. What are your "stories" about yourself, your beliefs about yourself?

You can identify your own outer circle by writing a short paragraph saying how you would introduce yourself to, for example, a prospective roommate whom you had not yet met. For example, "I'm five foot three, attractive but not gorgeous. I'm a pretty happy person most of the time. I'm very energetic. I like to make others laugh. I love children. I hate numbers and anything to do with business and finance. I love one-to-one conversations and am a good friend—generous, attentive, thoughtful. But I dislike crowds; I'm lousy at small talk," and so on. What is your personality, what are your skills, likes, dislikes? How do you believe others view you? How do you view yourself?

Sometimes your outer circle is completely true. You really are happy. You really are a good friend.

Most often, the outer circle is *partially* true. That was the case with my excessive smiling. My deeper, truer nature is enthusiastic and happy. But in my frenzy to cover up my insecurities, I *overdid* the "nice" me and felt I had to do it all the time.

Occasionally, the outer circle has very little truth in it. The person who acts like the life of the party all the time may really be a terrified child under all the studied glitz and urgent entertaining. People who have a lot to cover up often have a kind of compelling quality to their behavior. They seem to operate automatically, unconscious of their impact on others.

2. Just under the outer "layer" of you are the fears and insecurities that the outer layer is designed to hide.

When I became aware of my inappropriate smiling, I had to ask myself *why* I did that. I found out by experimenting with not smiling. When I didn't smile, I discovered I was terrified that people would not like me, would not even notice me. I realized I was compulsively manipulating everyone I met to pay attention to me.

So I had to *experience* that fear of being ignored (Circle 2). It was extremely unpleasant. And seeing how obnoxious my behavior had been made me hate myself (more of Circle 2).

All of that "stuff" is in the second circle. It can seem like a bottomless pit of self-hate. It is *all* the faces on the totem pole. It's all your regrets and unfilled dreams and unachieved goals. It's the truth about the parts of your past you have glossed over because they were miserable.

For some, all this reality is so painful, there is a reason they never choose to look at it. But these people will never be able to relax fully, for they will have to be constantly vigilant to keep all the pain covered up. They won't ever become deeply and fully satisfied with life.

Unfortunately, it is probably true that, in order to become genuinely self-loving, you have to go through some painful times. No pain, no gain. The reason is that the *only route* to the inner circle of self-love is through circle number 2.

Psychologist Carl Jung said that neurosis is a substitute for legitimate suffering. In other words, the outer circle—neurotic workaholism or criticalness or guilt or gushiness or whatever your neurotic tendencies are—is what you would rather experience than the "real" pain that lies underneath.

3. The inner circle on the map is self-love.

Self-love happens when you realize that all those awful parts of yourself in the second circle are part of you, and they are okay. Some of them you may want to change; and that's good. But some of them are unchangeable. To continue to fight them and hate them will only keep you miserable. Your only real choice is to accept your whole, entire self, with all your regrets and imperfections. Make peace with yourself. Let go of the struggle. You are fine, just as you are. You'll do.

The two outer circles are *still there*. But now you are familiar with them. You don't have to fear them or hide from them—or hate them.

For example, I still catch myself smiling inappropriately. But now when I do my reaction is *not* "Oh, rats! There's that ugly part of me again. I hate myself. I'll never learn." Instead, my reaction is, "Oh! There's my old friend, Smily Me. I better pay attention. What little ugly thing am I trying to cover up now? Ah ha! I see I just told a little lie to keep them from seeing how lazy I really am. Shall I tell them?" (Note that I have a choice. I don't have to tell.) "This time I will tell the truth." (When I do, I feel rewarded because two others admit how lazy they feel underneath, too, and we all feel better.)

The reason that self-love provides such serenity is that there are no more unknowns to fear. You know your whole self and you love your whole self. It's simple.

There is an irony about self-love. You can't will it to happen. You have to work for it—or work against the obstacles to it. But in the end, it will just be there. You have to be willing to keep paying attention, to look at unpleasant parts of yourself, even to experience some painful feelings of self-hate. But self-love is not something you can earn like pay at the end of a job. You don't deserve self-love because you worked for it. You deserve it because you are human. Every human deserves it. All religions tell us this in one way or another.

Self-love is a gift that will one day be yours if you are open to receiving it.

Once you have experienced total self-love, even if you have just glimpsed it, your life will never again be the same. For even if you are depressed, or you've been rejected, or you've failed and you feel awful, you will know what self-love feels like, and that knowledge will give your life a different character. You will know you can experience it again.

At first, your self-love may be fragile, like a tender green shoot in early spring. People and experiences in the cruel world will come clomping along and crush it. But the shoot will appear again and in time will grow into a sturdy plant that is impervious to outside influences of any kind. Gradually, you will become secure in your self-love.

Maybe you can get a glimpse of self-love through this experiment.

EXPERIMENT #19

The best way to do this experiment is to ask a friend to read it to you, slowly, with pauses between sentences. You should lie on your back, get comfortable and warm, and do the experiment with your eyes closed.

Relax.
There is no place you need to be going right now.
There's nothing you need to be doing. There's nothing to worry about.

Take a deep breath. As you breathe out, let go of all your tension. With each exhale, relax a little more. Feel yourself let go. Imagine you are standing beneath a warm shower of relaxation.

Relax your feet. Relax your lower legs. Relax your knees. Relax your thighs. Let your hips drop all tension. Feel your back completely relaxing. Let go of all tension in your stomach. Relax your chest. Relax your shoulders. Let your arms become completely limp and very heavy. Let go of all the tension in your neck. Let your head become very heavy. Relax all the muscles in your face. Relax your eyes, your cheeks, your jaw, your lips. Let go. Your whole body is very heavy, very relaxed.

Let a picture come into your mind of a very pleasant scene, any place in the world that you might go. It could be a place from your childhood. It could be the beach. It could be a mountain. It could be a meadow or a woods. Picture it in your mind's eye. Pretend that you are there. Bring it in clearly and vividly with all the senses. Hear the sounds around you there. Feel the feelings. See the colors and the movements around you. And most of all, let yourself feel the really good feeling of being in this most comfortable, relaxed place.

If any unnecessary thoughts come into your head, just let them float out again like clouds floating by, barely noticed.

As you continue to relax, let yourself recall a very pleasant experience, some time when you were feeling very good about yourself. You might have been active or quiet. It was a time when you felt really good—all over. There was a deep feeling that all's well. Perhaps you were with someone you really cared about. Maybe it was just a few days ago, maybe a month ago, or a year ago. Or maybe it was a time in your childhood. A time when you felt completely happy to be you. Let yourself go back there now. Maybe it was right after you accomplished something or when you got a pleasant surprise or your graduation day or wedding day. Whatever this time was, go back there now. Bring it in as clearly as you can. (Later, you might come up with an even better memory. But take the one you have now.)

Breathe easily, deeply.

Tune into that part of you that feels really good; the living part of you; the self-accepting part of you; the part of you that feels whole and complete; the part of you that can say, "I love myself." "I love myself fully and completely. I really feel good about who I am." You may find that these words repeat themselves in your head. "I accept myself. I feel good inside, all over. The good feelings I have about myself are totally unaffected by anyone else's opinions, attitudes, or judgments. I like me. I'm glad I'm me." Let this feeling fill you completely. Let it fill every cell in your body.

(Pause)

Now, very slowly, begin to become aware of the room you are in. Keep this feeling of self-love with you as you—very slowly—begin to move, first one foot, just a little bit, then one hand. As you move, keep your feeling. Slowly bring yourself back into the room, and after a while, open your eyes. Keep being aware of how you feel.

This feeling—this experience of self-love—is always within you. You may lose track of it sometimes. But you can always find it again—whenever you wish. And the more you go to this place within yourself, the more a part of your everyday life it will become.

You may lie here as long as you wish. There's no hurry to move.

Step Three: Change

Suppose you decide you want to change some of the things you become aware of as you begin paying attention to yourself.

It is critical to understand *how change occurs.*

When I first heard that people were uncomfortable with my smiliness, my initial reaction was to stop smiling. I would go into a meeting deliberately somber-faced. I felt unnatural and began to resent the people who didn't like my smile. I went back to smiling and decided they were wrong. I would be me and smiling felt better.

Then, a Gestalt therapist pointed out that, rather than try to change my behavior, I should simply *start paying attention to it.* As I did that over a period of time, I realized that smiling inappropriately felt uncomfortable to me. Then the behavior changed all by itself. What was more comfortable emerged, and that turned out to be not smiling so much.

Behavior changes only as belief changes. Remember the man who sprinkled gold dust on his lawn to keep the tigers away? As long as he believes he is in danger unless he performs his daily ritual, he'll keep doing it. He is trapped in his own belief system, which perpetuates itself by its own internal logic. Only when this man is able to change his belief about the tigers will his behavior change.

Whatever behavior you would like to change is tied to some internal belief system. For example, I believed that people would ignore me unless I smiled at them all the time. Only after I learned from experience that I could survive without perpetual forced smiling was I able to give it up.

Suppose you are a workaholic or a conversation hog or a shy person or a BTN junkie or you have identified any other behavior you would like to change. The steps to changing self-defeating habits are these:

1. Without changing your behavior, begin paying close attention to it. How do you feel when you do it?

2. Experiment gently with altering your behavior and see how that feels to you. It will probably be extremely uncomfortable. It may make you feel insecure, possibly even afraid. Pay attention to those feelings. What are you afraid of? Try to find out what underlying fear compels you to behave as you do.

3. Be patient with yourself. Don't force change. Rather, keep paying attention to how you feel when you do and do not engage in the behavior. Gradually, as you see the assaults that you fear are imagined or exaggerated, and as you experience yourself surviving and even feeling more

secure and more alive without your old habits, your behavior will change all by itself.

Programming yourself—or ordering yourself—to make a change is almost always doomed to failure. If you order yourself to change, you will not be able to find out why you were using the self-defeating behavior in the first place. What is it that you fear? This is critical information for you.

If you simply order yourself to change, you will be working against yourself rather than with yourself. Your Self has been surviving against big odds for many years, and you are not likely to defeat it with one simple New Year's resolution.

If you *really* want to change something about yourself, you will also need *support*. The best support is a partner who wants to make the same change you do. But anyone who understands what you are trying to do and is willing to offer you non-judgmental support will be an enormous help to you. More about the value of support and how to enlist it is in Chapter 12.

Expect backsliding. When you are changing a lifelong habit, it won't happen overnight. You will take two steps forward and one back, over and over. It is painful to discover that you are regressing after you feel you have made good progress. But it is inevitable. Don't be hard on yourself.

There are many things about yourself that you won't be able to change completely, for they are an integral part of your makeup. But awareness about an issue in your life can transform it.

I have a counseling client, Amanda, whose life seems to be run by guilt. If she doesn't have something to feel guilty about, she finds something. She has been paying attention to her guilt for some time now, and she has it in perspective. She told me, "I haven't completely eliminated these guilt messages that run through my brain all the time. But I've succeeded in turning the volume way down. I don't get so caught up in the guilt anymore. I don't choose to focus on it. But I think it will always be there. I accept it now. I just don't let it rule me."

Amanda hates her ongoing, ever-present guilt. But she has learned to love *herself*. She has changed her guilt messages as much as she can, given who she is. Sometimes her guilt is still painful to her, but just as often now she can

194

make jokes about it. She has accepted her guilt, and by accepting it, has been able to reduce its impact on her life.

Step Four: Self-Esteem

Self-esteem fluctuates. Some days it's up, some days, down.

Self-love, once you have achieved it, remains constant. You may be having a week in which your self-esteem is low, but your underlying self-love enables you to cope with the low self-esteem. You can know that you are a good, lovable person in spite of it all. You can hold onto a vision of what self-love feels like and know that you can and will return to that place. Self-love is the bedrock, the foundation. Low self-esteem is not nearly so painful or difficult if a solid base of self-love is there to start with. You simply accept that you are having a period of low self-esteem. It's not pleasant, but it's not a disaster. Periods of low self-esteem are part of the whole, lovable, acceptable package of you.

Self-esteem is how you feel about yourself. Generally speaking, when your life is going well, you feel good. When things are tough, you feel bad. Self-esteem is affected by life events, by how things are going with your job, your love life, your friends, by mistakes you've made and successes you've had. It has nothing to do with I.Q., achievements, status, or fame. Many famous, accomplished people feel terrible about themselves; many ordinary folks feel just great about themselves.

Self-esteem is not about who you are or what you have; it's about *how you feel about* who you are and what you have.

I want to make several points about self-esteem:

Some things that affect how you feel about yourself, you can't help. For example, if your lover breaks up with you, if you fail to get a promotion you wanted, if you lose a competition, if you inadvertently hurt someone or make a mistake you regret, you may feel bad for a while. You just have to get through it by loving yourself and letting time pass.

However, many things that affect your self-esteem, you *do* have control over. For example, if you spend much of your time in a job that gives you little or no satisfaction, or a career that does not let you use your best skills, you may have difficulty sustaining feelings of high self-esteem. *Feeling low is a normal, healthy response to any circumstance that steadily belittles you.* Many BTN relationships, in which one or both partners feel they are not getting all they want or all they deserve, contribute to feelings of low self-esteem.

You may not realize how much impact your day-to-day experiences are having on your self-esteem. You may think, "Work is really giving me problems. I can't stand my boss. *And* I feel awful about myself. If I could just feel better about myself, I could handle work better."

But if you are getting put down at work and you get little or no credit for the good you do there, or if you feel you aren't able to use your best skills, or if you can't get along with the people there, that will make a major impact on your self-esteem—little by little, day by day.

If your own self-esteem is being eroded by something you could change, *it is almost certainly worth any difficulty you have to endure to make the change.*

EXPERIMENT #20

1. Think about the past week of your life. Take a look at your appointment book to help refresh your memory.

   Now, for each day on this chart, put a dot opposite a number that characterizes your overall self-esteem for that day. Of course, your self-esteem may fluctuate during each day, but in general, was this a good day for you or a bad day? Think not in terms of the events of the day, but in terms of how you handled the events, how you felt about yourself.

   Connect all the dots with a line.

Self-esteem	S	M	T	W	Th	F	S
High 10							
9							
8							
7							
6							
5							
4							
3							
2							
1							
Low 0							

2. Now look back over the last year of your life—or perhaps
   the last five years if that seems more appropriate to you. You
   may fill in the horizontal headings for the graph. In addition
   to identifying years or months, indicate *specific events* that
   had an impact on your self-esteem. I have put examples on
   the chart.

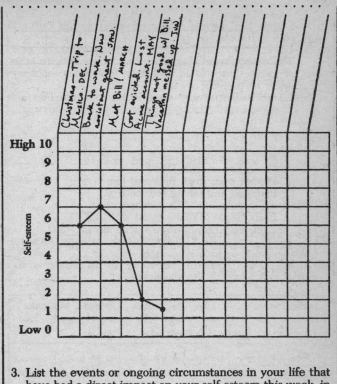

Handwritten column labels (top to bottom, left to right):
Christmas — Trip to Mexico. DEC.
Back to work. New assistant great. JAN.
Meet Bill! MARCH
Got switched. Lost Acme account. MAY
Things not good w/ Bill. Vacation messed up. Jun.

Vertical axis: Self-esteem — High 10, 9, 8, 7, 6, 5, 4, 3, 2, 1, Low 0

3. List the events or ongoing circumstances in your life that have had a direct impact on your self-esteem this week, in the past year, in the past five years. Again, refer to your calendar or journal if it will jog your memory.

For example,

Writing employee handbook at work.
Conversation with Dick.
Dinner party with Rick and Jan.
Planning and taking Mexico trip.
All interactions with my supervisor.
Early stages of relationship with Bill.
Events leading up to loss of Acme account.
Other.

4. Now go back over the list and place a code next to each item as follows:

. . . .

1—I have (had) a great deal of control over this item and could (did) change it.

2—I have (had) control over this item and could change it. The change would be difficult and would create other problems, but I would very likely feel better about myself if I made the change.

3—I have (had) little or no control over this item. I do (did) the best I could and it happens (happened) anyway.

For example,
Code
    1 Writing employee handbook at work.
    3 Conversation with Dick.
    1 Dinner party with Rick and Jan.
    1 Planning and taking Mexico trip.
    2 All interactions with my supervisor.
    1 Early stages of relationship with Bill.
    3 Events leading up to loss of Acme account.

5. Go back over the list a third time and circle the items you would like to or plan to change.

6. Finally, write the items you would like to change on this chart and fill in the other colums.

Items I want to change.	How I will make the change. First step I will take.	When I will make the change (or begin it).
1. Get out of my relationship with my supervisor.	1. Apply for transfer.	1. At end of current project — no longer than one month from now.

Remember, if you don't take action on the issues that affect your self-esteem, no one is going to do it for you.

Everyone needs continuing sources of affirmation. The most common sources are friends, lovers, clients/students/customers, bosses, employees/supervisers, relatives, and oneself. Most people cannot rely on *all* these sources, but you have a better chance of feeling good about yourself if you hear frequently from more than one source that you did well, that your thoughtfulness is appreciated, that you are attractive, that you are a great cook or a special friend. You need *some* positive interactions with the people and activities in your daily life.

EXPERIMENT #21

1. List all the sources of affirmation you have in your life now. It could be people who acknowledge, appreciate, like, love, or respect you and who let you know this in *any* way. It could be an activity in which you demonstrate competence and know you do well. It could be some way in which you take care of yourself. It could be some kind of recognition you have received. What helps you to feel good about yourself? Draw two columns out to the right of your list.

2. In column 1, indicate how frequently you receive this affirmation: D for daily, W for weekly, M for monthly, I for infrequently (less often than once a month).

3. In column 2, put an O if this source of affirmation is outside yourself and an I if it is something you do for yourself.

Ideally, you should see a balance of O's and I's in the second column and at least several D's and W's in the first column. If you don't, you may have a clue to what some of your self-esteem problems are. If you see only O's in column 2, do you rely too much on other people to make you feel good about yourself? Sample chart:

	How frequently I receive	O = Outside myself I = I do for myself
1. Tennis	W	I&O
2. Board committee I chair	W	I&O
3. Ted	D-W	O
4. My clients, esp. BC, TM	M	O
5. My daughter	W	I&O
6. Kiwanis award	I	O
7. Jogging	D-W	I

Even though your self-esteem is affected by external circumstances and affirmations (or lack thereof), the ultimate source of self-esteem is from within. If your bedrock of self-love is firm enough, if you believe in yourself, then you can withstand criticism, failure, and periods when your sources of affirmation have all but dried up.

A mistake many people make is to *rely exclusively* on external sources to make them feel good about themselves. They are "outer-directed." Their core of self-love is weak, and they can't rely on it. So they look to others for approval. They sometimes work very hard to manipulate their environment so that it props them up.

Some "outer-directed" people are ostentatious consumers; they surround themselves with material evidence of their success, sometimes in the hope that others will envy them. The feeling of being envied is the best feeling they can come up with.

Or they may be people who "fish for compliments," usually indirectly. "Oh, I didn't do a very good job." (Expected reply: "Oh but you did! It's marvelous!")

When an outer-directed person gets into an intimate partnership, problems can result. I interviewed a very troubled man, an attorney, age twenty-seven, who had just broken up with a woman who sounded to me to be quite outer-directed.

> "She was constantly asking me, 'How do I look? How did you like the vegetables? How did you like the meat? Do you still love me? Do you like my hair? Do you think I talked too much at dinner? Wasn't my comment funny?' It was sad. I didn't see this side of her at first. But it got to be too much for me. I told her, 'I can't make you feel good about yourself.'"

Comparison is the basis of all misery. You can *make* yourself feel bad if you dwell on people you see as more successful, more accomplished, more beautiful than you—or just people who seem to have a nicer life. Comparison, or playing "one-up/one-down," is toxic *whether you judge yourself to come out on top or bottom!* If you have to put someone else down in order to feel good about yourself, it is simply a sign that you are feeling insecure. And of course if you feel yourself to be worse off than someone else, you can really feel miserable.

EXPERIMENT #22

If you feel that you rely a great deal on other people's opinions of you in order to feel good about yourself, try this: Whenever you catch yourself asking someone's opinion of how you did or how you look, stop and ask *yourself* first. Pretend you are that other person, and give yourself an honest evaluation. Experiment with relying on yourself for opinions about yourself. See if you can begin to trust your own evaluation. Tell yourself what you would like to hear from others.

Also, practice complimenting others. Notice when they do well or look nice, and tell them the kind of thing you would like to hear. You may find that giving compliments to others will make you feel good, make others feel warm toward you, and contribute to a positive outlook on life.

Self-esteem is as important to life as food, water, and oxygen. Without it, you may exist, but you can't *be fully alive.* Yet many people go on for years, knowing their self-esteem is low and doing nothing to raise it. Low self-esteem makes finding a love relationship difficult, too. So if one of the "dybbuks" you carry around is low self-esteem, let me encourage you to take some steps to change this. Low self-esteem is one of the problems that responds well to therapy, so you might want to consider some kind of counseling. Or start with the suggestions in this chapter. Don't wait. Life is going on right now!

We have looked at the importance of expanding our self-awareness, of cultivating a foundation of self-compassion and self-love, and of working *with* ourselves to make changes we want to make. We have seen that the nature of self-esteem is that it fluctuates, and that there are things we can do to strengthen it.

But beyond all this lies yet another level, that of self-acceptance.

Step Five: Self-Acceptance

Imagine that each of us has two selves, the active self and the observing self. The active self is the one that eats breakfast, takes the kids to school, goes to work, makes decisions, has dinner with a friend, calls Mom, runs out of money, loses weight, gains it back, cares about the arms race, gets anxious, argues, makes love, has health problems, reacts to things.

While the active self is busy doing all these things, the observing self is standing some distance away watching, much as an audience watches a play. The active self is quite involved with whatever is occurring at the moment. The observing self sees the present activity as one scene in a much larger drama.

For example, take Jane. Let's suppose she's had a couple of dates with a man she likes very much. She's expecting to hear from him this evening. When he calls, he tells her that he feels he must come clean with her; he is in a relationship with another woman. He likes Jane a great deal, but he doesn't want to see two people at once, and he is already involved.

Jane is crushed. When she hangs up, she cries for a while. Then she calls her best friend but gets the answering machine. She tries to convince herself that he's not the only man left, that she'll get over it. She starts telling herself that she has terrible luck. She feels so unlucky that she can't believe it. She orders herself to *do something,* to turn on the TV or start a novel, or call someone else, or go out for a walk. But she can't make herself do any of these things. She just plain feels miserable. Her self-esteem is low. She doesn't really feel that this episode is her fault, or that he ditched her because he didn't like her. But she feels victimized, cheated. She feels she has the rottenest luck of anyone on earth, and that, try as she may, she can't make her luck change. She feels doomed; she is in despair. It's worse to know that she *is* a good person with a *lot* to offer a man, but that who she is doesn't seem to make any difference!

While all this is going on, Jane is also judging herself. She's thinking, "It's *good* that I'm sobbing like this. I'm sure it's *good* for me to let out feelings. It took *courage* to call my friend when I'm feeling so low. That's *good* that I did that. Hmm. I seem to be taking it amazingly well that she wasn't home. *Good.* Another pat on the back. But get off this now. Go out and do something. You're *stupid* to just sit here and feel rotten. You're *immature* to let this get to you. You're slipping into a pool of despair. Stop yourself, *dummy.*" (Now Jane feels despair *and* she feels stupid for feeling despair—two separate bad feelings.)

All of this is Jane's *active* self. She is very involved with herself, very intense. She is completely attached to all her thoughts and feelings. As far as she knows, she *is* her thoughts and feelings. She is all caught up in her little drama; it might be called "Jane and Her Pain."

Jane has no awareness of her observing self at this time. But her observing self is there, standing perhaps twenty feet outside her apartment, observing the scene as if she were a neutral outsider, not at all attached to Jane's feelings or thoughts, but simply *aware* of them.

The observing self might be saying, "Jane just got an awful blow. She's feeling terrible pain. Now she's sobbing, really letting herself get into it. On a pain scale of 1 to 10, this feels to her like a 10. It's *very* painful. Now she's telling herself she's a good girl for crying so thoroughly. Now she's feeling dreadful and telling herself she's *bad* for feeling despairing."

The observing self is not just more thoughts going on in Jane's head but a different "system" altogether. All Jane's thoughts and feelings are part of her active self. Her self-esteem, her ability to like herself, to have good judgments about herself—indeed, to love herself—are all part of her active self.

Jane's observing self doesn't judge. It *notices* her self-judgments and her level of self-esteem. It *notices* how intensely involved Jane is with herself. The observing self might say, "Jane is very involved with herself right now. Right now Jane believes that she has always been unlucky and she will always be unlucky. That is the *nature* of the feelings she is caught up with right now. And that's fine. That's what is. Of course *I* know this is not the case. Because I stand back at a distance, I am aware of more than just this intense drama going on right now. I know there are times when Jane has felt *very* lucky, and I know she'll feel lucky again. I know that one of her best assets—which she has totally forgotten about right now—is perseverance. I know Jane won't give up."

The observing self is a separate *system* from the active self, a separate level of awareness.

Awareness of the observing self is actually an extension of the "self-awareness" we spoke about in Step One. The more you pay attention to yourself, the more you will gradually become aware of your observing self. Your observing self is simply a part of you that you may or may not pay attention to, as you choose.

Why is awareness of the observing self beneficial?

Because the observing self is completely self-accepting. Everything the observing self sees *just is*. It's not good or bad, it just is. So the more you can identify with your observing self, the more self-accepting you can be.

Jane's active self was busy judging herself. "It's *good* that I'm crying. It's *bad* that I feel such despair." But her observing self simply observed. "Jane cries. Jane berates herself. Jane has a piece of bad luck." The event exists. The fact that it is bad or good does not exist. The judgment "good" or "bad" is something *Jane adds* to the event. It is how she experiences it. Since the observing self is always aware of a bigger context, it knows that in a few months, when Jane falls in love with someone else for example, Jane may view her "tragic" phone call as "good."

Jane's observing self accepts *all* of Jane. It accepts her judgments, her self-love, her self-hate, her triumphs, her mistakes—the entirety that is Jane.

Awareness of the observing self is beneficial for another reason: expanded self-awareness is an integral part of maturity.

Children are completely self-absorbed. Teenagers often exhibit little ability to see beyond themselves; they "know it all." They are so caught up in their own earthshaking dramas that they can't even broaden their perspective enough to see the needs of members of their own families.

Some people never mature very much. In fact, plain old immaturity is the basis of many of the marital and relationship conflicts I see. People just don't have a very broad perspective of things. They can't develop enough of an observing self to become aware of their own self-defeating processes.

For example, John often belittles his wife. It is pointed out to him over and over. But he can develop no awareness that he does this. He feels he is simply commenting on situations that need to be commented on. He defends his behavior. He can't stand back from himself enough to see how his "comments" affect his wife. His world is only as big as he is, and he is completely absorbed in it. If there were a

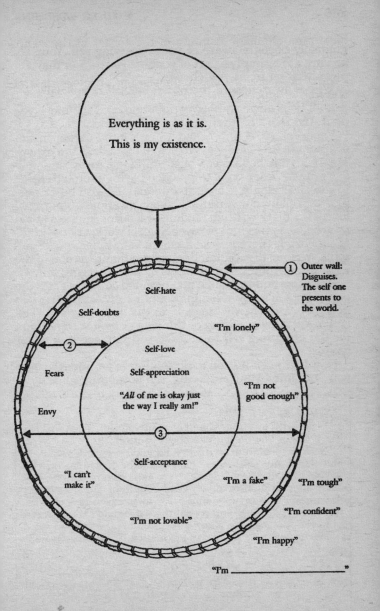

huge pink elephant standing in the corner of the room, John would not be able to see it. He would just go on defending his behavior.

How does one go about developing an awareness of one's observing self?

It all boils down to *paying attention,* and the more you do it, the more natural and easy it becomes.

Experiments #16, 17, and 18 presented earlier in this chapter are excellent ways to begin. Indeed, all the experiments in this book have been designed to expand self-awareness. Other ways to practice paying more attention to the observing self include interactions with other people (especially conversations about awareness), personal journal or diary writing, reading or hearing lectures about awareness, some kinds of psychological work, various kinds of support or therapy or consciousness-raising groups, and some spiritual disciplines. Regular meditation is one of the most direct routes to awareness of the observing self.

It is important to realize that both the active self and the observing self are functioning continuously. The active self does not *stop* when it tunes in to the observing self. The active self is always doing or thinking or feeling something for the observing self to observe and to place in a wider context.

Now let me invite you to do another experiment to help you "tap into" your observing, self-accepting self.

EXPERIMENT #23

1. Make a list of things you like about yourself. Then make a list of things you do not like about yourself.
2. Read the first item on the first list and afterwards say, ". . . and this is my existence." Now read the first item on the second list and afterwards say, ". . . and this is my existence." Keep alternating lists. Slowly read each item and after it say, ". . . and this is my existence." You may decide to stick with just one or two items and repeat them over and over with the phrase, ". . . and this is my existence."

This experiment is a kind of meditation. Try it—maybe with just one item that really bugs you about yourself—over and over for a long time, ten or even twenty minutes. Even if you do it only five minutes, do it every day for seven days.

You may find as you do this little meditation that you will

soften toward yourself. Your feeling about a quality you regarded as a major flaw may be transformed within you. You
may be able to experience the meaning of the term "self-
acceptance" in a whole new way. However, it is critical to
involve yourself totally in the experience itself and to free
yourself from specific expectations about the result. Just *do it*,
and see what happens.

Getting in touch with your observing self, experiencing
yourself as totally acceptable just as you are, is actually a
spiritual discipline in the sense that it involves more than
mind and body. It goes beyond rational, cognitive, and
even emotional experiences.

Many people *never* have any knowledge whatsoever of
their observing selves. They are completely attached to
the importance of what is going on in their own lives—
they are "self-centered." When these people get into arguments, they become consumed with their point of view.
They have no ability to stand back and smile at themselves
and say, "My, you surely are caught up in this thing. It
certainly does matter to you!"

Other people are vaguely aware of an observing self—
because they occasionally experience it. For example, suppose you see yourself getting really mad at your lover.
Suddenly, you realize you are about to have the same fight
you've had fifty times before, and you make a joke about it.
You label the disagreement and choose not to trot it out at
this time: "Let's not have our money argument now,
okay?" Your observing self has "caught you." A certain
pattern has become so familiar that you have become
aware of the habitual nature of it.

Still other people, a small group, become extremely familiar and friendly with their observing selves. They have
made an active decision to do so, and they devote time and
energy to it. Some of these people become spiritual teachers; they are simply farther along the path of awareness
than the rest of us.

Now let us look more closely at how all this relates to
relationships.

As we said at the beginning of the chapter, in assessing
why you are still single, you have to look not only at the
strategies you use—or fail to use—in running your love life,

you have to look at *yourself*. What do you have to offer another person in an intimate relationship? What qualities in you might a potential partner find undesirable? What belief or behavior of yours keeps defeating you in your quest for love?

If the reason you are single has to do not with your strategies but with yourself, then in order to find love, you must make some changes in yourself.

If you are a person who likes yourself, you will be more appealing to a partner. This is not to say you can't work on your self-esteem while you are in a relationship. But my point here is that if you are still single because of a lack of self-awareness and self-acceptance, then all the strategies and techniques in the world won't be very useful to you.

A good relationship with yourself is a prerequisite for a successful relationship with the person you love. If you don't love yourself, you will place an unfair and impossible burden on your partner: you will try to get him or her to make you feel good about yourself. No one else can do this for you.

Good self-esteem is the foundation of all the strategies we have discussed in preceding chapters. For example, it is difficult to look for high standards in others if you don't maintain high standards in yourself. Your ambivalence may be based on a fear that you aren't good enough to get what you want. Or you may be hanging around in a BTN relationship because you believe that's all you deserve.

If you are indifferent to yourself, or you don't know or like yourself, how can you expect someone else to get to know and like you?

Great relationships—with oneself and with others—begin with self-awareness, which itself is an ongoing, ever expanding process. So figure out what your dybbuks are, and make peace with them. You have nothing to lose but your own naïveté. And what you have to gain is love.

Chapter 11

Special Challenges of Involuntary Singlehood: Loneliness, Balance, and AIDS

Every lifestyle has its delights and its encumbrances, and involuntary singlehood is no exception. On the plus side, singles have freedom and independence. On the other hand, involuntary singles are always on the lookout for love, and, much of the time, looking for love is not especially pleasant. Even for the most social of singles, loneliness can set in, and discouragement can be a problem. Life sometimes seems unfair; a positive, optimistic attitude can be as elusive as love itself. And now singles must cope with the constraints that the fear of contracting AIDS has placed on their sex lives.

Involuntary singlehood has its own unique set of challenges. To keep life pleasant while you are looking for love, you have to know how to leap over certain inevitable hurdles that will arise. In this chapter, we will consider three of them: loneliness, lack of balance, and sexually transmitted diseases.

The "Why Me" Blues

Being alone when you wish you weren't can get you down, and being down leads to an inevitable vicious circle. When you're down, you don't feel like going out and you stay home and get lonelier. Or, if you do meet someone, you can't hide your desperate longing, and others find that unappealing and back off. And you tell yourself, "Of course they back off. Who would want to be with such a depressing person!"

So what's the way out?

Ironically, you have to begin by *accepting* your depression. It is a mistake to fight it, because the more you resist it, the longer it will persist. Let yourself feel depressed.

A common reaction to depression is self-loathing. "I hate feeling this way! Why don't I just snap out of it! Most people could handle this better. If I weren't such a worthless slob, I'd be able to pull myself out of this black hole."

Now, not only are you depressed, you are depressed *and* self-hating. You now have two problems where you might have had only one.

We may judge depression as "stupid, unhealthy." Depression is *unpleasant*, but it is not stupid. Indeed, it is a normal human experience and an appropriate response to certain situations—like being lonely. So instead of putting yourself down when you feel lonely or depressed, pamper yourself. See if you can feel kindly toward yourself for getting depressed occasionally. "It's okay if I feel depressed. I'm pleased to know I don't feel complacent about being lonely."

I don't mean to be glib about depression. It's painful; it's unpleasant. It can be dreadful. But when you feel depressed, you have two choices: You can hate yourself for it and fight it, or you can let it happen and reassure yourself that you are normal. The latter strategy is likely to move you through your depression sooner. (Obviously, I am not speaking about chronic, "clinical," or pathological depression, but about the blues that most of us feel from time to time, often related to a specific experience like feeling lonely or being rejected.)

Needy, depressive times are probably not a good time to put yourself out in the world (unless you know that this can help pull you out of your blues). It is better to stay home and pamper yourself. Or spend time with friends with whom you are completely comfortable and who won't mind listening to you complain for a while.

Depressive, needy, panicky feelings come with the territory of being involuntarily single. And when they come, they are painful. But they do usually run their course. The illusion that if you were "more together" you wouldn't have to feel this way is destructive. People who are so "together" that they never feel lonely or needy probably don't feel very much else, either.

In my workshops, I have encountered a great deal of confusion about the notion of taking responsibility for oneself. The basically sound principle that you can be an active agent in your own life rather than letting life happen to you is widely misunderstood; it does not mean that everything bad that happens to you is your fault! One woman told me, "I'm creating my own aloneness by staying depressed all the time. If I can take responsibility for my depression and end it, I'll probably meet someone. I know I have no reason to feel depressed, and I'm going to get out of it."

This woman had everything backward. It is not possible to end depression by making a New Year's resolution about it. You can't order your feelings around. While she felt that her depression was contributing to her aloneness, the reverse was probably more accurate: her aloneness was contributing to her depression.

You are not "responsible" for your single status. Many factors contribute to it, *one* of which is the amount of initiative you take to meet people and to overcome your relationship problems. I have seen people engage in vitriolic self-judgment because they think self-responsibility means self-blame. They turn a valid insight, "I have choices in my life," into a rod with which they repeatedly beat themselves: "It's my fault that I'm alone. It's my fault that I'm depressed. What a child I am. I should just snap out of it. If I were a better person, I'd be in love now."

Self-responsibility can be taken to a ridiculous extreme. Don't use your depression to make yourself feel worse.

The Someday Syndrome

"I'm not ready for love. First I have to get my act together."

Probably the reason there are so many singles today is that we are all off in our private corners getting our acts together and getting ready for love later on!

It is dangerous to put your search for love on hold until you accomplish certain goals because that moment when you feel you have it all together may be very elusive. Life does not divide itself into neat compartments; it is going on all at once.

A woman who had not been in a significant relationship for four years explained to me why she was not dating and not planning to date. She told me, "I have some other issues I have to deal with first. I'm just not ready for a man in my life. I want to lose some weight, and the truth is, I'd like to quit my job. And I don't know what I want to do then."

There is a serious flaw in the idea that you first get a tidy little self all ready and then walk out onto the stage to audition for love. Getting your life together and finding a person to spend your life with are two separate issues; they may *or may not* be causally connected, and they can occur in any sequence. After all, what if the perfect mate for you happens to show up right now?

You assume that pulling your life together will help you to meet the right person. But it is just as logical to assume that meeting the right person will help you to pull your life together! And you'll be having more fun while you're at it. As long as you are not depending on your new partner to make you feel good about yourself, there is no law in the universe that says you have to have your job, your finances, your living situation, your weight, your physical fitness routines, and your friends all neatly in place before you can open yourself up to being loved.

In fact, having your life all together may make you less desirable as a mate. "Perfection" is intimidating. And you may become so set in your ways you'll have no room for love any more. Falling in love will probably upset all your carefully established routines anyway, so why bother to get yourself all set *first?* (When I fell in love, I stopped jogging, folk dancing, singing in a choral group, and playing the piano—for a while at least.)

Supporting each other in achieving personal goals is a wonderful way to build a relationship. You will be depriving yourself and your mate-to-be if you achieve all your goals ahead of time. Leave something for him/her to give you.

Here is one woman's revelation:

I have not been interested in men for a long time because I just don't feel very together. I've never settled on a career. I just don't feel anyone would be interested. But my friend Sally was worse off than I am. She had even started using drugs. Then she got sued for a car accident, and she fell in love with her lawyer! He's a wonderful man, and he gave her a lot of help. They have a fabulous relationship now. She's a great lady. She had just gotten real depressed. Well, I saw this happen and I just said, "If she can fall in love when she's so down—if someone can fall in love with her—what am I sitting around waiting for?"

The worst part of getting your life together first and then hoping love will find you is that after you finally pull it all together, you discover that all your new-found strengths and successes don't make any difference in the strange drama of love. After you make changes and feel more "ready," you are still the same person facing the same singles scene and the same challenges. If you want love in your life, no time will ever be better than right now.

There *is* such a thing as deciding to be alone for a time that is quite different from the scenario I have just described.

The experience of living alone and being entirely on one's own resources is undeniably enlightening. A person who has never had this experience as an adult may have a strong desire to discover the riches of living alone and to become acquainted with the self that emerges under these circumstances. It is quite common to desire a period of being alone following the end of a relationship.

But being alone because you prefer being alone—either for an interim period or forever—has a different quality to it from being alone as a way to get ready for a relationship. The latter is a kind of self-deception that contributes to your negative self-image and simply defers issues you will eventually have to face anyway about dealing with the opposite sex.

The whole notion of "getting your act together" is just postponing life. Getting your act together *is* life. It is the process that is important, not the end result. Feeling at loose ends is not especially pleasant, but it doesn't make you into an undesirable person. It makes you human. And your humanness is exactly what you want to share with a loving partner.

Should You Buy a Stereo?

The opposite of putting love on hold until you clean up your life is putting your life on hold until you fall in love; both are problematic. Listen to Rachel:

> I've been putting off buying myself a good stereo for five years now—because I always have the feeling I'm about to fall in love with someone who has one. I can see I'm depriving myself, but it's symbolic. Somehow, buying a stereo is a way of giving up—admitting defeat.

I have heard Rachel's dilemma expressed by many singles, and sometimes the stakes are higher. Some singles fear that they are giving up on love if they buy a house by themselves, or if they decide to enter into parenting without a mate.

For singles who clearly have their hearts set on a relationship at some time, these questions represent a genuine dilemma. *But the pivotal factor is not what you do but how you do it.* Some people give up on finding love without making any major life decisions. And others can remain open to love even with a stereo, a house, and a baby!

Winnie put the problem this way: "How can I *both* live my life fully as a single *and* keep actively looking for love? If I'm always looking, it's as though I'm saying I'm not happy being single. I want to get on with my life right now. But I don't want anyone—most of all me—to get the message that I've settled in. I'm having a good time being single—but I'm not content with it!"

There is a way out of the dilemma: think "both/and" rather than "either/or." Not "I can enjoy being single *or* I can be looking for a relationship," but "I enjoy being single *and* I want a relationship."

After I had been single for about three years, I found myself caught in the "either/or" mentality, anguishing over which path to take: settle in or keep looking? Quite suddenly, I had an insight that eliminated the dilemma for me. I decided to behave as if I had only a limited period of time to be single. I simply assumed that after some unknown period of time I would fall in love and marry. I realized I didn't want to look back on my years of being single and have the feeling that I had somehow missed out, that I had not taken full advantage of the freedom, the independence. That meant that I had to be single with a vengeance! Suddenly, my life acquired a kind of urgency. I fixed up my apartment exactly the way I wanted it. I entertained more, I traveled alone, I dated around, I expanded my household and business skills, and I spent my money and planned my time more consciously, making sure I was being true to what I wanted since I had only myself to consult. I consciously enjoyed the experience of making all my decisions myself, assuming that I would not always have that luxury.

But all the while, I was actively looking.

Of course, "being single with a vengeance" can lead to yet another danger: You can become so involved with being self-sufficient that you give up on love altogether. I call this "overadapting to singlehood."

Dolores, an executive secretary, age thirty-nine, was a case in point. While she *said*, "I want someone to love," she was obviously not giving herself fully to this desire. She told me that she felt a part of her needed to prepare for the possibility that she might *not* find a man for herself. But Dolores was contributing to the fulfillment of her own prophecy because, in most cases, an unequivocal desire for love is a prerequisite for finding it! She didn't have such a full, exciting life that she wouldn't have had room for a man; indeed, she spent a lot of time watching TV. She had simply overadapted to singlehood.

Dolores had been divorced for several years when I met her. She dated, but she kept meeting one baffling and discouraging obstacle after another. Then I noticed she began talking about whether or not she was "marriage material." She would emphasize the aspects of being alone that she enjoyed, although she also talked about feeling lonely and missing intimacy. She seemed to be very drawn to books and singles groups that assured her that it's okay to be single.

I only saw Dolores every few months, but I saw a subtle change take place in her. She began shifting her conversation from finding ways to overcome the problems she'd had in relationships to preparing herself for the possibility that she might never find her ideal mate. This task took a lot of her attention. She talked about the grief of letting go of her dream, and about having to change her identity to that of a "single." Since she chose to devote herself to these psychic tasks, she turned her attention away from working on her communication skills or her fear of intimacy—which in turn made the relationships she did have more discouraging. It seemed to me that, by trying to make a healthy adaptation to living alone—by trying to prepare herself that she might always be alone—Dolores was unwittingly defeating herself.

Singles groups sometimes inadvertently contribute to the "over-adapting syndrome." They work so hard to establish legitimacy for singlehood that they verge on giving coupling-up a bad name. This "single-ism" has given rise to a group of people who have adapted to being single—*but not as a genuine preference*. Rather than asking themselves, "How can I get around my obstacles and achieve my goal of a lasting relationship?" they begin convincing themselves that intimacy is neither possible nor desirable.

Most singles groups subtly reinforce singlehood. By providing singles with a "family" and with a whole range of social activities, singles groups fill short-term needs for companionship and a sense of belonging. They make life comfortable enough for many singles that, even though they may clearly want a relationship, they become less deliberate, less purposeful, about finding one. Singles groups hold out a positive and appealing model of what it is to be single. Though most of the people in the group may not feel that they fit that happy-go-lucky model, they all assume that everyone else in the group fits it. Whenever I ask a group of singles how many of them hold a committed intimate relationship as an ideal for their lives, the vast majority raise their hands. Yet the programs these groups offer are things like "Financial Planning for One" and "Human Sexuality and Singles Lifestyle," rather than "Looking at Our Fears About Intimacy" or "Communication Skills for Great Relationships."

Obviously, all of the features of singles groups I have mentioned have positive sides to them, too, and I would surely *never* suggest that singles avoid these groups. On the contrary, they are a fine way to meet people and they fill other needs as well. I would simply suggest that, if you are serious about finding love, you be cautious about getting lulled into complacency by these groups. They may be more likely to reinforce your hesitations about intimacy than they will be to confront them.

The challenge for involuntary singles, then, is to maintain a balance between both enjoying life as a single and keeping up an active search for an intimate partner. It is a mistake to put off your life until you meet someone. But it is also a mistake to get so involved with your singlehood that you get lazy about your search for love—or put it off until some magic day in the future when you "have it all together."

If I were going to do a bumper sticker for singles, it would say, "Keep the Balance." This balance: I'm enjoying my life 100 percent and I want intimacy in my life 100 percent.

The Sexual Revolution Was Great While It Lasted: Sexually Transmitted Diseases

Without doubt, the biggest challenge ever to face single men and women is the alarming rise of sexually transmitted diseases, especially AIDS.

Suddenly, the days of carefree, casual sex are over. And for a generation who came of age with the Pill and the sexual revolution it spawned, the change is a shock. We grew up feeling that the freedom to make choices about our sexual activities was a right as natural as choosing a restaurant or a movie for the evening. Now it seems that right has been taken away from us. Many singles feel resentful that a lifestyle to which they had become accustomed is no longer an option. The awkwardness that herpes victims have known for some time is nearly universal; fear and caution are now part of virtually every new amorous encounter.

Most of the AIDS news we get focuses on the public health aspects of the epidemic, leaving to us the problem of how to handle it in our personal lives. We hear about high-risk *groups* (gay and bisexual men, prostitutes and the men who see them, intravenous drug users, and people who have had many sexual partners). We are assured that AIDS can be transmitted *only* through exposure to the blood or bodily fluids of infected people. We hear of the need to reduce ignorance about the disease and prejudice against its victims. And inevitably, we are cautioned to have "safe sex"; that is, (a) to use condoms and contraceptive foams, jellies, or creams that contain the spermicide nonoxynol 9, or (b) to be certain that our partners have tested negative for the AIDS antibody.

But the most urgent question for most sexually active singles is this one: how am I *personally* supposed to handle these exasperating restrictions that have suddenly been placed on my sexual life? How am I to cope with them both emotionally and socially? Especially when I loathe condoms!

First, it is important to realize that for people who do *not* fall into high-risk groups, that is, for most heterosexuals, the risk of contracting AIDS is relatively low. This doesn't mean you don't have to be cautious, but it does mean you don't have to be paralyzed with fear. For heterosexuals, becoming celibate is an extreme measure, because straights account for just 2.3 percent of all AIDS cases in the nation. Also, even though the AIDS virus may remain asymptomatic for eight or more years after a person has been exposed to it, there is still one very firm piece of ground we can stand on: if you test negative for AIDS, go three to four months with absolutely no possible exposure to AIDS, and then test negative again, then you absolutely do not have AIDS. If you practice safe sex from then on and you never share an I.V. needle, you will not get AIDS.

But it is the whole idea of "safe sex" that gives singles their biggest headache. Sex with condoms, dental shields, and rubber gloves leaves a great deal to be desired!

One solution many singles seem to be choosing is to restrict themselves to what I call "social sex." "Social sex" includes all kinds of affectionate and erotic exchanges *except* oral and anal sex and intercourse. The hugging, snuggling, kissing, and petting of social sex is entirely safe. Orgasm is not necessarily excluded but has to be accomplished with hands. During "social" sexual exchanges, partners politely keep their bodily fluids to themselves. (Although many people fear that AIDS can be transmitted through saliva, at this writing, not a single case transmitted by contact with infected saliva has been reported.)

"Social sex" is different from "safe sex." The term "safe sex" implies intercourse with lots of precautions. But many singles I have spoken with prefer "social sex" to "safe sex." That is, they would rather stop short of any potentially unsafe activities; they specifically avoid the awkwardness and risk of intercourse-with-precautions. Intercourse—especially with a casual acquaintance—just isn't worth it, they feel.

"Social sex" is the same thing that, at the height of the sexual revolution, we called "technical virginity," but the connotation of the two terms is entirely different. The term "technical virginity" suggests, "why bother to stop short of intercourse? If you are doing everything else anyway, it's just a silly technicality."

The term "social sex" has a dramatically different feeling and philosophy behind it. It suggests something more like, "Not only might intercourse expose me to a fatal disease, but in addition, I prefer to differentiate *with my sexual behavior* between casual sex and sex with a person with whom I have become genuinely close. I *want* to save intercourse, both so that I can enjoy dating without a lot of sexual pressure, and because I do feel that intercourse is something special. I want to put the mystique back into intercourse."

Limiting yourself to "social sex" is one possible solution to the problem of dating in the post-AIDS era. About the only other possibilities are complete abstinence; "safe sex," that is, intercourse with heavy safeguards; or getting tested and insisting on a blood test from any potential sexual partner.

Getting tested works for some singles, but this route can also present problems. Some people are simply too afraid to get tested because a positive test result would ruin their lives. People surely have a right to decide whether or not they want such information about themselves.

The testing solution can raise other issues: Can you trust that a potential sexual partner who claims to have a negative test result is telling you the truth, or that that person has absolutely *not* taken a risk since the time of the test?

For a couple who have decided to make a lifetime commitment to each other, testing is an obvious answer. But for all the dating that goes on short of that, testing may or may not be a solution.

Clearly, the first step you need to take in the wake of the AIDS epidemic is to decide what course of action you want to take for yourself.

Will mutual testing work for you? Do you want to limit your casual sexual encounters to "social sex?" Do you feel comfortable having "safe" sex? Are you going to abstain from sexual activities altogether?

Setting your own parameters for your sexual activity is only half of the problem; the other half is communicating your limits to your partner.

AIDS is so much on everyone's mind these days that the subject is usually fairly easy to bring up. Often resolutions are relatively easy to come by—even if neither party is very happy about the options available—because your self-interest and your interest in the well-being of your partner are usually served by the same course of action.

It's best if you can have a conversation with a potential partner and agree on a course of action before the two of you become involved in sexual activity. For one thing, major disagreements about how to proceed sexually might signal other areas of incompatibility as well. And of course, you can be freer and easier sexually if you have agreed on what to expect from each other beforehand.

Nevertheless, it is definitely a good idea to *memorize* a few phrases so they are readily available in the event that an awkward moment does arise. For example, "I'm not comfortable taking this any further right now." Or "I need to tell you, I'm enjoying this very much, but I am firmly committed to safe sex." Or ". . . but I am very sure I don't want to go beyond this stage."

But suddenly, the scene is beginning to sound familiar. Even before the AIDS epidemic, women were often in the position of asking men to "slow down," to wait until the "friendship" part of the relationship had progressed a bit before making love. Since the beginning of the sexual revolution, many of us have been having sex on what's been considered "men's" time schedules (the first or second date). The AIDS epidemic may mean that we are simply going to shift to having sex on "women's" time schedules (get to know the person first and move more gradually into sex, savoring the pleasures of anticipation and heightened sexual desire along the way). For decades, women accommodated men in many different arenas. But since the women's movement, men have had to do a great deal of adapting themselves. Placing sex more in the context of giving and loving is one more change that men are being called upon to make, even more so now that we must contend with AIDS.

I submit that we were on the verge of a "second sexual revolution" anyway, and that AIDS has simply accelerated its onset.

The sexual revolution of the sixties brought sex out of the closet. We learned to talk openly about sex and to treat it as a positive, pleasurable aspect of life, not something to be ashamed of or embarrassed about. Many people broadened their range of acceptable, pleasurable activities. Women affirmed their own right to sexual pleasure. Premarital sex and sex among singles changed almost overnight from a taboo to a norm, and non-monogamy was widely tested by reasonable people with varying results. Parents were encouraged and coached to provide their children with a solid education in sexual facts and values.

But the excesses of the sexual revolution soon became apparent. Too often, sex was divorced from love, from intimacy, even from affection. At worst, it became a substitute for love and intimacy. One-night stands came to be about as significant as a handshake, and sex became frivolous. No longer an integral part of the package of love and commitment, sex was now a recreation to be enjoyed—like going out to eat, getting a massage, or smoking marijuana. It became a meeting of genitals that were only remotely connected to human beings with an emotional life, a past, and a future.

For some of us, sex didn't separate so neatly from the rest of our lives, and trying to make it separate was painful. The unfettering of our bodies to follow every sexual urge to completion led to a demystification of sex, and this felt like a big loss. When sex lost its sacredness, it was missing the very quality that made it so pleasurable; when sex became commonplace, it could no longer express specialness.

Ultimately, many people discovered that the trivialization of sex was too great a price to pay. The sexual revolution lost momentum.

The "second sexual revolution" of the eighties is another

leap forward. We have retained from the first sexual revolution open, unashamed attitudes about sex and the elimination of old-fashioned Victorian taboos. But now, at least in some segments of the population, we are again reserving sex for special relationships. Falling somewhere between the Victorian ideal of sex in marriage only and the sixties obsession with no limitations on sexual activities at all, we are re-evaluating both extramarital sex and entirely casual sex. We have rediscovered the pleasures of petting, teasing, and what some call "outercourse," and we can enjoy these activities with friends and casual acquaintances. But intercourse is something many singles now reserve for love relationships. Sex is becoming reunited with intimacy, of which it is seen as an expression and an extension.

AIDS is a hideous nightmare come true. Its effect on our social lives—and on our sociological evolution—seems hardly an issue at all compared with the tragedy it has wrought in so many families and among so many friends. Yet each of us must make a decision about how to conduct our social lives in the wake of this disaster.

Look realistically at your own alternatives. If you remain ambivalent or full of denial on this issue, you could pay dearly. Even if you have a strong conviction, acting on it may present you with a challenge every time you have to do it. Thinking clearly about this issue *before* you confront a difficult situation may be the best protection available to you.

EXPERIMENT #24

1. How do you feel about AIDS? List as many adjectives as you need to complete this sentence: "With regard to the affect of AIDS on my personal social life, I feel _____." (For example: frustrated, cautious, resentful; or supported in my desire to slow things down at first, etc.)
2. Rate the following courses of action:

	Very inclined to follow this course of action	Not sure	*Not* inclined to follow this course of action

a. Total abstinence			
b. Restricting my sexual activity with others to "social sex."			
c. Engaging in "safe sex" (intercourse with condoms and contraceptive jelly or cream).			
d. Getting tested and insisting on negative tests from anyone I relate to sexually.			
e. Other _____ _____ _____			

I strongly encourage you to invite a few friends to join you in doing this experiment and to discuss your responses together.

We have looked at quite a few attitudes, strategies, and ways you might consider changing the way you run your love life.

Now we shall review it all. You will have a chance to see what fits for you and exactly how you might proceed from here if you have decided you would like to make your search for love more active.

Part IV

Making It Happen: How to Put the Strategies to Work

Chapter 12

Summing Up:
Why Are You Still Single,
and What Do You Plan
to Do About It?

Let's consider these two questions separately. First, why are you still single?

You may recall that you were invited to answer that question for yourself at the very beginning of this book in Experiment #1. Find the list of reasons you made at that time, and let's look at it again.

EXPERIMENT #25

Look at every item on the list you made for Experiment #1, the list of reasons you are still single. Try regarding every reason you have listed as an "excuse." Now that you have read this book, see if you can answer every excuse. Write down a reason why your excuse won't work for you anymore.

Do this for yourself before you read further.

I have been asking involuntary singles why they are still single for years now at my workshops, and I think I've heard every reason in the world. But what I hope has become clear in the preceding chapters is that if you genuinely want a lasting intimate relationship in your life, none of these reasons is reason enough to stay single!

Let's look now at some of the most common "excuses" involuntary singles give for their continuing single status. Along with each excuse, we will draw upon material presented in the foregoing chapters to "zap" the excuse; that is, to demonstrate the fallacy in it.

I'm too busy; I have no time to meet new people.
ZAP: Using networking, the "time management" system of scheduling activities to meet new people, and the Two-Hour Date, even the busiest
person can find time to "screen" lots of new
people. The two *best* methods—work-related
activities and being introduced by friends—
don't require extra time so much as extra attention. Keep reminding your friends to think of
people, and mention your desire to everyone—
in a light but determined way.

I don't know of any ways or places to meet new people.
ZAP: Dating services give you a steady supply of pre-
screened, available members of the opposite
sex. Every week hundreds of personal ads appear in several local publications in virtually every city, and in many highly respected national
publications as well. If these methods do not
appeal to you, simply figure out a method that
does appeal to you—or at least that you are willing to try.

I'm not the kind of person who uses personal ads or
dating services.
ZAP: They have a name for your "kind of person":
single. Every imaginable category of single uses
personal ads and dating services these days.
Both are entirely respectable. (You might even
say in your ad, "I'm not the kind of person who
does this," or "I never thought I'd be doing
this," if you feel that would be more likely to
attract your type.)

I've had several bad experiences with blind dates and
personal ads. I've never met anyone the least bit inter-
esting.
ZAP: You may have to be willing to put up with a little
unpleasantness, just as you do when you are job
hunting. Don't give up because it didn't work
the first few times. If you figure there are nine
*un*interesting people for every one who turns
you on, then the more lousy dates you have, the

closer you are to a good one! Stick resolutely to two-hour dates (or shorter). Then, should a date turn out to be a drag, at least it won't last very long.

My standards are too high. I'm afraid what I really want is unrealistic, but I can't make myself compromise.

ZAP: Your high standards are a great asset. Clarify what your *essential* requirements are, and then stick to them. Trust your intuition. You may have to look *harder* and *longer* than others, but your search will be worth it. You are not so unusual a person that absolutely no one exists who would be a good match for you. If you hold out for the very best, you are likely to get it. Above all, don't settle for someone who isn't quite right for you. Keep looking!

(Women): All the men I meet are either married, gay, or confirmed bachelors.

ZAP: It is true we are in a period of history when men and women are at "different phases." It's a challenge to find "good men." That only means you need to look harder. Remember, there are always new men entering the scene: getting divorced, coming home from abroad, moving from a different city, getting out of a BTN. You have to be active and out there, so you'll be in the right place at the right time when a "good man" becomes newly available.

(Women): There aren't enough men to go around. There's a shortage of men and an even greater shortage of men who are truly available for a committed relationship.

ZAP: Statistics about a "population" are *entirely irrelevant* with regard to your personal odds of finding love. Even if some women *may* be left out in the vast game of musical chairs, there is absolutely no reason why you need to be one of them. You can affect your own odds of finding love *dramatically* by meeting the challenges discussed in this book: identifying your ambivalence and being willing to act in spite of it, keeping your standards high, devising a plan for "screening" lots of men, avoiding commitmentphobes and BTNs, learning to say no to the wrong men, working with your fears so you will be able to say "yes" at the right time, and getting to know yourself better.

I'm too intense. I intimidate all the potential partners I meet. I scare them away.

ZAP: What you are seeking is a man who loves you for *who you are.* So whatever people you intimidate, you aren't interested in anyway. This can get discouraging to be sure, but it's no reason to give up. Discouragement isn't pleasant, but it's virtually inevitable. It will pass.

Don't make the mistake of trying to attract dates by putting a damper on yourself. Be yourself with a vengeance so you'll attract a person who likes the real you. Just because there are lots of people who aren't "your equal" doesn't mean there aren't also some who *are.* They may be harder to find, but they are *there.* Pass up the ones you intimidate, and keep looking.

I don't feel great about myself right now. I need to work on myself before I start looking for love.

ZAP: Implementing the plans outlined in this book will almost certainly *help raise your self-esteem.* And finding a loving relationship will, too. Being alone *may* be a major contributing factor to your "blues," for it means that one source of continuing positive input that many people have is missing from your life. So both looking for and finding love can help you raise your self-esteem. For example: When you read "dreadful statistics" reports, tell yourself you will be one of the allegedly few people who *will* match up successfully. If you invest yourself in this belief, it will make you feel better.

Raise your standards about what you seek in love and, whether you truly believe it or not, act as if you will achieve what you want. This "pretend" can lift your spirits incredibly!

Go for volume. Meet lots of people—*briefly*. Know that there is an abundance of single people for you to meet, not a scarcity. Even if the people you meet are not quite right for you, know that with each one you are getting closer to your true love. You will *feel good* because you'll know you are doing all you possibly can for yourself. Doing the right thing—even if it is not "working" for you at the moment—feels much better than doing nothing. Also, you stand a good chance of meeting some people who will boost your self-esteem!

If you are in a BTN relationship, consider getting out of it. Freeing yourself from a mediocre or deadening situation can do wonders for your self-esteem.

Let yourself look at your fears, and try doing something you are afraid of anyway. Remember how Bruce felt when he tried calling the woman he was attracted to? He said he felt better than he had ever felt in his life!

I haven't gotten over the pain of my last relationship, and that's why I just can't connect with anyone.

ZAP: Only the passage of time—sometimes even three or four years—can heal some wounds. There's nothing "wrong" with you because you still grieve your loss or feel angry at the way you were treated. You may believe that you can't connect with anyone new because you haven't let go of your last relationship. But an equally reasonable theory is that you haven't let go of your last relationship because you haven't connected with anyone new yet! Try using the latter belief system. Be easy and loving with yourself and your pain, but keep looking!

I give up too easily and too soon on a person. Maybe if I were willing to go on a few more dates, something would happen.

ZAP: Don't let go of a new acquaintance until you are

sure the person isn't right for you. But *do* trust your own judgment. You can't be certain it's the *right* person in the first half hour, but often you can be certain it's the *wrong* person. Trust this.

If your goal is a long-term, committed intimate partnership, you should deliberately avoid relationships which are obviously terminal. Don't begin building a history and telling all your secrets to one more person who is clearly going to disappear after three months or six months or two years. When you first pick up clear signals that the relationship won't be forever—either from your point of view or the other person's, bow out. That could be after one two-hour date, or after one or two months.

One single woman, forty, told me in an interview, "I dated around for several years and had many brief relationships. Now I have become both more careful to avoid painful endings and less tolerant of low-quality intereactions. When I avoid short-term relationships now, I know what I'm missing, and I have no regrets."

I'm too needy. Whenever I date, I'm afraid my desperation shows through and people find it unappealing; it scares them off.

ZAP: If you find it painful that you are alone, you can't pretend that pain isn't there. You can hide it sometimes. You can even keep it below the level of your own awareness by staying busy and involved, but you can't make it go away. If you deeply desire intimacy and you are without it, it is *appropriate* for you to feel deep longing.

But the secret is to distinguish between *desire* and *anxiety,* and to keep the former and let go of the latter. This will be discussed in greater detail at the end of this chapter.

I'm too critical. After an hour with a person, I start finding fault.

ZAP: You must determine whether you are maintaining high standards, which is a productive approach, or whether your criticalness is a defensive habit that you use to cover up fear or ambivalence. If you think it may be the latter, then start paying very close attention whenever you begin to be critical. How does it make you feel inside? Try pretending that the quality of which you are critical does *not* bother you. How does that feel? If you discover fear or ambivalence, then you need to ask yourself whether you are willing to experiment by proceeding with the relationship anyway. You may decide you would rather give in to your fear or ambivalence—a *perfectly valid choice*. You'll still be way ahead because you'll be conscious of the choice you are making, not simply repeating old habits without examining them.

I'm always attracted to the wrong people—or to the right people but at the wrong time. (Variations: I love him, but he won't commit to me. She's a wonderful woman, but she puts me down sometimes.)

ZAP: The world is full of wonderful "wrong" people! There is nothing wrong with you because you fall in love with them. But if you know they are "wrong" for you for whatever reason, or if they are clearly unavailable, even though "no" may be extremely difficult and painful, *say no.* Keep yourself available for the *right person.* You deserve your perfect match. And if you are willing to keep looking—actively—you will find it!

Remember, finding the right person but at the wrong time is exactly the same as finding the wrong person. It's sad, but what you seek is the right person at the right time! Don't give up!

I fear a relationship. This excuse has many different variations. Some of them are:

- I fear rejection.
- I fear I'll lose myself.
- I fear I'll be too vulnerable.
- I fear I'll become too dependent.

- I fear my partner will become too dependent on me.
- I fear I'll lose my freedom.
- I'm afraid to commit myself because someone better might come along.

ZAP: One or more of these fears may be very real for you; I don't mean to make light of them by calling them excuses. But if your fears, however great, are keeping you from finding love, and if you would rather be in love than be afraid of love, then you have to find a way to overcome your fears. If you want to badly enough, you can.

Start by paying a lot of attention to yourself when your fears emerge. Talk about your feelings to trusted friends. Begin to experiment with taking risks, and see how you feel. Know that your fears will probably not disappear altogether, but that if you choose to, you can act in spite of them. Your fears do not have to control you.

I'm not sure what I want. I keep putting off looking for love.

This excuse also comes in many different forms:

- I love my life the way it is.
- I'm involved in my career, and I love it. I don't know when I'd squeeze a relationship in.
- I feel good alone, so maybe I'd rather be alone—but I'm not sure.
- I enjoy my privacy and my freedom a lot.
- It's taken me six years to prove it's okay to be single!
- I'm set in my ways. I like my apartment, my routines.
- I'm not sure what I'll gain will be worth what I'll have to give up.
- I'm not sure I believe really good relationships exist. I've never seen one. I'm better off alone than with someone who drains my energy.

ZAP: As long as you let these doubts be in control, they will keep you single. Maybe that's what you want, and if so, that's fine. At least now you *know* the answer to the question, "If I'm so wonderful, why am I still single?"

But realize that your ambivalence will probably not go away. So if you lean toward wanting to be in love for keeps, you will have to be willing to mount a deliberate campaign, to "screen" lots of people and see what happens—in spite of your ambivalence. Of course, you can leave it up to fate; if you blunder into a terrific relationship, *then* decide what to do. If you don't, be happy alone. But if you do nothing to advance your cause, the chances of finding your all-time great match are probably not as great as the chances of people who know what they want and mount a deliberate, systematic effort to achieve it.

I don't want to want love too much because what if I never find it? I need to prepare myself for that possibility.

ZAP: If you want love in your life badly enough and you are willing to make an effort to find it, *you will find it.* Being alone is *not* an issue like infertility, where eventually you may have to accept the fact that you *will never* have your own child. To the extent to which you "prepare" yourself to remain single, to that degree you are sabotaging your chances of finding love! As was stated earlier, one of the prerequisites for finding love in most cases is precisely *deciding that you want it!*

If you prepare yourself that you might not find love, you are contributing to the fulfillment of your own prophesy.

I just haven't met the right person yet.

ZAP: No zap.

This "excuse" is probably the only one that is a legitimate reason and not an excuse. If you have corrected all the mistakes we have discussed in this book and you are doing everything right, it may really be the case that you haven't met the right person yet. Don't worry about it. Keep doing all the right things, and you will!

I'm single because I want to be!
ZAP: Again, no zap.

If you are single by choice, great! You are a "voluntary single," and most of what we've discussed in this book for "involuntary singles" probably does not apply to you.

Some of the suggestions I am making in response to "excuses" take quite a bit of time and effort. I do not intend to imply with my laconic "zaps" that the solutions are quick and easy—only that, to any excuse you can raise, there *is* an answer—if you care enough about having love in your life.

Do you have an excuse that does *not* appear on this list? If so, be your own consultant. Tell yourself how to "zap" your own excuse. There is no reason you have to remain single if you don't choose to. Remember, the secret to success boils down to one word: perseverance.

EXPERIMENT #26

Now, to see whether, for you, this book has answered the question it posed, complete the following sentence in as many ways as are appropriate:
"I am still single because _____."
Compare your answers now to the list you made in Experiment #1, before you read the book. Chances are, you already knew why you are still single; you just hadn't paid attention to it!

. . . And What Do You Plan to Do About It?

Now that you have some idea *why* you are still single—and how you may be fooling yourself with your excuses—let's look at the second half of our chapter title: What do you plan to do about it?

Actually, only *you* can write this section. Only you know what mistakes you have been making and what you need to do to get yourself on the right path. What are you going to do to turn your love life around? Below are some experiments to help you formulate your own personalized plan.

EXPERIMENT #27

Below I have listed the most common ways singles inadvertently defeat themselves in their seach for love. As you will see, each "mistake" is simply a failure to employ a strategy we have discussed at length.

By circling the appropriate numbers, give yourself two scores on each of the ten major strategies we have discussed. Using two different colors, give yourself one score for your past behavior and another score for the way you plan to behave— or think you will behave—in the future.

Self-defeating belief or behavior	Extremely	A lot	Some-what	A little	Not very much	Not at all
	5	4	3	2	1	0
1. I believe there is a *shortage* of good men (or women) available for committed relationships *and* that this affects my chances of getting what I want for myself.	5	4	3	2	1	0
2. a. I am ambivalent about what I want for myself.	5	4	3	2	1	0
b. I want love, but my competing priorities are _____.	5	4	3	2	1	0
c. I have over-adapted to singlehood. I'm so set in my ways I probably won't change.	5	4	3	2	1	0
d. I have put my search for love on hold until						

Self-defeating belief or behavior	Extremely 5	A lot 4	Some- what 3	A little 2	Not very much 1	Not at all 0
I achieve certain other goals.	5	4	3	2	1	0
3. I lower my standards. I feel I have to take what I can get. I reach for what I think I can have, not what I truly want.	5	4	3	2	1	0
4. a. I believe there are no good ways to meet people.	5	4	3	2	1	0
b. I never do anything designed specifically to meet new people.	5	4	3	2	1	0
c. I behave as if there is a scarcity of members of the opposite sex. I do not keep a volume of new people flowing through my life.	5	4	3	2	1	0
d. I think that meeting new people always has to be enjoyable.	5	4	3	2	1	0
e. I forget to ask about a person's "lifestyle preference" early on.	5	4	3	2	1	0
5. I get seduced by pseudo-intimacy—by sex, infatuation, or the closeness game. I spend time "playing" rather than holding out for genuine intimacy.	5	4	3	2	1	0
6. I get involved with com- mitmentphobes. I naïvely walk right into their traps.	5	4	3	2	1	0
7. I try to "make" people						

Self-defeating belief or behavior	Extremely 5	A lot 4	Some-what 3	A little 2	Not very much 1	Not at all 0
love me, using one or more methods that never work. I find it hard to accept that I'll never get what I want from *this* person.	5	4	3	2	1	0
8. I stay in BTN relationships longer than I should. I don't say "no" soon enough. I don't ask for what I want, and then if it is not forthcoming, get out.	5	4	3	2	1	0
9. I let my fears stop me from doing what I want to do.	5	4	3	2	1	0
10. I could work more on my self-esteem and my self-acceptance.	5	4	3	2	1	0

Later on, I will suggest a way for you to make use of your scores.

How to Achieve Your Goals

We have established two central principles for finding love:

- Become clear about what you want.
- Persevere toward your goal.

Now, I want to become much more specific about *how* to persevere *effectively*, how to work toward your goal in a way that maximizes your chances of achieving it.

Why is it difficult for us to make desired changes in our lives? To use a simple example, suppose you have decided that you want to start jogging. But months after you made this resolution, you still aren't jogging. Why?

Most people make the mistake of visualizing only their final goal; for example, jogging five miles every day. They don't think about the process they will need to go through on the way to achieving their aspiration. All a goal is, really, is a good intention, and human nature being what it is, good intentions often lead nowhere. Relying on good intentions alone is the most common reason for failure to achieve desired goals.

The second reason is, as a colleague of mine puts it, the urgent always drives out the necessary. In other words, you have to go to work; the children must be fed; the bills have to be paid; your house guests must be entertained—there are always urgent tasks requiring your immediate attention. Fitting in something necessary or desirable—but new—means finding a crack in your established routines. And to combine this with the first problem, your good intention is probably so major a change that you'll never find a big enough crack.

A third common reason for failure to achieve goals is that we erroneously assume we can make big changes in our behavior all by ourselves. In fact, making a significant change without the support of at least one other person is extremely difficult. The proliferation of successful self-help groups based on the Alcoholics Anonymous model is evidence that people *can* make enormous life changes if they do have support. But if you make a promise to yourself and you can break your own promise with no dire consequences, then the urgent may go on driving out the necessary in your life for years.

Does the following scenario describe you at all?

You hope someday to be part of a long-term intimate relationship. But you are very caught up with the urgent tasks of your day-to-day life, and you seldom give thought to what you are going to do to realize this hope. You assume it will just happen some day. Also, it has never occurred to you that you could ask a friend to support you in achieving your goal of finding love.

If you recognize yourself in this picture, I have some suggestions that could make a difference in your life. The program I am about to outline is *simple,* and it overcomes the three most common reasons for failure to achieve goals. If you move with me, step by step, you will end up with a specific, realistic, custom-designed recipe for achieving a loving connection with another person. Get out your notebook, and let's go.

Step One

What is your overall purpose, your intention, your long-range hope for yourself? At the top of a clean page write "Purpose: _____"

Some examples might be these:

Purpose: To get married.
Purpose: To find a person I really love—and like—without reservations, who loves me in the same way, and to make a life-long commitment to that person.
Purpose: To find a person I love who loves me also, who wants to share companionship but not live together or get married.

Figure out why you are doing this exercise at all, what you hope to achieve—whatever that is for right now—and state it all clearly in a simple sentence.

Step Two

Now return to Experiment #27 on page 239. Circle each item where you identified a gap between what you have done in the past and what you plan to do from now on. For each circled item, write one or more sentences which state your goals with regard to that mistake. You may find it useful to review each chapter summary where there is a discussion about how to apply the strategy identified in that chapter. List your goal statements under your purpose statement. Make as many statements as necessary with regard to each mistake you wish to correct. Some examples:

Goal: To let go of the belief that an alleged man/woman-shortage affects my chances.

Goal: To increase my own personal odds of finding love.

Goal: To pay close attention to my ambivalence and how it affects what I do.

Goal: To increase the flow of new people through my life.

Goal: To meet new people even though I'm ambivalent about what I want.

Goal: To start doing things to look for love right now and not wait until I feel in a better place.

Goal: To keep my standards high.

Goal: To let go of my scarcity mentality and believe that the right person does exist for me.

Goal: To stop my fears from controlling my love life.

Goal: To work actively on improving my self-esteem.

Step Three

Rank your goals in the order in which you believe they will help you obtain your overall purpose. You may find that some goals must be attained first before you can go on to other ones. Do not eliminate any goals; they are all important.

Now, write each of your first three goals at the top of a clean page.

Step Four

Goals are achieved by breaking them down into specific intermediate objectives. In order for the objectives to work, that is, to achieve the desired goals, they must meet certain criteria: Each objective must be manageable, meaningful, measurable, and monitored.

a. Manageable—Your objective must be realistic for *you*. Choose a small task that you know for certain you can actually achieve, something you are willing and able to do, and that, knowing yourself as you do, you believe has a high probability of actually being accomplished.

b. Meaningful—On the other hand, your task must be substantial enough that accomplishing it makes you feel a sense of progress. Don't set up a task so insignificant that it is meaningless.

c. Measurable—Your objective must be both specific and time-bound so that you will know with certainty when you have or have not achieved it.

d. Monitored—You must enlist the support of another individual who will agree to serve as your monitor. That person will put your objective deadline on his or her calendar and check with you to see whether you have achieved your objective. Also, your monitor will work with you to evaluate your progress and encourage your efforts. This monitor, or support person, can be a friend or possibly a member of a support group to which you belong. Often, two people serve as monitors for each other.

I will say more about the importance of support later in this chapter.

To complete Step Four, then, under the goal you have written at the top of each page, draw four columns, two wide and two narrow, like this:

Goal: _____

Objective	How: Tasks Needed	By When	Discussed w/Monitor?

Now, select some manageable yet meaningful objectives that will move you toward achieving your goal. For example, suppose your goal is, "To meet new people, even though I'm ambivalent about what I want." Your page could look something like this:

Goal: To meet new people even though I'm ambivalent about what I want.			
Objective (including target date)	How: Tasks needed*	By When*	Discussed w/Monitor?
1. Meet one new eligible person every week for two months for a total of eight by December 1 (a conservative objective, by the way).	1. Join a dating service.	Oct. 4	Yes—Joan
	2. Answer five personal ads.	Oct. 8	Yes—Joan
	3. Put a personal ad in ____ Magazine.	Oct. 12	Yes—Joan
		Oct. 12	Yes—Joan
	4. Ask five people to think seriously about introducing me to someone.	Nov. 8	Yes—Joan
	5. Have a Trivial Pursuit party with people from work.		

* Be sure to write these dates and tasks on your calendar.

Here is another sample page:

Goal: To get out of my BTN with J. and avoid BTNs in the future.

. . . .

Objective (including target date)	How: Tasks needed	By When	Discussed w/Monitor?
1. To change relationship with J. to a friendship by December 1.	Tell J. I want a two-week moratorium and then I want to see each other a lot less.	This Sunday	Yes—Bill
2. To increase my awareness and ability to say no when appropriate. Every evening for the next 3 weeks, think through the day and *list* every incident when I should have said no but didn't or when I did say no even though it was hard.	Actually take 10 minutes and write something down every evening.	Oct. 25	Yes—Bill

Step Five

Make a date with your monitor to evaluate your objectives.
It should be on or very soon after your target date.
   Together, discuss these questions:

1. Did you achieve your objective by your target
   date?
2. If not, why not?
3. In retrospect, do you think your objective actually
   was both manageable and meaningful? How would
   you modify your objective as a result?
4. Have you made progress in moving toward your
   goal?

The two of you together can now establish a new objective or set of objectives and a new evaluation date.

Change does not come easily. Human nature seems to
have a strong innate tendency to revert to the status quo.
So, especially if you are working to change long-estab-
lished habits, you should expect yourself to hit plateaus
when you don't seem to be moving forward, and even to
backslide at times. But, especially when you feel discouraged, the important thing is to persevere, to move ahead
with patience and persistence—and with the help of your
support person. People do make miraculous changes. And
people who have been single for years do fall in love and
get married. If you choose to, you can be one of them.
   If you glossed over this experiment and said to yourself,
"I don't need to do all this; I get the idea," let me encourage you to take the few minutes you'll need and a
pencil and paper and actually jot down some notes to yourself. For what I am trying to convey is that things don't
happen because they ought to happen, and things don't
happen because you want them to happen. *Things happen
only when you make them happen.*
   When you complete your personal program for finding
love, I believe you will make several encouraging discoveries:

- Mounting a deliberate effort to find the kind of relationship you most want *does not require a great deal of time*.
- Leading a full, satisfying life as a single *is not mutually exclusive* with keeping alive your search for a romantic partner.
- Virtually everything you do to further your goal of finding an intimate partner will enhance your self-esteem at the same time.

Persistence and patience are truly a winning combination.

Putting Your Plan Into Action: The Value of Support

You can't know the power of support in your life until you have experienced it.

Alcoholics Anonymous is the most widely known support group. It has been so successful in transforming lives that people with other problems have patterned support groups on the AA model. One can find support groups now for overeaters, people who are grieving, adults who were abused as children, smokers who want to stop, adult children of alcoholics, former mental patients, ex-cons, parents of teenagers—the list goes on and on. Whenever people want to make changes in their lives, they find they can do so more easily if they join together with others who are seeking to make the same change.

In the late sixties and early seventies, women formed support groups in unprecedented numbers and found so much inner strength—just by discovering and supporting *each other*—that they spawned a revolution. One reason the women's movement has progressed so much faster than the men's movement (insofar as a men's movement exists at all) is precisely that women discovered the power of joining together in small groups and talking about what was true for them. For the first time in large numbers they stopped talking about what was *supposed* to be true. The women's movement was really thousands of individual, personal "movements." In living rooms across the country, women began expanding their self-awareness and developing strategies for change.

What is it that makes support groups so empowering? Why can people turn their lives around in support groups when they have sought in vain to do it alone? Why do support groups have an almost miraculous effect on people over and over and over?

Actually, it's not all that mysterious. Let's look at what a support group can provide that no one can experience alone.

1. The first thing you discover when you join a support group is that you are not alone. Even if you know this intellectually, the actual experience of hearing others say what you've been feeling can provide enormous relief. You find you don't have to explain yourself; everyone else understands what you are going through. People often report that they have a feeling of community after one meeting of a support group that they haven't felt for years—even with their friends.

2. You also discover that each person's experience—with this same problem you all have—is different. You find out that there is no *right way* to experience or to solve your problem, that, in other words, no matter what your own experience is, *it is valid.*

Abby was twenty-eight when she joined a support group in which the participants wanted to help each other look at their relationship issues. After her first meeting, Abby told me,

I thought there was something wrong with me because my dream relationship is with someone who wants to be *married*—by which I mean committed and monogamous—but we would each continue to live separately. I figured I was just weird. You can't imagine how good I felt to hear other people's ideal relationship-styles! One liked the idea of a three-year commitment; one wanted a partner who was a primary person but *not* monogamous; one wanted *not* to live together *unless* she was married; one said she would not *ever* marry, but would consider living together. Just by hearing all these differences, it hit me that there's no one right way to do it. I suddenly realized that my idea was no more stupid or weird than anyone else's. It helped me to stop putting myself down for what I wanted. It was an enormous relief.

3. Probably the most important benefit of support groups is that people tend to be honest there, to drop their pretenses and masks, and to tell the truth. For many people, a support group is one place where they can let go of their "I've-got-it-all-together" acts and be honest with one another.

Often in our day-to-day lives, we are too bound by convention—and simply too busy—to talk with each other about what we are feeling inside. But that's *all* that happens in support groups. For many people, it takes time and practice, but in a support group, you can learn how to find out what is true for you and to talk about it. And you learn in the best possible way: by hearing other people discuss discoveries they have made about themselves.

Of course, you never have to say more than you are ready to say, either. Many people do most of their learning by listening—listening to people just like them talk honestly about the most difficult things in their lives.

In short, support groups help you to expand your awareness about your life. They give you "input" and an opportunity to pay attention.

You cannot see your own "mask" if you are wearing it. Someone must look at it from the outside and tell you what it looks like. This is just as true of symbolic "masks"—defenses—as it is of the Halloween variety. Most of us are not aware that we are wearing masks at all; much less can we see what they look like. Because of the nature of the problem, outside viewers of some sort are required as a part of the solution.

A second piece of information you can never acquire by yourself is how others perceive you. You can't know what they see or how they feel about what they see. Since what you are seeking to improve is your interaction with other people, this is essential information. People who are around you all the time may see a great deal more about you than they ever tell you. But only in structured settings with established safeguards and ground rules—where you have specifically asked for this information—are people willing to give you these observations, which may be incredibly useful to you.

4. As you work on making changes in your life, your support group gives you someone besides yourself to be accountable to. If you promise yourself you'll sign up for a

singles weekend, you can easily talk yourself out of it. But if you commit to your group that you will do it, you'll find it harder to wiggle out of. Support groups *work* in helping people make difficult changes they want to make.

5. When you are working on self-exploration and change, you need the right kind of friends. Serious self-exploration is never a painless process. When you learn things about yourself that you don't like, when you are working on making changes but find yourself reverting to old habits, when you feel the frightening void you will feel when you give up the old "you" but haven't yet discovered the new "you," you will need people around you who understand what you are experiencing *and will let you experience it.* Well-meaning friends who don't understand the process and try to smooth it over and make you feel better are not being supportive. Your support group will provide the *kind* of support you need.

6. The support group itself is a "laboratory" for practicing human interaction. The group is a microcosm of the real world, where you get to see under a microscope how you behave. Everything that goes on in the support group is "grist for the mill." If you get angry or you feel hurt, your group will help you look at how it happened. They will validate your feelings and help you look at what part of your behavior is productive for you and what is counterproductive.

7. A support group can be a good place to meet people and to make new friends. It can provide a sense of continuity and community in our fragmented world, and can help overcome the feeling of isolation so common in our frenzied urban lives.

Support is a powerful experience for which there is virtually no substitute; serious self-exploration or change is probably impossible without it.

So if you have decided you want to employ some of the strategies we have identified in this book, where can you turn for support?

One close, trusted friend is a good start. If you agree that you want to offer each other "support" in the sense we have discussed here, you can. Experiment #16 (see page 180) is a good way to start.

But a support *group* actually has advantages over a one-to-one relationship, such as the following:

1. Since you have regular meetings, you will be more disciplined in getting input and paying attention. Friends can easily let these things slide.
2. Part of your learning comes from hearing other people discuss their own personal discoveries. This is a critical experience that two friends can provide only in a limited way.
3. The group gathered together creates a certain atmosphere or "energy" that two people can't create by themselves. There's more creative tension in a group, more excitement, more vitality, more experience and intelligence to apply to a certain problem. A group holds the potential of becoming a community, an antidote to our fragmented world with its emphasis on rugged individualism.
4. The group provides a way to expand your circle of friends and to learn to be honest—to be your more genuine self—with more people.

Now, how do you go about starting a support group? In the Appendix, you will find Guidelines for Forming a "Making It Happen" Self-Help Support Group. They are comprehensive, including everything from finding members for the group to possible formats for meetings and ground rules for participation. As you read through them, you will discover that starting a support group is not at all difficult, and can be enormously rewarding. A support group—even a very small one—could make the difference between your using the suggestions in this book effectively —and *intending* to do something about them but letting them slide.

A Final Word: The Secret of Letting Go

I interviewed a strikingly beautiful woman, Wendy, who, at thirty-four, had achieved remarkable success as a painter. She told me this:

I want love in my life. I want it a lot. But everyone says you'll find romance after you let go of needing it. When you give up your search, love walks in. So I'm trying to let go of wanting a relationship—so I can get one.

There is a lot of wisdom in Wendy's statement, for letting go *does work.* But what a contradiction to say this at the end of a book in which every chapter admonished you to get busy and *do something!*

If you understand what letting go is, it turns out it's not a contradiction after all.

Letting go does not mean giving up on love or adapting to being single. It does not mean you are in fact no longer looking for or wanting a relationship. *It simply means that you are no longer anxious about finding a relationship.* This is a pivotal distinction.

Letting go is a state of mind—and body. It is a light, easy feeling of being free of a burden, a quiet that settles over you like a cosmic tranquilizer. It is the *feeling* that you will find a good mate when the time is right, a sense of inner peace, of accepting life just as it unfolds. What you are letting go of is the struggle, the panic, the longing for things to be other than they are.

Letting go means that, for the time being, your worry, your discouragement, your apprehension have all vanished. You are who you are, life is what it is, and somehow it is all okay. Letting go is a kind of deep trust that things will work out as they should. It's like putting down your sail and your oars and casting yourself adrift on the sea, rather than rowing as hard as you can in one direction.

Letting go is relinquishing control, giving up the effort to force your boat in one direction by manipulating your situation and the people around you. It is turning your boat over to fate, recognizing that fortune never comes in the form you expect, and trusting the natural flow of the universe. To let go is to assume an attitude of patient optimism, to be sure, not exactly where your boat is headed nor when it will arrive, but that you are moving in a positive direction, and that—when the time is right—you will discover the particular lush shore toward which you are most certainly headed.

Letting go is recognizing that you don't have all the

answers. You don't know enough to be able to control everything. You can work *with* the forces in the universe that make things happen, but you don't have to make everything happen yourself. Trust that things will work out beautifully for you. Know that, no matter what happens, it will all work itself out for the best. Believe that whatever is in store for you is right and good and as it should be.

But here's the rub: letting go is not something you can achieve by willing it, as Wendy tried to do. It is something that happens to you. Like grace, it comes to you not because you earned it or because you did anything in particular to "get" it. Rather, it steals unobtrusively over you, and one day you take a look and discover that—sometime, you aren't sure when—you let go. You gave up. You gave in. You stopped struggling. Or something let go of you.

It helps to hold "letting go" as a vision of where you'd like to be. It helps to become aware of your anxieties and your loneliness and experience them fully. For some people, it helps to pray or meditate or exercise. It helps to be open to letting go. But you can't make it happen. In fact, the more you work at it, the more you defeat yourself. I once heard a therapist say to a very driven man, "Don't just do something; sit there!"

It may be the case that love is more likely to find you when you are in this state. But that is a side effect. The best thing about feeling better is that *you feel better*. You realize that your anxieties, your worries, your depressions are not getting you anywhere. You can give them up.

So continue in your determined effort to find a relationship, but leave behind the desperation that makes the whole thing so unpleasant. Move ahead with your plan, but let go of your anxiety and enjoy your life as it unfolds before you each day.

Never sacrifice your present life for your future dreams. Remember the all-important balance between living a full, satisfying life as a single at the same time you patiently but persistently look for an intimate partner. Life is going on right now. Don't miss it! Let your motto be "Determination Without Depression."

And good luck!

Appendix

Guidelines for Forming a "Making It Happen" Self-Help Support Group

The following guidelines will show you exactly how to go about setting up and participating in a self-help group that can support you in making whatever changes you desire to make in your love life. These groups are an excellent way for members to expand their self-awareness and to develop and improve the intimacy in their lives.

1. *Getting Started.* One or two people should decide what they want the purpose, composition, and format of the group to be. Then they should invite others to join a group with their predetermined goals and format.

Much less successful is convening a group and then spending several meetings deciding as a group what the goals and structure of the group will be. Since ten people will have ten different ideas, decision-making can be arduous, and people will begin the group feeling frustrated.

A statement of purpose could be something like this: "Our purpose in this group is to

- support each other to talk honestly about our desires and our fears
- to support each other in establishing and achieving goals and objectives for our lives
- to listen to each other nonjudgmentally
- to share insights and feelings and keep advice to a minimum."

2. *Composition.* Decide whether you want a women's, men's, or mixed group. One format which combines the

advantages of single sex and mixed groups is, each month the men and women meet separately for the first two weeks and jointly for the last two weeks.

3. *Inviting Participants.* One successful way of inviting people to join is to start with two people. They each invite a friend. Then the two new recruits each invite a friend, and those two recruits each invite a friend. This avoids "cliques" of people who already know each other well. Also, some people prefer the anonymity of a group in which no one is a close friend. For their recruit, these people can ask an acquaintance rather than a close friend.

4. *Size and New Members.* No support group should be larger than twelve. A group can be as small as four or five people. For the format suggested above, the women's and men's separate groups should be no larger than six people if they plan to meet jointly sometimes. A group should set its membership at a specific size, whether small or large. Then when someone new wants to join, he or she must wait until an opening occurs.

5. *Frequency of Meetings.* Groups are most effective if they meet once a week. Weekly meetings provide continuity and a sense of community which is hard to achieve with less frequent meetings. Also, if people are willing to meet weekly, they are more likely to have a serious commitment to the work of the group.

6. *Length of Meetings.* Meetings should have a set beginning and ending time. Two hours works well; two and a half for a larger group. Meetings that ramble on all evening run the risk of being undisciplined. If you limit your time, you'll find you can accomplish what you need to in less time, and absenteeism will be reduced. The two hours can be tucked into convenient times, like 5:00 to 7:00 P.M., which leaves the evening free, or even 7:00 to 9:00 A.M.

Limited-time meetings also allow for group members to socialize or continue talking informally in smaller groups after the formal meeting is ended.

7. *Location and Refreshments.* Groups can meet in members' homes, although a neutral setting is preferable

because no one has the burden of hosting. A meeting room in a church, community center, or even a business conference room is ideal.

Refreshments—food or drink of any kind—should be avoided. On special occasions, the group can socialize after the meeting with food. But the pressure for food every week becomes a burden. More important, food can be a distraction, even a little "defense" for a person to hide behind. Food can get in the way of the deep, honest sharing you are trying to promote.

8. *Leadership.* The one or two people who convene the group should offer a little structure for the first three or four meetings to get things off to a positive, well-organized start. Nothing can destroy a group faster than spending time on logistic discussions in the early meetings: "Well, now we're here. What shall we do?" is deadly.

But after the group is off and running, the "leadership functions" should rotate. If the group is basically leaderless, anyone who wants to bring up an issue about the group's process can do so. The group may want to designate a "co-ordinator," and rotate the position every month or so.

Many self-help groups do have leaders who have received special training in skills such as helping members understand and adhere to the group's ground rules, keeping the discussion productive, keeping participation somewhat equal, suggesting special activities, etc. A group could look for such a leader or obtain leadership training for one of its members. Or, leaderless groups can also work well.

9. *First Meetings.* The two group convenors should decide how they want to get the group started. They could select anything from the format list which follows. One plan that has been very successful in the past is:

  a. Members introduce themselves by telling what their relationship history is and what they hope to get out of the group.
  b. Each member is given the opportunity to tell his or her life story. This should probably be done in the smaller, single-sex groups, because it can take several meetings to get through everyone's story. Opening

with biographies is useful because it gives members practice in talking about themselves, including some parts that may be difficult or unpleasant, and it gives everyone in the group a context in which to place present-day issues the person will be discussing later.

10. *Format.* A support group can be structured in a variety of ways. Many groups combine two or more of the suggestions below. Almost anything will work as long as the members talk about their own personal feelings instead of broad generalities. Here are possible formats to choose from:

a. One person gets "the floor" for a half hour or forty-five minutes. The whole group focuses on that person's problem or topic, helping the person to talk it through, listening, offering insights, and keeping "advice" to a minimum. The person might choose to get help setting up or evaluating goals and objectives. When he or she is finished, other group members should have a chance to say how the discussion affected them, especially if it touched off something for them personally. Of course, not everyone will get the floor every time. But over a period of several weeks everyone should have approximately equal time.

b. The group selects a topic like sex, money, competition, intimacy, fear, saying "no," BTNs, self-esteem, etc. That's the topic for the evening, but members must talk about it *personally*, not in a general way.

c. The group could decide on an article or book to read together and discuss it, again, not philosophically, but personally.

d. The experiments in this book provide an excellent way to structure a "Making It Happen" Self-Help Support Group. Using one or two experiments each evening, members can take fifteen to thirty minutes —whatever is required—to do the experiment individually. Then, especially if the group contains ten or more people, members should pair up and spend several minutes talking with just one other person about what the experiment was like for them. Finally, the whole group can share their experiences together.

e. At the beginning of each meeting, every member can be given an opportunity to "check-in," that is, to say briefly how he or she is feeling and report what has gone on in the past week. Care must be taken to keep the "check-ins" brief, lest they take up time that was to be allotted to another format. Some groups do not do check-ins every time but devote an entire meeting to them *occasionally*.

It is important for members to keep up-to-date with each others' lives. On the other hand, telling stories and reporting news is the least useful way to spend support group time. So "check-ins" must be kept brief.

11. *Ground Rules.* There are productive and counter-productive ways to participate in a support group. Members should become familiar with the ground rules for helpful participation and encourage each other to stick to them. You will all find yourselves slipping up from time to time, but you can give each other friendly reminders to get back on track.

a. Gestalt therapist Fritz Perls identified three types of conversation which are always designed to avoid the truth and are generally counterproductive in a support group (Fritz Perls was not a delicate kind of guy):
   - Chickenshit is small talk, trivia, gossip, throw-away remarks.
   - Bullshit is lies, usually self-aggrandizing; rationalizations, exaggerations.
   - Elephantshit is broad, philosophical generalizations: "All men . . ." or "Most people . . ." It is discussing a theory rather than personal experience; intellectualizing.

Whenever group members hear each other verging on any of these, they should gently remind each other to speak *personally* and *honestly*.

b. Keep advice-giving to an absolute minimum. Members can share their own experiences and talk about what works *for them*. Advice can too easily become patronizing; besides, what works for one person may not work for another. When you are tempted to give advice, realize that you will be far more useful if you can support your friend in coming up with his or her own solution.

c. Never criticize another group member. And never give feedback or input to another group member unless he or she has asked for it.

d. Avoid storytelling and simply reporting events. Support group time is not social time.

e. When a member begins to experience some emotion —anger or tears, for example—let the person's emotion come out fully. Don't try to "help" your friend or "make her (or him) feel better." Your quiet, attentive presence will let her know you are with her as she cries or yells or feels fear or whatever. Sometimes touching or holding is an appropriate show of support.

f. Use "I" statements whenever possible. Very often in American speech, we say "you" when we mean "I." For example, "When you feel sad sometimes, you want to cry, but you just can't." What the speaker means is, "When I feel sad sometimes, I want to cry, but I just can't." Speaking in the first person will help you to focus on what you mean and to say it accurately.

We also tend to substitute "it" for "I" sometimes. A person may say "It feels wonderful!" when she means "I feel wonderful!" Remind each other to say "I" when you mean "I."

g. Members should be encouraged to talk about what they are *feeling*. Again, Americans are not in the habit of using "feeling words." An easy formula for talking about feelings is, "I feel ____," and the blank is filled in with one or more adjectives. For example, "I feel excited, sad, tense, etc."

If a group member is being invited to talk about how she feels, two things should be discouraged: (1) the words "good" and "bad." They simply aren't very specific. What *is* your good or bad feeling? (2) "I feel *that* . . ." should be disallowed because what follows probably won't be a feeling. "I feel that I was interrupted and that John wasn't listening to me," is a *thought*, not a feeling. "I feel hurt and annoyed" is a feeling. Very often, "thoughts" tend to be about other people. Feelings are always about yourself. A feeling statement is often the most direct way to say what is true for you.

h. Absolute confidentiality must be agreed to by everyone. Nothing that is said during a meeting should ever be repeated outside the group by *anyone anywhere*.

Once you become familiar with the ground rules, they will become a habit for you as a group. Don't be obsessive about them; sometimes it's far more important not to interrupt than to bring up some ground rule. But in general, remind each other gently when you notice slip-ups.

Once again the ground rules are:

- Avoid chickenshit, bullshit, and elephantshit.
- Avoid advice giving, criticism, and storytelling.
- Let people experience their emotions.
- Use "I" rather than "you" or "it."
- Talk about feelings.
- Maintain strict confidentiality.

12. *Duration of the Group.* Initially, members should commit to remaining in the group for eight weeks. The group itself can decide to "self-destruct" after a period of time, say sixteen weeks. But groups can continue meeting weekly for years and years. The longer people meet together, the better they know each other and the more useful they can be to each other. Also, trust and intimacy deepen over time. Very often people make breakthroughs in their awareness or in their experience of themselves all along throughout three or five or seven years in a support group. Members stick together through weddings, babies, family deaths, divorces, new relationships—they are there to support each other. People may join as singles, marry, invite their spouses to join, and stay in the group as couples. The process of expanding awareness never stops. And the other purposes of the support group continue to be met over time, too: the feeling of community and continuity, the development of friendships, and, what one group member called "mental health maintenance."

"Whenever I hit a difficult situation at work or with my

kids or in a relationship," she said, "I have a place to go with it, to get ideas, perspective, and support."

The concept of "mental health maintenance" is a useful one because it makes it clear that you don't have to be "sick" to find a support group helpful. Support groups work well for people who have the normal, garden-variety ups and downs of life that most of us have but who find that they feel better when they have reliable, trustworthy friends with whom to share them.

13. *Managing Problems.* Surprisingly infrequently but occasionally, self-help groups develop internal conflicts. A group member may prove to be insensitive to the needs of others or otherwise unable to adapt to a group setting. Often these conflicts are resolved as the group brings its collective resources to bear on the problem and works it through.

If a group decides that a certain problem is beyond their ability to resolve it, they may invite a therapist to visit the group for one or two meetings. When the cost of a visiting therapist is divided among group members, it is usually manageable.

14. *Leaving the Group.* All members should agree to give the group at least three weeks advance notice if they plan to leave the group. This gives people time to complete any "unfinished business" they have with the departing member, and it gives everyone a chance to say good-bye to what was almost certainly an intense relationship. Most groups develop a little ritual to say good-bye to a departing member. For example, a person leaving goes around to each member separately. With each person, the two exchange what they appreciate and—if appropriate—don't appreciate about each other.

Notes

Introduction

p. 5, For a study of leisure time see, for example, Jay B. Nash, *Philosophy of Recreation and Leisure* (Dubuque, IA: Brown Co., 1960).

p. 5, Statistics on leisure time from "Working at Relaxation," *Wall Street Journal* supplement, "Corporate Leisure," April 21, 1986.

p. 6, Daniel Yankelovich, *New Rules: Searching for Self-Fulfillment in a World Turned Upside Down* (New York: Random House, 1981), see p. 79.

p. 6, I am indebted to Paul Schulze for the idea of the seesaw metaphor.

Chapter 1

p. 23, I first heard about "class B membership" from Berkeley, California, psychologist John Enright.

p. 30, Ralph Blum, *The Book of Runes* (New York: St. Martin's Press, 1982), p. 79.

Chapter 2

p. 31, See "Too Late for Prince Charming," *Newsweek*, June 2, 1986.

p. 32, Katha Pollitt's article, "Being Wedded Is Not Always Bliss" in *The Nation*, September 20, 1986, provides an analysis of the Bennett-Bloom-Craig study which I have drawn upon.

p. 34, The San Francisco area singles magazine is *Trellis Singles Magazine*, published in Sunnyvale, California.

Chapter 4

p. 67, Definition of "intuition" from *Random House College Dictionary,* Revised Edition, 1975. Quotation from "If You're So Smart, How Come I'm Still Single?," *Philadelphia* magazine, December 1986.

Chapter 5

p. 87, The story about the rats in the maze is adapted from a story which was told at an est seminar in 1978.

Chapter 6

p. 105, Definition of "infatuation" from *Random House College Dictionary.* Revised Edition, 1975.
pp. 105–106, For discussion of the biochemical aspects of infatuation, "What Scientists Think They Know—Isolating the Chocolate Factor," by Jane O'Reilly, *Ms.,* August 1980.
p. 110, Thomas C. Oden, *Game Free: The Meaning of Intimacy* (New York: Harper & Row, 1974).

Chapter 7

p. 115, See Daniel Goldstine, et al., *The Dance-Away Lover* (New York: Morrow and Co., 1977).
p. 117, I am indebted to Dorothy Wall for the imagery of the splinter.

Chapter 9

p. 138, The word "flove" was coined by Judye Hess and Lorraine Bahrick.
p. 139, The story about the boy walking across hot coals is told by Tolly and Peggy Burkan, who conduct workshops designed to help participants overcome fear (Box 1738, Twain Harte, CA 95383).
p. 142, John Powell, S.J., *Why Am I Afraid to Tell You Who I Am?* (Niles, IL: Argus Communications, 1969), pp. 13–14.

p. 155, Marilyn Ferguson, *The Aquarian Conspiracy* (Los Angeles: J. P. Tarcher, Inc., 1980).

Chapter 10

p. 185, Aldous Huxley, *Island* (New York: Harper & Row, 1962).
p. 188, I am indebted to Santa Barbara, California, therapist Clive Cazes for the idea behind this map of the self.
pp. 192–193, I am indebted to Emmett E. Miller, M.D., for this meditation, which has been adapted with his permission (P.O. Box W, Stanford, CA 94305).

Chapter 11

pp. 219–223, Source of AIDS data: "AIDS: At the Dawn of Fear," *U.S. News and World Report*, January 12, 1987.

Chapter 12

pp. 241–249, I am grateful to Loren Cole for his assistance with the section "How to Achieve Your Goals."
pp. 254–255, Robert A. Johnson uses the metaphor of the boat drifting at sea in his beautiful book *We: Understanding the Psychology of Romantic Love* (San Francisco, Harper & Row, 1983).

Suggested Reading

The following books were useful to me in preparing the text and may be of interest for further reading.

Brandon, Nathaniel. *The Psychology of Romantic Love.* New York: Bantam Books, 1981.

———. *The Romantic Love Question and Answer Book.* New York: Bantam Books, 1983.

Ferguson, Marilyn. *The Aquarian Conspiracy.* Los Angeles: J. P. Tarcher, 1980.

Goldstine, Daniel, et al. *The Dance-Away Lover.* New York: William Morrow and Co., 1977.

Johnson, Robert A. *We: Understanding the Psychology of Romantic Love.* New York: Harper & Row, 1983.

Keen, Sam. *The Passionate Life: Stages of Loving.* New York: Harper & Row, 1983.

Leonard, George. *The End of Sex.* Los Angeles: J. P. Tarcher, 1983.

Marshall, Megan. *The Cost of Loving: Women and The New Fear of Intimacy.* New York: G. P. Putnam's Sons, 1984.

Mornell, Pierre, M.D. *Passive Men: Wild Women.* New York: Ballantine Books, 1979.

Novak, William. *The Great American Man Shortage.* New York: Rawson Associates, 1983.

Oden, Thomas C. *Game Free: The Meaning of Intimacy.* New York: Harper & Row, 1974.

Paul, Jordan and Margaret. *Do I Have to Give Up Me to Be Loved By You?* Minneapolis, MN: CompCare Publications, 1983.

Peck, M. Scott. *The Different Drum.* New York: Simon & Schuster, 1987.

Powell, John, S.J. *Why Am I Afraid to Tell You Who I Am?* Niles, IL: Argus Communications, 1969.

Rubin, Lillian B. *Intimate Strangers.* New York: Harper Colophon Books, 1983.

Rubin, Theodore Isaac, M.D. *Reconciliations: Inner Peace in an Age of Anxiety.* New York: Viking Press, 1983.
Schaef, Anne Wilson. *Women's Reality.* Minneapolis, MN: Winston Press, 1981.